THE ₿ITCOIN SAGA

THE ₿ITCOIN SAGA

A MIXED MONTAGE

Rachna Singh

BLOOMSBURY

NEW DELHI • LONDON • OXFORD • NEW YORK • SYDNEY

BLOOMSBURY INDIA
Bloomsbury Publishing India Pvt. Ltd
Second Floor, LSC Building No. 4, DDA Complex, Pocket C – 6 & 7,
Vasant Kunj, New Delhi 110070

BLOOMSBURY, BLOOMSBURY INDIA and the Diana logo are trademarks of
Bloomsbury Publishing Plc

First published in India 2019
This export edition published 2020

ISBN: PB: 978-93-88271-84-4; eBook: 978-9-3882-7185-1

Typeset in Manipal Digital

Printed and bound in India by Replika Press Pvt. Ltd.

Dedication

To those who have the courage to embark upon the bitcoin-blockchain rollercoaster ride. Cheers!

Acknowledgements

A thumping thanks to Anhad and Kainaat who threw much needed light on the complexities of blockchain technology and cryptocurrencies.

Hats off to Shreya Chakraborti and Yash Sharma of the Bloomsbury team who whipped my manuscript into perfect shape.

Last but not the least, a special thanks to my 'better half' who encouraged me to wade into unfamiliar 'cryptocurrency' waters.

Every informed person needs to know about bitcoin because it might be one of the world's most important developments.

—Leon Louw
Executive Director of South Africa-based Free Market Foundation

CONTENTS

A Missive to the Reader

Dear reader,

Bitcoin has taken the modern-day world by storm. The unprecedented and meteoric rise in the value of bitcoin has intrigued investors looking for a quick profit as well as the coder fraternity and the man on the street. The media has discussed it ad nauseum, peppering the discourse with half-baked and sometimes inaccurate facts. Myths and fallacies have taken centre stage in the bitcoin opera.

I'm sure most of you, at some time during this bitcoin brouhaha, tried to understand the concept of virtual currency and the technology underlying it. YouTube videos and talks on the subject are a dime a dozen. Articles on different aspects of bitcoins elbow for attention on the internet. Print media has also taken the bitcoin bull by the horns and published a slew of write-ups on the subject. With a surfeit of information available, it becomes difficult for a person untutored in blockchain technology or cryptography or finance to make sense of this fledgling currency and technology. I have worked in finance for 27 years and have handled taxation policies and regulatory mechanisms but even I occasionally have difficulty in separating the bitcoin grain from the chaff. This admission was the starting point of my Homeric journey (there is no other metaphor to explain the long and strife-torn path of discovery) to unravel the nuanced complexity of a cryptocurrency like bitcoin. The journey, let me assure you dear reader, had all the thrills and spills of an exciting adventure. So, I decided to share the excitement of my discovery. My book *Financial Felicity: Making Sense of Money Matters (2017)* featured two articles on bitcoins. I also wrote in a couple of national dailies with widespread circulation and some magazines. Much to my consternation, I realised that such forums offered a very limited space to share the intricacies of bitcoins. That is when I decided to write *The Bitcoin Saga*.

The Bitcoin Saga: A Mixed Montage, as the name suggests, comprehensively chronicles the bitcoin story. The book is divided into six sections. The first section, 'A Promising Prelude', dwells on the subprime crisis, the historical event that triggered the genesis of a peer-to-peer decentralised and self-regulated currency. This 2008 event caused a trust crisis in banks and financial institutions and egged on several cryptographers or 'cypherpunks' to look beyond the banking systems to an alternative ecosystem of financial transactions that would not involve a third party. This 'Trust Trampoline' set the stage for the advent of the master wizard, Satoshi Nakamoto.

The second section of my book, 'The Tech Tales', explains the Ps and Qs of bitcoins and then goes on to elaborate upon the Bible of bitcoins—Nakamoto's brilliant white paper 'Bitcoin: A Peer-to-Peer Electronic Cash System'. During my research, this was the point of 'no return'. This was the point when I realised I was completely and immutably (forgive the pun) hooked to the bitcoin paradigm. Here, I would like to acknowledge and thank Anhad Jai Singh, a software engineer working with a multinational company in Gurugram, for reviewing the technical aspects of my book to ensure there are no technical 'bloopers' to tip me up. The technical diagrams used in the book were also put together with his help.

Section III is simply called 'The Rant and the Rave'. As the name indicates, this section is more of a balancing act. What caused the bitcoin juggernaut to roll to a mind-boggling $20,000? Who set up the Silk Road, an anonymous market that allowed the sale of drugs, porn, guns and ammunition? Is it possible to overcome the Byzantine General's problem? Who will be the ultimate winner in the crypto turf war? Is bitcoin caught in a bubble that will self-destruct? You will find the answers to such questions in this section. I promise you, dear reader, this section will read like a racy bestseller. So, curl up in your rocking chair with a cup of your favourite brew and enjoy the bitcoin rollercoaster ride.

The fourth section, 'Judicial Jargon', was perhaps the most difficult to write. I call it my Scylla and Charybdis section. Those of you who are familiar with Homer's classic, *The Odyssey,* will know that it refers to a situation where Odysseus (the protagonist) was caught between the 'devil and the deep blue sea'. This section describes the legal stance of the international community towards bitcoins as well as other sibling currencies in a chapter called 'Legal Laminate'. It touches upon the somewhat dry issues of regulation ('Regulatory Reckoning') and tax frameworks of different countries ('Taxing Matters'). It also dwells on the aim of some countries to mint their own cryptocurrencies ('Minting Mores'). The intention of this section is not to inundate you with unnecessary government policies. The objective is to ensure that you understand the tightrope walk between a policy that monitors and a policy that strangles the growth of the technology. I tried to keep the interest alive in this section without being Scrooge-like in my description of the virtual currency laws and regulations in force globally. Those with an academic inclination would enjoy it. Those with more 'bestseller' tastes may gripe about the academic overload. So be it.

The penultimate section, Section V, is 'A Motley Mix'. It is an interesting but miscellaneous collection of articles on altcoins ('Others of the Ilk'), myths that have rightly or wrongly become a part of the bitcoin narrative ('Moribund Masala') and the future of bitcoins ('Future Fables'). To this heterogeneous mix I have added a chapter called 'The Chat Room'. Here you will find illuminating quotes and comments on various aspects of bitcoins and blockchain technology by coders, bankers, economic experts and so on. Hold on! A Google search will not throw up these comments for your ready consumption. This is because these views have been generously but exclusively contributed for the book by compatriots, peers and experts.

The final section comes with a 'Twist in the Tale'. Most of us look at bitcoins as a mode of payment or investment. So, we have conveniently placed it in a niche with a 'financial instrument' glow sign on it. Don't worry! I did the same juggling and categorisation. But hey! We are being somewhat hasty in this 'naming and shaming' business. The blockchain technology that underpins bitcoins and others of its ilk can be applied to sectors like healthcare, agriculture, entertainment, humanitarian skills, governance and so on. The chapter, 'Future of Blockchain Technology', opens up new vistas of blockchain applications. The potential and promise to improve and simplify the voting processes marred by allegations of ballot fixing, the ability to ensure that 'identity theft' by hacking the 'Aadhar' portal is a thing of the past, the capacity to disburse money and tokens to Syrian refugees, a technology that enables front row seats to an IPL match or a Coldplay concert—these are some of the inherent benefits that the blockchain offers. However, there are glitches. Scalability, internal strife among the coder community, government policies that are aimed at controlling a disruptive technology and, of course, ignorance—these are some of the factors that will be the death knell of a futuristic and promising technology. For the potential to transmute into day-to-day reality, we need to iron out these creases and make the blockchain ecosystem hardier and more robust. 'Steering the Titan' mulls over the ways and means of stewarding the technology so that its potential is not belied.

Dear reader, as you can see, *The Bitcoin Saga* is an attempt to encompass all aspects of the bitcoin domain. It is another 'block' in my initiative to demystify subjects that wear the 'keep away' sign. I started with *Penny Panache: Piecing the Economic Puzzle* and went on to *Financial Felicity: Making Sense of Money Matters* where I endeavoured to simplify all things economic. With *The Bitcoin Saga*, I am striving to bring the subject of bitcoins, with its concomitant technical, financial and social complexities, to the table of the common reader with an intellectual palate. After reading the book if you, dear reader, can say with certainty, 'I know what makes bitcoins tick', I will know I have achieved my goal. If you find the subject exciting enough to mentor others on bitcoins, I'll pop a celebratory bottle of champagne. So, enjoy your very own virtual journey to the Bitcoin 'Ithaca'.

Bon voyage. Happy reading.

—Rachna Singh

SECTION I

A PROMISING PRELUDE

Chapter 1

The Trust Trampoline

> *The problem, in a nutshell, is that our money currently depends on trust in a third party for its value. As many inflationary and hyperinflationary episodes during the twentieth century demonstrated, this is not an ideal state of affairs.*
>
> —Nick Szabo, Founder of Bit gold

The global economy of 2006 was thriving as never before. The housing sector in the United States had scaled dizzying heights. The world was on a buying spree. All and sundry were purchasing houses, hoping for a fat profit on a subsequent sale. Banks were happy to lend and cash in on the credit surge. This lending, however, lacked due diligence and loans were handed out like free candy. There was absolutely no verification of the loan repayment capacity of the borrowers. As a result, the real estate market was flourishing with subprime borrowers leading the accelerated property purchase. The year 2007 saw a shift in balance. The real estate supply inched up slowly but steadily as more and more purchasers decided to tap profits by selling property. By mid-2007, the supply far exceeded the demand. Borrowers were caught between the Homeric Scylla and Charybdis. On the one hand, they were faced with loans they could not pay off at adjusted interest rates (read higher interest rates). On the other hand, they had to square off with a property market that was inundated with sellers with nary a purchaser in sight. A tough face off.

Saddled with unpaid loans and mortgaged properties, borrowers began to default in repayment of instalments, resulting in a slew of bank foreclosures. The foreclosed properties were the proverbial albatross around the bankers' necks. They were unable to sell the foreclosed properties and make good on the unpaid loans of subprime borrowers. The inevitable happened. The credit bubble burst and bank credit slowly but surely dried up. Things came to such a pass that banks were unable to meet their day-to-day obligations and liabilities. Almost 100 banks filed for bankruptcy in 2007 alone.

Figure 1.1: The Genesis of the Subprime Crisis

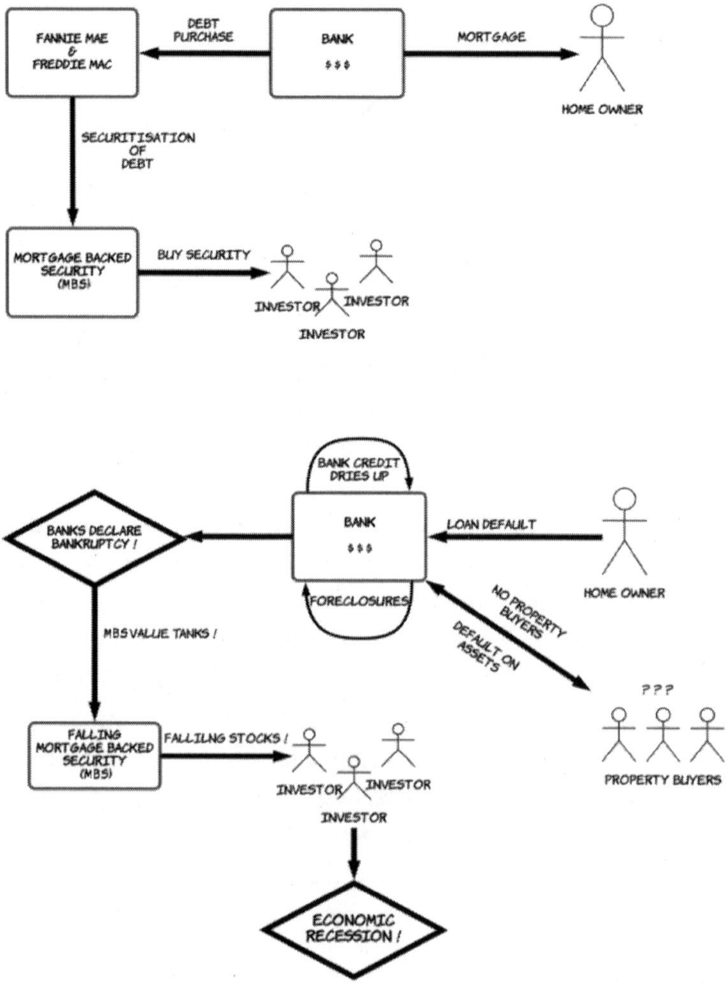

Source: Author

Two major mortgage-backed banks, Bear Stearns and Lehman Brothers, that were listed as the success stories of 2006, found themselves weighed down by a mountain of liabilities they could not discharge. In the first half of 2008, they filed for bankruptcy, sending shock waves to the economy that looked ready to sink into recession. This event became the immediate trigger for the 2008 meltdown of an economy that had been precariously teetering on the brink of collapse for more than two years.

Far-reaching and global consequences ensued. Mortgage-backed securities (MBSs) muddied the global economic waters some more. But first, a word about what MBSs entail. An MBS is a type of asset-backed security that is secured by a mortgage or collection of mortgages. The mortgages are sold to a group of individuals (a government agency or investment bank) that securitises, or packages, the loans together into a security that investors can buy. To put it simply, MBSs were nothing but shares of home loans sold to investors and packaged as government-guaranteed securities. As these were issued by government-authorised agencies like Fannie Mae and Freddie Mac, they were believed to be sovereign guarantees that were a safe bet for the investors. With the subprime loan/ mortgage defaults, the property prices plummeted and it was but natural that MBSs backing such assets would also go into free fall and lose much of their intrinsic value. Which they did, much to the consternation of even the most hardened and wary investors.

The realty slump along with the concomitant fall in value of government-sponsored securities triggered a panic in the equity market resulting in the frenetic sale of equities on a global scale. The stock markets of the world tanked as never before. This started the inevitable domino effect. Consumption fell and unemployment levels rose. And so, the world was caught in the throes of a recession that took almost eight years to shrug off.

There was significant collateral damage that most economists and historians refuse to dwell upon. This not-insignificant damage greatly impacted the thinking processes and economic practices of the subsequent years. The major fatality of the 2008 recession was the childlike trust in financial institutions. Until 2008, the sanctity of banks was never doubted. Banks were revered as the sanctum sanctorum of all economies, the safe that would keep the money of the common hard-working citizen intact and out of harm's way.

Government-backed securities were considered the Holy Grail for investors. These beliefs received a death blow from the events that led to the recession of 2008.

Thinkers and professionals all over the world put on their thinking caps and began to explore ways to make banks and financial transactions through banks safer. This led to a spate of measures that involved stringent checks on borrowers. Bank protocols were tweaked and regulatory frameworks were tightened. The United States saw the implementation of the widely acclaimed 'Dodd-Frank Wall Street Reform and Consumer Protection Act'. This was, as President Barack Obama explained, 'a sweeping overhaul of the US financial regulatory system'. It encompassed within its ambit the consolidation of regulatory agencies, tweaking of consumer protection provisions, comprehensive regulation of financial instruments, tools for financial crisis management and so on. As a consequence of the mania of 2008, it mandated the requirement of approval from the US Treasury before the Federal Reserve could consider extension of credit in 'unusual and exigent conditions'. Proposals were mooted to ensure tightening of regulations and accounting practices of credit-rating agencies.

As we can see, most of the changes suggested were within the existing frameworks and were aimed at plugging the loopholes that had led to the economic meltdown of 2008. However, there were rebels and innovative thinkers who were not satisfied with these minimalist and by-the-book changes. They were looking for a systemic change that did away with third-party intermediaries, like banks, completely. This set the stage for the debut of 'cypherpunks'.

Chapter 2

The Cypherpunk Crypto Cauldron

> *We, the Cypherpunks, are dedicated to building anonymous systems. We are defending our privacy with cryptography, with anonymous mail forwarding systems, with digital signatures and with electronic money.*
>
> —'A Cypherpunk's Manifesto'

Today, in the year 2018, when we toast the meteoric rise of bitcoin and its mainstream acceptability, we must honestly acknowledge that the underlying technology that powers virtual currencies is not of recent origin. It is, in fact, a concept that has evolved as a result of more than four decades of dedicated effort by various individuals and organisations. At the heart of this revolution were the libertarians and privacy proponents who passionately believed in 'privacy' as opposed to 'secrecy'. The tenet that empowered their belief was simple. They believed that 'privacy is the power to selectively reveal oneself to the world'.[1] For these privacy promoters, privacy was not synonymous with secrecy. Privacy was the desire to disclose to the world only what they wanted to reveal and was not a need to hide that which reeked of the nefarious or illegal.

It all started in the 1970s with the US government's publication of the Data Encryption Standard. Quick on the heels of this publication came the publication of 'New Directions in Cryptography'[2] by Dr Whitfield Diffie and Dr Martin Hellman which was the first publicly available work on public key cryptography. Up until now, cryptography was confined to the realm of the defence sector. With these publications, the concept of cryptography was brought into the public realm.

In 1981, came the research paper 'Untraceable Electronic Mail, Return Addresses and Digital Pseudonyms'[3] by Dr David Chaum. This laid the groundwork for the field of anonymous communications research. Chaum's proposal called 'mix networks' allowed a group of senders to submit an encryption of a message and its recipient to a server. On receiving a batch of images, the server reordered and obfuscated the messages so that only the server stored the messagesender link. The batch was then forwarded to another server which followed an identical process. Eventually, the messages would reach the final server where they were fully decrypted and delivered to the recipient. A mechanism to allow return messages was also proposed. Mix networks became the conceptual ancestors to modern anonymous web browsing tools like Tor. At a more primary level, it could be compared to the 'incognito' browsing tool allowed by Google Chrome today.

From anonymous communication Chaum took the inevitable but short step, applying the concept of anonymity to financial transactions. He established and delineated a cryptographic methodology which allowed obtaining digital currency from a bank and spending it in a manner untraceable by the bank or any other party. Sounds impossible? Nope. Dr Chaum's paper entitled 'Security without Identification: Transaction Systems to Make Big Brother Obsolete'[4] discusses the modus operandi of anonymous transactions through a bank. He introduced the concept of a 'blind signature'. Dr Chaum has explained his idea through the use of a 'carbon paper-lined envelopes' analogy. A carbon paper-lined envelope with a slip of paper inside it would ensure that a signature mark made on the outside of the envelope would transfer to the slip inside the envelope. So, would it be possible to make payments using such envelopes without letting Big Brother into the secret? The good doctor thought so.

Let us imagine a scenario where a bank had a special signature mark that it guaranteed to be worth $1, meaning thereby that the bank would pay $1 for any piece of paper with that mark on it.

Harry decides to test how this works. He takes a carbon-lined envelope containing a plain slip of paper to the bank and asks to withdraw $1 from his account. The bank deducts $1 from his account, makes the signature mark on the outside of his envelope and returns it to him. The signature is 'blind' since the bank cannot see the slip through the envelope. Upon getting the unopened envelope back, Harry verifies that the proper signature mark has been made on it. He then removes the slip (with the signature mark) and goes to a grocery shop to purchase a bun worth $1. The shop verifies the carbon image of the bank's signature on the slip and accepts the payment against the purchase of the bun. The bank, on the other hand, verifies the signature on the slip submitted for deposit, just as the shop did and puts $1 in the grocer's account. This gives rise to a rather piquant situation. Since the bank has used an identical signature mark on several envelopes each day for its innumerable account holders, it cannot correlate a specific slip with a specific account-holder. The bank cannot determine which withdrawal corresponds with which deposit. Voila! The payments are now untraceable.

In 1988, Dr Chaum extended this idea (with Amos Fiat and Moni Naor) to allow offline transactions that enable detection of double-spending. In 1990, he founded DigiCash, an electronic cash company, in Amsterdam to commercialise the ideas in his research. DigiCash recorded its first electronic payment in 1994. Here was the use of electronic payment that had all the characteristics of anonymity of the present-day cryptocurrencies, albeit with a somewhat primitive prototype.

Over the next several years, these ideas came together under the banner of what is widely known as the 'cypherpunk movement'. In late 1992, Eric Hughes, Timothy C. May and John Gilmore founded a small group that met monthly at Gilmore's company Cygnus Solutions in the San Francisco Bay Area. The group was jokingly baptised 'cypherpunks', an amalgam of 'cipher' and 'cyberpunk'. On 9 March 1993, they issued what has been christened 'A Cypherpunk's Manifesto'. This manifesto was penned by Eric Hughes and was based on the principle that 'an anonymous system empowers individuals to reveal their identity when desired'[5] and that an 'anonymous transaction system is not a secret transaction system'.[6] Later, this concept of privacy became the sine qua non of the blockchain technology framework—so dear to the bitcoin developer community. The manifesto lays the groundwork for the anonymous transaction rationale and asserts that although technologies of the past did not allow strong privacy, modern-day electronic technologies most certainly do. It makes for an interesting read, which is why I have reproduced an extract from the manifesto:

> We cannot expect governments, corporations, or other large, faceless organisations to grant us privacy out of their beneficence.
>
> We must defend our own privacy if we expect to have any. We must come together and create systems which allow anonymous transactions to take place.

This manifesto became the cornerstone of the present-day blockchain technology-based cryptocurrencies that aimed for transactions that were transparent within the blockchain but otherwise completely anonymous.

In 1997, Dr Adam Back, an active cypherpunk, added his bit to the seething cauldron of protocols that advocated complete privacy of financial transactions. He proposed the concept of 'Hashcash'. This did not need the creation of an account and also was more resistant to 'double-spending' than the concept and protocol involved in Chaum's DigiCash. Hashcash is a cryptographic function that behaves like a magic box that scrambles anything that goes into it. So, if I put 'Rachy' into the Hashcash magic box called SHA-256 (hash function), it would come out looking like this:

```
A1A75458CE0DA2D9080581265 72A3C0D69A3C00C0C2345A
5E80973C7A8C336F1
```

SHA-1 (another hash function) would spew out an alphanumeric string looking like this one:

```
450D93240EF1992E095C61F0A5273449B9176F93
```

Try it on for size. If you don't believe me, just click on the Hash256 Generator or SHA-1 generator site and you have your very own magic box. To move back from this alphanumeric string to 'Rachy' would be near impossible, especially with the longer and therefore more secure SHA-256. Such a string makes a loud statement of anonymity which is why it became an indispensable part of the blockchain technology underlying bitcoins and other cryptocurrencies. The magic box flowchart has been embellished and clarified by Satoshi Nakamoto in his white paper.

Figure 2.1: Satoshi's Transaction Diagram

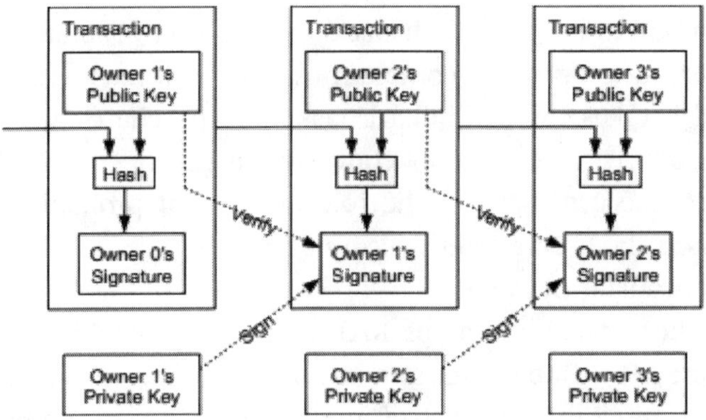

Source: https://bitcoin.org/bitcoin.pdf

In 1998, Wei Dai, another privacy adherent, published a proposal for 'b-money'[7], a practical way to enforce contractual agreements between anonymous actors. B-money propounded a protocol in which every participant maintains a separate database of the quantum of money belonging to a user. Wei Dai also established a variant of the first system where the accounts of money users are kept by a subset of the participants who are incentivised to remain honest by putting their money on the line (proof-of-stake). He described the first protocol as 'impractical'.

However, it was this first protocol that transmuted into the 'proof-of-work' concept that is used in the contemporary cryptocurrency protocol. If we look at the original proposal of Wei Dai, we would be able to zero-in on the similarities. Wei Dai's proposal details four major steps involved in the process. This protocol, in fact, became the precursor of the present-day protocol of bitcoins. It also laid the framework for the smart-contract protocol programmed into the current-day Ethereum blockchain. Let us take a look at the threads of the original protocol:

1. The creation of money

   Anyone can create money by broadcasting the solution to a hitherto unsolved computational problem. The only prerequisite is that it should be possible to ascertain the computing effort needed to arrive at the said solution and the solution should be denuded of any practical or intellectual value. The number of monetary units created would then be equal to the cost of the computing effort in terms of a standard basket of commodities. Wei Dai explains this with an example. So, if a problem takes 100 hours to solve on the computer that solves it most economically and it takes three standard baskets to purchase 100 hours of computing time on that computer in the open market, then upon the broadcast of the solution to that problem everyone credits the broadcaster's account by three units.

2. The transfer of money

   If Alice (pseudonym of KA) wishes to transfer X units of money to Bob (pseudonym of KB), she broadcasts the message, 'I give X units of money to KB'. Upon the broadcast of this message, everyone debits KA's account by X units and credits KB's account by X units, unless this would create a negative balance in KA's account, in which case the message is ignored.

3. The effecting of contracts

   A valid contract must include a maximum reparation in case of default for each participant party to it. It should also include a party who will perform arbitration should there be a dispute. All parties to a contract including the arbitrator must broadcast their signatures of it before it becomes effective. Upon the broadcast of the contract and all signatures, every participant debits the account of each party by the amount of his maximum reparation and credits a special account identified by a secure hash of the contract by the sum the maximum reparations. The contract becomes effective if the debits succeed for every party without producing a negative balance, otherwise the contract is ignored and the accounts are rolled back.

A sample contract might look like this:

KA agrees to send KB the solution to problem P before 0:0:0 1/1/2000.

KB agrees to pay KA 100 MU (monetary units) before 0:0:0 1/1/2000. KC agrees to perform arbitration in case of dispute. KA agrees to pay a maximum of 1,000 MU in case of default. KB agrees to pay a maximum of 200 MU in case of default. KC agrees to pay a maximum of 500 MU in case of default.

4. The conclusion of contracts

   If a contract concludes without dispute, each party broadcasts a signed message, 'The contract with SHA-1 hash H concludes without reparations' or possibly, 'The contract with SHA-1 hash H concludes with the following reparations…' Upon the broadcast of all signatures, every participant credits the account of each party by the amount of his maximum reparations, removes the contract account, then credits or debits the account of each party according to the reparation schedule if there is one.

5. The enforcement of contracts

   If the parties to a contract cannot agree on an appropriate conclusion even with the help of the arbitrator, each party broadcasts a suggested reparation/fine schedule and any arguments or evidence in his favour. Each participant makes a determination as to the actual reparations and/or fines and modifies his accounts accordingly.

This protocol, however, remained unused as the proposal came with the rider that it was 'impractical'. It was only later that Satoshi Nakamoto picked up this protocol and melded it into the structural framework of his paper and the rest is history. The contracts were not a part of the bitcoin protocol but were adopted for the Ethereum blockchain.

Some years later, in 2004 to be exact, Hal Finney created what is called reusable proof-of-work (RPOW) which was based on Back's Hashcash. The RPOWs were something like unused cryptographic tokens and are similar to the unspent transaction outputs in bitcoins. The drawback of using a central server for protection against double-spending, remained in this system. Nick Szabo, in 2005, took it upon himself to build on Finney's RPOW proposal. His concept of 'bit gold' was strongly based on the proof-of-work concept. So, what did he mean by proof-of-work? Let us take a look at his own proposal in this regard:

> My proposal for bit gold is based on computing a string of bits from a string of challenge bits, using functions called variously 'client puzzle function', 'proof-of-work function', or 'secure benchmark function'. The resulting string of bits is the proof-of-work.[8]

Nick Szabo envisioned the following steps in his bit gold protocol:

1. A public string of bits, the 'challenge string', is created.
2. A user, say Harry, generates the proof-of-work string from the challenge bits using a benchmark function.
3. The proof-of-work is securely timestamped.
4. Harry adds the challenge string and timestamped proof-of-work to a distributed property title registry for bit gold. This string also creates the challenge string for the next-created string.
5. To verify that Harry is the owner of a particular string of bit gold, Rachy checks the unforgeable chain of title in the bit gold title registry.
6. To assay the value of a string of bit gold, Rachy checks and verifies the challenge bits, the proof-of-work string and the timestamp.

Szabo was strongly aware of bit gold glitches and he mentions them clearly in his treatise, but he also strongly believed that bit gold would be a firewall against insecurities that mar financial transactions such as counterfeiting and theft. He believed that:

> In summary, all money mankind has ever used has been insecure in one way or another. This insecurity has been manifested in a wide variety of ways, from counterfeiting to theft...bit gold may provide us with a money of unprecedented security from these dangers.[9]

Bit gold did not make much of a dent in cyberspace or in the financial transactions realm but it made the debut of bitcoin a possibility.

Figure 2.2: The Cypherpunks

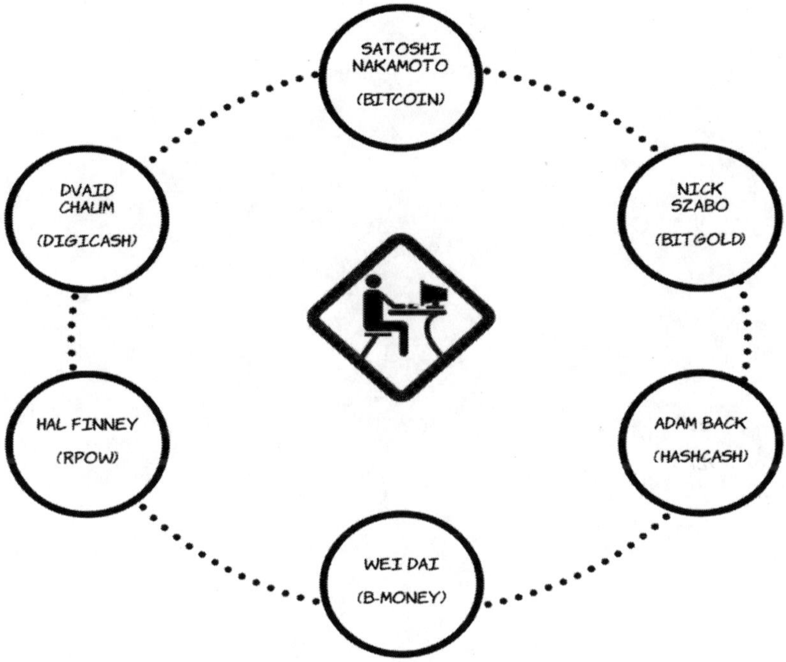

Source: Author

The protocol and tenets enunciated by the cypherpunks finally coalesced into the 'peer-to-peer' white paper published by the phantom of the bitcoin opera, Satoshi Nakamoto. Satoshi's paper is structured around Adam Back's Hashcash function and the first protocol enunciated by Wei Dai in the b-money proposal. The paper also adopted the proof-of-work function proposed by Finney and enlarged by Nick Szabo. Satoshi's paper and identity analysis deserves a larger stage so let's wait with breathless anticipation for the debut of the master wizard. We'll talk about the intricacies of Nakamoto's paper in the chapter 'Phantom of the Bitcoin Opera'.

SECTION II

THE TECH TALES

Chapter 3

The Ps and Qs of Bitcoins

> *What is needed is an electronic payment system based on cryptographic proof instead of trust, allowing any two willing parties to transact directly with each other without the need for a trusted third party.*
>
> —Satoshi Nakamoto, Founder of Bitcoin

You must be wondering at my unseemly jump from a treatise on cypherpunks to modern-day crypto jargon... from 2004 to 2018 in one fell swoop. Let me assuage your concerns. Before we step into the somewhat complicated realm of Satoshi Nakamoto's white paper, it would be appropriate to pause and understand how the bitcoin protocol works in the contemporary scenario. This would not only help connect the dots but also enlarge the scope of our understanding of cryptocurrencies and the way the distributed ledger works in the blockchain. This self-governing and self-regulating technology can be best understood using a bank analogy that we are all familiar with.

Banks have a transaction ledger which records all transactions. Banks also have individual ledger accounts of clients that record transactions specific to the clients or account holders. Like banks, the bitcoin blockchain maintains a digital public ledger that records every bitcoin transaction and updates the ledger every time a new transaction occurs. A copy of this ledger is also distributed on a network of computers (nodes) of all the participants of the network. All transactions are verified through a process of consensus by all the nodes. Once such transactions are approved by all nodes, the public distributed ledger is updated i.e. the verified transaction is then reflected in the public ledger. So, what are the Ps and Qs of such a consensus-based transaction?

Here again, the bank analogy that we are familiar with can be used to explain this process. If we want to use a bitcoin to make a transaction, we first need to have a bitcoin wallet which is nothing but an application or a programme that connects us with the bitcoin digital ledger. It is similar to setting up a bank account. Sort of. For those who are computer savvy, setting up their own private wallet would be a lark. This would have the added advantage of not needing to go through the stringent 'know your customer' (KYC) parameters that have to be followed by all wallet providers. For those who are not well-versed in computer dynamics or are too lazy to make the effort to set up their own wallet, we have a host of altcoin wallet providers to choose from. But here is the downside: if we set up this account through a service provider, it would mean handing out of personal details under the aegis of a KYC protocol. Here, the anonymity that is crucial to the bitcoin technology is lost completely. While we are on the subject of bitcoin wallets, a little snippet of information that will not go amiss is the nature of the wallet.

A bitcoin wallet may be a 'hot' wallet or a 'cold' wallet. A hot wallet is an online wallet. Hot wallets are suspect as they are more vulnerable to a network-based theft as the private key of the bitcoin owner is stored online and can be accessed by a smart hacker. Coincheck, a Japanese cryptocurrency exchange dealing in NEMs (a cryptocurrency), lost $534 million worth of NEMs stored in a hot wallet in January 2018.[1] Similarly, NiceHash—a Slovenian website that allows users to purchase and sell time for mining cryptocurrency—was robbed of $77 million in December 2017.[2] So, it would be safer to use a 'cold' wallet that is stored offline. That, of course, is no guarantee that it is theft resistant.

Coinsecure, an Indian bitcoin exchange found to its disquiet that bitcoins worth ₹20 crore stored in a cold wallet were siphoned off by an insider who leaked its private key to a hacker. Does that mean 'paper wallets' are a better idea? Paper wallets are documents that store the code to generate the private key to access a cryptocurrency wallet. A document stored on an online PC is again not secure as it may be subject to a malware attack. Jotting the private key on a piece of paper might mean that it gets lost or gets into the wrong hands. Maybe you could stash the private key in a safe. Grim humour aside, cold wallets are probably the safest. We can just send up a prayer that a disgruntled insider does not trade it for personal benefit.

I have been talking on and on about private keys. You must be wondering how the private key works. Bitcoin wallets keep a secret piece of data called a private key or 'seed', which is used to sign transactions, providing a mathematical proof that they have come from the owner of the wallet. This key is a part of an asymmetric key encryption scheme, where anyone with a public key can encrypt a message but the decryption of the information is possible only through a private key. Let me elaborate. Asymmetric cryptography, also known as public key cryptography, uses public and private keys to encrypt and decrypt data. One key in the pair can be shared with everyone; it is called the public key. The other key in the pair is kept secret; it is called the private key.

Now that we have our crypto-jargon ducks in a row, let us see how the actual transaction on the blockchain looks like. If Harry wants to pay Rachy bitcoins (I hope Alice and Bob will forgive my temerity in replacing their names with impunity), he will make a public announcement of the proposed transaction on the blockchain. This entails recording the transaction (wherein a bitcoin is removed from Harry's wallet and the corresponding bitcoin is added to Rachy's wallet) in a public ledger that is visible to all participants of the network. For this update to be recorded, every network node or participant computer examines the transaction to ensure it is legitimate.

Figure 3.1: Bitcoin Made Easy

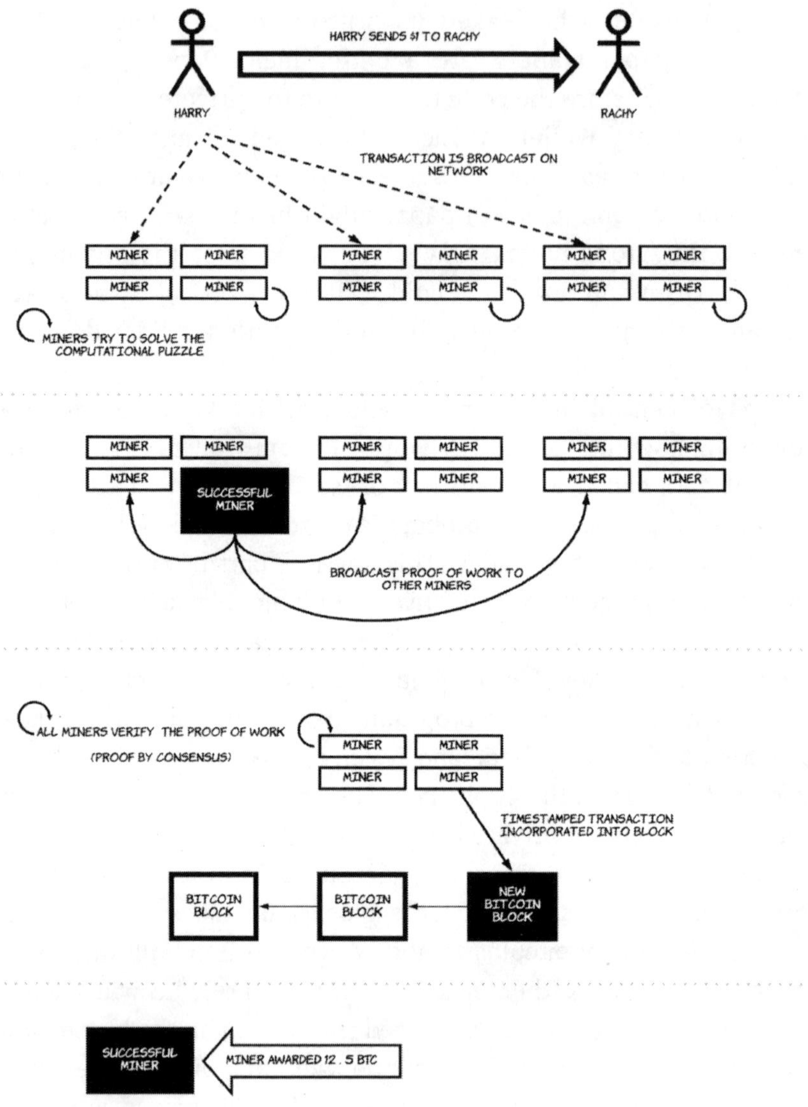

Source: Author

This involves ascertaining that the requisite bitcoin is actually owned and available for use by Harry. It also ensures that Harry is not attempting to defraud Rachy by double-spending the bitcoin.

In order for the new transaction to be approved by the network of participating computers, the nodes try to solve a computational puzzle or algorithm known as 'proof-of-work'. This is nothing but a decryption of the encrypted transaction between Harry and Rachy. Nodes that try to solve this algorithm are called 'miners'. As soon as the algorithm is solved, the miner sends it to the rest of the network for verification. Once the solution is verified by the entire network through a process of consensus, it is added to the blockchain. Just so you know, a block is made up of several verified transactions that total 1 MB in size. Unfortunately, the transaction-processing capacity of a bitcoin blockchain is just seven transactions per second. This transaction-processing capacity is further limited by the block creation time of 10 minutes. Ethereum claims that it can handle about 15 transactions per second. But considering that Visa handles as many as 1,500 transactions per second, the blockchain has still a long way to go as far as scalability is concerned. For blockchain technology to become viable on a large scale, this block size needs to be increased several times over. There is plenty of bickering on this issue in the blockchain fraternity but we will discuss that at length in subsequent chapters.

Each individual transaction is nothing but a string of characters having certain cryptographic values that are produced by applying a function, propounded by Adam Back, called 'Hashcash' (remember, we discussed the 'magic box' analogy to explain the Hashcash function in the chapter on cypherpunks).

These individual values of various transactions are combined in a sequence called a Merkle tree. Before you look askance at this new term, let me explain. The Merkle tree is nothing but an upside-down tree where each node represents values of individual transactions. The individual values represented go through a further 'hash' function forming one 'hash' value also called 'root' for all the set of transactions that form a new block. So, the new block is a combination of the new hash value, the hash value of the previous block, a timestamp and a solution often called 'nonce'. Since the new block is approved by the entire network, it is accepted as a part of the chain. The digital ledger is, in fact, a chain of approved blocks. Simple.

Now that we are able to make sense of the blockchain technology underlying bitcoins, let me introduce you to the three main protagonists in the bitcoin saga—the miners, the developers and the users. The developers write the code which is essentially a framework of rules within which the blockchain functions. They are like advisors or consultants that give you a solution to a problem. In the case of bitcoins, the developers write the code that allows transactions on the blockchain. The sequential hashing protocol and proof-of-work that the developers have incorporated in the blockchain protocol makes it secure and nigh impossible to hack or reverse. The miners are tasked with finding a random value called 'nonce' that fits the designed bitcoin protocol. Once a miner finds the nonce that satisfies the protocol, it sends the solution to the network for validation, upon which the block is added to the chain. The nonce is found through trial and error and requires tremendous computing power. For example, if the rule in the protocol is that the output hash must begin with 10 zeros, it would take 10^{12} trials, before finding a nonce satisfying the rule. In fact, solving for the nonce requires so much computing power, the miners actually compete with each other to solve it and the winning miner is incentivised. When bitcoin was first introduced, the miner solving the 'proof-of-work' was awarded 50 bitcoins. Today, the miner is awarded 12.5 bitcoins for every solution. Users are the most important actors in this saga as the user community establishes the credibility and acceptance of the blockchain. If users do not accept the integrity of a chain and transact on it, the chain will decline into oblivion in no time. The acceptability of the blockchain depends on what user needs it fulfils. For some user groups it may be a means of making investments, for others it may be a means of making transactions like that seen in PayPal or Paytm. The blockchain technology that powers bitcoins fulfils both these needs which accounts for its current popularity.

Figure 3.2: Bitcoin Trinity

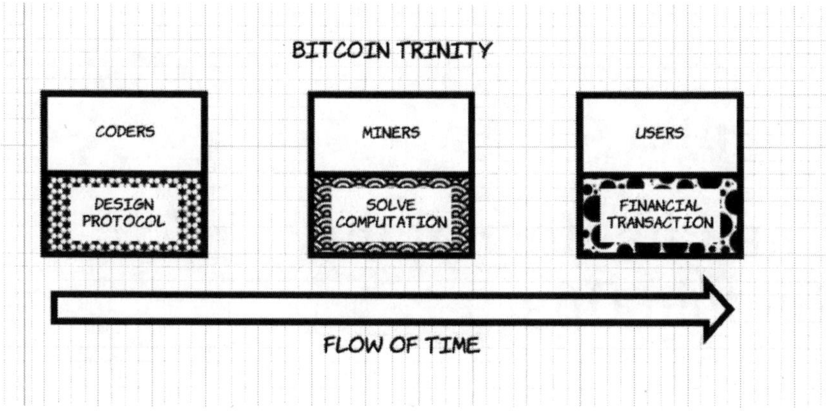

Source: Author

The blockchain technology underlying Ethereum has added the concept of a smart contract to the blockchain and may appeal to those who are conducting business transactions of huge volumes. This may include sale or purchase of commodities at a global level. Whatever the variations instituted in the code by the developers, the implementation has to be made by miners and eventually adopted by users. This trinity of stakeholders has to work in tandem for the blockchain to be successful. The man who made the impossible look like child's play was the mysterious Satoshi Nakamoto. There is, however, nothing secretive about the bitcoin protocol propounded by the bitcoin wizard. His white paper 'Bitcoin: A Peer-to-Peer Electronic Cash System' has become the Bible for the bitcoin community.

Chapter 4

The Phantom of the Bitcoin Opera

We have proposed a system for electronic transactions without relying on trust...We proposed a peer-to-peer network using proof-of-work to record a public history of transactions that quickly becomes computationally inpractical for an attacker to change... The network is robust in its unstructured simplicity.

—Satoshi Nakamoto, Founder of Bitcoin

The identity of the bitcoin founder, Satoshi Nakamoto, is shrouded in mystery and intrigue. There are several interesting stories on the internet as well as in the media archives of this 44th richest man of the world with a bitcoin ownership of roughly one million bitcoins valued at $19 billion as on 17 December 2017.[1] It was initially believed that he was a Japanese cryptographer but this theory was discarded as his paper on bitcoins and his various emails and posts were worded in perfect English. The use of the exclamation 'bloody difficult' had researchers dubbing him as a man of Commonwealth origin. As Satoshi's paper on bitcoins had some tenets of Wei Dai's b-money proposal, it was speculated for a while that he was Wei Dai. As Satoshi also used Nick Szabo's proof-of-work concept (although surprisingly no specific reference is made to Szabo in the bitcoin paper), for a while it was believed that he was none other than Szabo. This was, however, denied forcefully by Szabo who referred to the emails he had received from the incognito stalwart himself.

What made things difficult for all those sniffing out Satoshi's identity, was that the trail went cold when the great man handed over the reins of bitcoin development to others of the bitcoin developer fraternity in 2010. They have attempted to examine the timestamp on his posts and speculated that Nakamoto was located in North or South America. Many have attempted to make sense of Satoshi's internet presence between 2008 and 2010 hoping it would give them some clues about his identity. There have been instances where bloggers have claimed that his identity has been ascertained based on an analysis of his handwriting (through stylometry) by the NSA. Recently, attempts have also been made to identify this coder as Elon Musk of SpaceX fame but Musk has vigorously denied this conjecture as being completely baseless. Although several theories are floating around, no credence can be given to any hypothesis that comes without evidence or substantiation.

Be that as it may, away from the intrigue and thrill that a search for such an identity may generate, let us look at the contribution of this brilliant coder and out-of-the-box thinker. In October 2008, Nakamoto published a white paper entitled 'Bitcoin: A Peer-to-Peer Electronic Cash System' laying down the foundation of bitcoin currency of today. On 9 January 2009, he released the first bitcoin software that launched the network and the first cache of the cryptocurrency, aptly named bitcoin. He then created a website with the domain name bitcoin.org and continued his collaboration with other bitcoin developers until mid-2010. Thereafter, he handed over the control of the 'source code repository' and network key to Gavin Andersen. He also transferred bitcoin related 'domains' to other prominent members of the bitcoin developer community and withdrew from any direct or indirect involvement in the bitcoin ecosystem. It is believed that before handing over the reins of his pet project, Nakamoto made changes to the source code himself. It is also believed that he mined the first block on 3 January 2009. The genesis of the block is timestamped at 18.15.05 GMT on this date. This genesis block was mined with the code written and implemented by Satoshi. As a sole miner of the genesis block, he was awarded with bitcoins at the genesis and for 10 days afterwards.

Such titbits may make for interesting reading but what is more important is the technology that Satoshi engineered and implemented that made peer-to-peer anonymous transactions possible. Let us start by looking at what Satoshi has to say in his white paper on bitcoin appropriately entitled 'Bitcoin: A Peer-to-Peer Electronic Cash System'.[2] Even today it is considered recommended reading for anyone trying to make sense of how bitcoins work.

It is a technical paper which is deceptively simple and may not appeal to a non-technical reader. And yet, it is necessary to understand the basic principles of this paper in order to get a handle on the genesis of this cryptocurrency. So, I'll slowly go through the bitcoin technology protocol envisaged by the founder with a generous sprinkling of 'Satoshispeak'. Before we get into the nitty-gritty of the process of mining and transacting of bitcoins, we need to ascertain the necessity of anonymous electronic transactions. The subprime crisis of 2008 shook the foundations of trust in third-party institutions like banks. The rationale for implementing a peer-to-peer cash system is best delineated by Satoshi in the introduction to his paper wherein he rues the fact that no mechanism exists to make payments over a communications channel without a trusted party and that a certain percentage of fraud is acceptable in the current financial ecosystem. He envisaged an electronic payment system based on cryptographic proof instead of trust, allowing any two willing parties to transact directly with each other without the need for a trusted third party. Satoshi's white paper proposes a solution to the double-spending problem using a peer-to-peer distributed timestamp server to generate computational proof of the chronological order of transactions. The whiz-kid believed that this system would stay secure as long as honest nodes collectively controlled more CPU power than any cooperating group of attacker nodes.

So, here is a proposal that seeks to do away with third party trust which is essential to all modes of existing financial transactions. Let us take a quick look at how current-day financial transactions are implemented. All cheque transactions are verified and recorded by the intermediary bank in a common ledger alongside the accounts of the transacting parties. Things are not any different in the stock market space. The purchase and sale of securities happens through a stock exchange within a purchase/sale protocol framework that involves a trusted intermediary. The investors and traders submit orders to buy and sell stock shares, either through a broker or by using an online order-entry interface. The buyer bids to buy shares at a particular price while the seller bids to sell it at a specified price. When the two prices match, a transaction occurs and both orders are filled. A clearing house works as an intermediary and settles trades and ensures delivery. In this system, intermediaries have the tacit trust of the transacting parties who in essence were putting their hard-earned money in the hands of these 'middlemen'. The subprime crisis of 2008, however, saw a major third-party trust crisis. With major global banks going insolvent, the banking system and other such financial intermediaries lost the blind trust of the common man who lost money on account of the credit caprice of such intermediaries. This subprime crisis led several astute thinkers to consider an electronic payment system that bypasses the necessity for a trusted third party. The result was Nakamoto's peer-to-peer electronic cash system.

Satoshi's paper describes virtual currency as an electronic coin. This electronic coin is nothing but a chain of digital signatures. The transfer is defined in somewhat technical terms:

> Each owner transfers the coin to the next by digitally signing a hash of the previous transaction and the public key of the next owner and adding them to the end of the coin. A payee can verify the signatures to verify the chain of ownership.

This explanation would be easy for computer-science engineers or cryptographers to absorb but for the ordinary mortal it would be a bit of mouthful. But where there is a will, there's always a way, as I found out. A research of the terminology used made things a lot clearer. To understand the crux of Satoshi's argument we need to understand the function of 'hash', or in the bitcoin context, 'Hashcash'. I have already explained the bare bones of the 'hash' function in the previous chapter. Remember the 'magic box'? Now for the technical sting in the tail. The 'hash' function was originally proposed by Adam Back in 1997 as a protection against email spammers and 'denial of service attacks'.

Hashcash is a relatively simple algorithm. It is considered secure as it is hard to invert or reverse. To put it simply, you can compute y from x using $y=H(x)$ but it is hard to find x given only y. This can be done only through 'brute force' running time which means it can be done only through 'put and check' method which is tantamount to putting in an infinite number of variables till one magic number yields the desired and correct solution. The optimal time for such a solution is 10 minutes. If the time taken is less, the code automatically increases the difficulty level so that the solution is generated within the 10-minute timeslot. Similarly, if the time taken for this process is more, the difficulty level is tweaked to achieve the optimal time level. There are various kinds of 'Secured Hash Algorithms' or SHAs but the one that is being used in bitcoins is called SHA-256. This is a more secure two-hash iteration which was used extensively after the Mt Gox bitcoin heist. So, the transfer of an electronic coin would involve signing the previous as well as subsequent transaction with a hash which would then be verified by the payee.

The problem that Satoshi envisaged in such a transaction was the possibility of a 'double-spend'. This in essence means that the same electronic coin may be fraudulently used to pay for two different services or to two different payees. In the real world, the security against such a double-spend was a trusted third party. How would such an electronic transaction be possible without a trusted intermediary? Satoshi came upon a brilliant way to circumvent this problem. Publicly announcing transactions would be the ideal way to discourage all attempts to double-spend. The methodology or the protocol is explained by Satoshi who writes:

> To accomplish this without a trusted party, transactions must be publicly announced and we need a system for participants to agree on a single history of the order in which they were received. The payee needs proof that at the time of each transaction, the majority of nodes agreed it was the first received.

The tricky part would be, of course, for the participants to agree on the history and chronology in which transactions are received. To circumvent this problem, Satoshi proffered a solution based on the concept of a timestamp server. This works by taking a hash of a block of items to be timestamped and widely publishing it. The timestamp is evidence of existence of data at that specific point of time. Each timestamp also includes the previous timestamp in its hash. Thus, this data forms a chain with each additional timestamp reinforcing the ones before.

A public announcement of each transaction makes the transaction foolproof against double-spending. The timestamp on every transaction records the cyber time of the transaction so that only the first correct transaction will be accepted after due verification. To implement the timestamp server on a peer-to-peer basis, Satoshi adopted the proof-of-work concept propounded by Markus Jakobsson and Ari Jules. It was later used by Nick Szabo in his bit gold protocol. Let us make some sense of the proof-of-work concept. A proof-of-work is a piece of data that is difficult to generate but easy to verify. Generating a proof-of-work is a random process which involves a lot of trial and error.

Hashcash proofs-of-work are used in bitcoin for block generation. Miners have to complete a proof-of-work pertaining to data in a block before the block can be accepted by network participants (also called nodes). As I have already mentioned, the difficulty of the work is adjusted so as to limit the rate at which the new blocks are generated by the network to one every 10 minutes. Each block indicates that work has been done generating it. Each block also contains the hash of the preceding block and creates a chain that contains a large amount of work of the various participants or miners who have generated the blocks. Changing a block (which can only be done by making a new block containing the same predecessor) requires regenerating all successors and redoing the work they contain. This protects the blockchain from tampering. As I have said in the preceding paragraphs, the most widely used proof-of-work scheme is based on SHA-256. Some other hashing algorithms that are used for proof-of-work include SHA-1, scrypt, BLAKE-256, CryptoNight, Quark, SHA-3, scrypt-n and combinations thereof.

The network protocol has been explained at length by Satoshi in his paper where he delineates six necessary steps in the blockchain as follows:

1. New transactions are broadcast to all nodes.
2. Each node collects new transactions into a block.
3. Each node works on finding a difficult proof-of-work for its block.
4. When a node finds a proof-of-work, it broadcasts the block to all nodes.
5. Nodes accept the block only if all transactions in it are valid and not already spent.
6. Nodes express their acceptance of the block by working on creating the next block in the chain, using the hash of the accepted block as the previous hash.

Once these steps are complete, the miner whose block has been accepted after due verification is then awarded for his work with a new coin. The award of this incentive is similar to miner coming across a nugget of gold. The steady addition of a constant amount of new coins is analogous to gold miners expending resources to add gold to circulation, which is why those generating coins are also called miners. This incentive may also be in the form of transaction fees. So, if the output value of transaction is less than the input value, the difference is a transaction fee that is added to the incentive value of the block containing the transaction. Satoshi, in his wisdom, decided that once a predetermined number of coins have entered circulation, the incentive can transition entirely to transaction fees and be completely inflation free.

Satoshi also believed that such an incentive system would also incentivise the nodes or participants of the network to remain honest as the benefits accruing to the participants were more than incentives arising from turning rogue. Here was an intriguing situation where if a greedy attacker is able to assemble more CPU power than all honest nodes, he would have to choose between using it to defraud people backing his payments or using it to generate new coins. Any financially savvy individual would prefer to follow the rules and opt for a situation where he is rewarded with more new coins.

This protocol taps into a human psyche that would prefer accretion of wealth to undermining the system and validity of his own wealth.

Satoshi further innovated by establishing a protocol for saving disc space being used by spent coins. He proposed the use of the Merkle tree. He suggested that only the root pertaining to a spent coin transaction be included in the blockchain. You are familiar with the term as we have discussed it at length in a previous chapter. So how does this work? To put it simplistically, the Merkle tree saves data. Let me explain this with a simple example. Say we need to store four transactions: W, X, Y and Z. These transactions will not be saved in the tree. Instead, hashes of these transactions will be stored as nodes of the binary tree. As we go up in the Merkle tree, the next step would be a concatenation of consecutive nodes. Concatenation is a simple process where character strings are connected end to end, such that concatenation of words 'end' and 'game' would be 'endgame'. The concatenation of consecutive nodes or hashes may be represented as HWX and HWY. This concatenation continues till only one node is left which is called the Merkle root. This root is a summary of the four transactions of the Merkle tree. This node is a part of the blockchain and is like a digital fingerprint (or footprint) of all the transactions in the Merkle tree. Instead of including thousands of transactions in a Merkle tree, the data block or the chain of data will include only the Merkle root of these transactions. This not only records all transactions but also saves disc space. This concept was first propounded and patented by Ralph Merkle in 1979 and was thereafter incorporated in Satoshi's paper that we are discussing. This concept also makes verification of a transaction easier as it allows the user to obtain the Merkle branch linking the transaction to the block it is timestamped in.

Satoshi established a protocol that makes financial transactions completely intrusion proof or identity resistant. The traditional banking system achieves a modicum of privacy by limiting access of information to parties involved and the trusted third party. The peer-to-peer protocol disrupts the third-party model. It announces all transactions publicly but maintains privacy by keeping the actual identity of persons transacting, anonymous. So, the public can see that a transaction is happening between two parties but information linking the transaction with an actual identity is not available. This is similar to the level of information released by stock exchanges, where the time and size of individual trades, is made public, but without divulging who the parties were. As an additional firewall, he talks about the use of a new key pair for every transaction, involving the same owner, so as to ensure that they are not linked to a common owner. Some linking, he admits, would still be unavoidable with multi-input transactions, which necessarily reveal that their inputs were owned by the same owner. The risk is that if the owner of a key is revealed, linking could reveal other transactions that belonged to the same owner.

Nakamoto, thus proposed a system for electronic transactions that was not dependent on a trusted third party. He created a framework of coins made from digital signatures which provides a process of ownership as also a method to prevent double-spending. This was done within a peer-to-peer network using proof-of-work to record a public history of transactions that becomes 'computationally impractical for an attacker to change'. The best thing is the simplicity of the structure of the framework which allows new rules and incentives to be imposed by a consensus mechanism. This framework has been the basis of the bitcoin system of transactions and has been working well for almost a decade. Some changes in the protocol have been made over the years to take care of any glitches that have happened. But for the most part, this system is robust and is still working well.

SECTION III

THE RANT AND THE RAVE

Chapter 5

The Hobgoblins: Cons and the Deep Web

> *We find that approximately one-quarter of bitcoin users and one-half of bitcoin transactions are associated with illegal activity... Our findings suggest that cryptocurrencies are transforming the way black markets operate by enabling 'black e-commerce'.*
>
> —Sex, Drugs and Bitcoins*

The bitcoin naysayers have cobbled together a strong, if mixed, lobby. It includes bloggers whose off-the-cuff remarks do not add a rational observation to the bitcoin discourse but are merely aimed at garnering attention of netizens. A three-year-old post on Reddit under the pseudonym Eazyg2002 said, 'bitcoins...a phoney baloney internet currency, that a lot of nerds are into...to buy drugs'[1] without explaining the reasons for the diatribe. Such anonymous quotes may be shrugged off but there are others whose voices are heeded because they are experts in their fields. It seems that Richard Thaler, the Nobel Prize-winning behavioural economist does not hold 'bitcoins and its sisters'[2] in very high regard either. If truth be told, he is not

* 'Sex, Drugs and Bitcoins: How Much Illegal Activity is Financed Through Cryptocurrencies'. A Paper by Sean Foley, University of Sydney Business School, Jonathan R. Karlsen, Talis J. Putnins, University of Technology, Sydney. 15 January 2018.

the only Nobel Prize-winning economist who has reservations about the newbie cryptocurrencies. Joseph Stiglitz, who won the Nobel Prize in 2001, apparently does not consider cryptocurrencies as having any useful function and is in favour of regulating them out of existence.[3] Robert Shiller, who won the Nobel Prize for his work in 'Trendspotting in Asset Markets' considers these digital currencies heading for an emphatic downslide. Some other sane voices in the global markets also have an axe to grind with bitcoins. JP Morgan Chase CEO, Jamie Dimon, openly decried bitcoins, calling them a 'fraud'.[4] In the initial years, Jordan Belfort, the Wolf of Wall Street, described bitcoins as a 'Ponzi scheme'. That both Dimon and Belfort ate crow later does not completely negate their bitcoin-belittling pronouncements.

So, what has outraged the economic community as well as the man on the street resulting in a bitcoin rant? Let us take a look. There are undoubtedly several inherent disadvantages in the use of these cryptocurrencies. The extreme volatility of this currency would make any self-preserving investor green around the gills. In July 2011, it was valued at $31 (fell to $2 in Dec 2011). It then clipped its merry way to $7,000 in November 2017. Thereafter, the world saw its meteoric rise to almost $20,000 in December 2017 and then a slow and steady slump to $7,000 in January 2018. Some market watchers have demurred and insist that this rise in the value of bitcoins in December and fall in January[5] is not indicative of an irrational volatility but is in fact a pattern or a 'trend' that has been repeating itself over the last three years. However, the fact remains that if bitcoins had a volatility index, it would more often than not hit the glass ceiling. This, in part, is on account of the limited number of bitcoins available in the market as well as the cap of 21 million bitcoins until 2140.

The bitcoin worrywarts also believe that if a major chunk of bitcoins fall into the hands of speculators, there may be a deflationary trend that would adversely impact the value of the bitcoins. Also, there would be spending surges and declines with increase and decrease in the value of the bitcoins. The unpalatable fact is that the current price of bitcoins is not wholly demand driven. Although the demand of bitcoins did see a spike in December 2017, when the

CBOE futures exchange announced it was open for bitcoin trading, the more perceptive bitcoin observers believe that there is rampant manipulation in the bitcoin trading ecosystem. The absence of airtight regulations undoubtedly makes it easy for rogue elements to strong-arm the bitcoin market into submission. Mathew Unger, CEO and founder of iComplyICO makes a very pertinent observation in this regard when he says:

> Now, some institutional major players are flooding the network with new cash and creating what appears to be market manipulation. Now that bitcoin futures are available, it is easy to buy into futures market first and then create a massive number of buys or sells of bitcoin to ensure the price swings in favour of your futures contract.[6]

There is more than a grain of truth in such fears. The bitcoin market today is sitting atop a tinderbox ready to self-ignite. So, caveat emptor 'let the buyer beware' would set the right note as far as bitcoins are concerned.

Another disadvantage that the buyers and bitcoin investors need to be wary of is the fact that the blockchain technology underlying bitcoins does not allow for reversal of transactions. Although this is touted as an inbuilt security protocol, there is a downside to this reversal resistant function. If the bitcoins are transferred to scamsters or some rogue nodes in the network, the currency is lost forever. Also, there is no centralised redressal forum and no remedial action clause for a heist or a fraud within the network. Moreover, the possibility of a security breach cannot be ignored. The story of the Mt Gox heist is a case in point. It caused irreversible damage to credibility of bitcoin.

The Mt Gox saga reads like a cryptograph version of a James Bond thriller. The only difference being that the heist happened in the real world with large-scale financial fallout. It would be a good case study to ascertain the 'dos and don'ts' for cryptocurrency exchanges. Mt Gox, a Tokyo-based bitcoin exchange, was originally established by a US programmer Jed McCaleb in 2010. In March 2011, Mark Karpelès, a French developer and a bitcoin proponent, purchased this exchange. June 2011 saw the first Mt Gox hack. There are several theories floating around about the cause of the hack. Some believe the hack was the result of a 'compromised computer' belonging to an auditor of the company. Others believe that the unencrypted private key was the cause. So, whether it was a cloned private key or a rogue insider, nobody knows for sure how the hackers manged to access the exchange. Be that as it may, on that occasion the hackers used this access to artificially alter the value of bitcoin to $0.01. The next step was to initially purchase 2,000 bitcoins and subsequently another cache of 650 bitcoins at this artificially lowered price of $0.01 and transfer them out without the exchange administrators being any the wiser. Having lost bitcoins on account of weak security protocols, the exchange attempted to plug the gaping security holes. They made arrangements to store a substantial amount of its bitcoin in cold storage (offline). Despite the June 2011 hack, the exchange managed to re-establish its credentials and was back to wheeling and dealing in bitcoins.

But the Mt Gox woes were not over yet. In February 2014, the hackers struck again with a renewed vengeance. The hack was initially kept under wraps presumably to avoid a public outcry and to recover some of the lost currency. On 7 February 2014, Mt Gox stopped all bitcoin withdrawals claiming that it was pausing requests 'to obtain a clear technical view of the process'. It was only on 24 February 2014 that the exchange finally admitted defeat, suspended all trading and went offline. Then came the death blow. An internal corporate document came to light that gave details of how the 744,408 bitcoins belonging to Mt Gox customers and 100,000 bitcoins belonging to the company were siphoned off by hackers. On 28 February 2014, Mt Gox formally filed for bankruptcy protection, initially in Japan and then in the United States. Subsequent investigations revealed that the insidious hack had been ongoing since September 2011. Some sources reveal that 80,000 bitcoins had gone missing from the exchange even before the exchange was purchased by Karpelès in 2011.

Investigators are still sniffing around but have not been able to ascertain how the hackers managed to gain access to the cold storage bitcoins as well as the hot wallet bitcoins. It is speculated that the bitcoins that were stolen from Mt Gox were taken from its online (or hot) wallets, including all of the currency being held in cold storage, due to a 'leak' in the hot wallet.

There are several theories about this hack. One that rings truer than others is the 'Norry theory'. Andrew Norry, a blogger, believes that the bitcoins were siphoned off from wallets without detection by simply reusing the address of the copied file. So, whenever a transfer of bitcoins was made, the Mt Gox system interpreted the transfer as a deposit being moved to a safer and more secure location. Norry gives a credible sequencing of the heist in his article, 'The History of the Mt Gox Hack: Bitcoin's Biggest Heist'. He says:

> Once the file was hacked, the hacker(s) were able to access and cipher bitcoins gradually...The shared keypool of the copied file led to address reuse...Whenever the wallets emptied, the Mt Gox system's interpretation of the theft as deposits resulted in an additional 40,000 extra bitcoins being credited to multiple user accounts.[7]

The mystery of how the hacker managed access to the bitcoins that Mt Gox held in cold storage has still not been solved. There are several theories doing the rounds. Some speculate that the storage may have been compromised by an individual with on-site access while others suggest that the cold storage coins were gradually deposited into the Mt Gox exchange system when a hot wallet ran low. The most obvious reason for the undetected hack seems to be the somewhat negligent approach of the staff. Lack of accountability and ignorance of the hack, allowed the hackers to siphon off coins with impunity over a period of three years without exposure.

'Mt Gox and the Surprising Redemption of the Bitcoin's Biggest Villain',[8] an article by Jen Wieczner published in the online edition of Fortune on 19 April 2018 talks of how Kim Nilsson, a Swedish software engineer, followed an arduous trail that led him to the perpetrator of the Mt Gox hack, Alexander Vinnik, a 38-year-old Russian IT specialist.

Despite its far-reaching impact, most bitcoin observers have shrugged off the Mt Gox hack, holding that security measures were lax and were tantamount to leaving the vault unguarded. Meaning thereby that the possibility of such a hack was now remote as there were more stringent security measures in place in all the bitcoin exchanges. However, the fear factor generated by the Mt Gox hack is stalking crypto users even today. When Kraken—the San Francisco-based popular bitcoin exchange—went dark for more than 48 hours starting 11 January 2018, the investors went frenetic with anxiety. A Twitter user, Colin Brogan, tweeted:

> To say 'Going Dark' is misleading. They have been talking about this new trading engine release for months and that it would take their site down for a while. They have regularly updated the reason why it is taking longer than expected.

Another Twitter user, using the pseudonym, MacroFxjunkie, tweeted:

> I agree with you in principle but the delay is truly crazy. I'm an actual user who has been with them for ages and I have been sleepless with worry. This is the kind of shenanigan than no one would tolerate in a bank or brokerage company.

The loss of cryptocurrency can also happen if the computer drive holding the bitcoin wallet crashes or if a virus corrupts data or the bitcoin wallet file. The loss of a wallet and the consequential 'orphaning' of coins is known to happen even if there is a flaw in the code. A critical code flaw resulted in freezing of $160 million worth of Ether in November 2017 in 'Parity', an Ethereum client.[9] This resulted in the loss of 584 wallets and the Ether stored in it. Some of these belonged to high profile start-ups including Parity founder Gavin Wood's 'Polkadot' which had $98 million in Ether. The Parity hack saw the deletion of the code library which supports Parity's multi-signature wallets (those that require multiple keys to issue transactions). Although this concern was flagged in August itself by Github, it was shrugged aside or considered too insignificant to matter. Hence, the catastrophe. As the access is lost, the cryptocurrency Ether is lost. Parity, on its part, continues to reassure its users that it intends to 'follow the will of the community' in deploying code fixes to release the locked millions. The release has not happened yet. In the meanwhile, Parity announced that it had done away with the functionality that allowed users to deploy multi-sig 'until we feel we have the correct security and operations procedures in place'.[10]

More and more cryptographers now feel that a security breach and subsequent crypto theft is also possible using digital QR codes. This was proved by two bright French hackers. Roger Ver, an entrepreneur offered $1,000 to viewers but the QR code that was needed to access money was deliberately blurred to discourage any attempt to win the booty. This did not deter Michael Sassano and Clement Storck. The keen-eyed pair noticed the top of the QR code and part of the key written in letters and numbers that was not blurred sufficiently, making them readable with software. They managed to zero in on the two valid keys that would match the bitcoin private keys. The whole exercise took the duo between 12 to 16 hours, Sassano told the BBC:

> The process to decode the private key from the moment we watched the show to when we entered it in the wallet took, I think, between 12 and 16 hours...most exciting was when we found the private key and the algorithm told us this was the one.[11]

Another big drawback of bitcoin mining is the use of huge amounts of energy. A large number of computers are used to solve strings of algorithms to arrive at the correct solution. These computers work all hours of the day, as an almost infinite number of trials have to be run to arrive at the nonce that signifies the correct computational solution to a complex problem. To start with, mining was done by individuals using a limited number of machines but with the meteoric rise of this cryptocurrency, mining has become a large-scale commercial enterprise with pools of miners single-mindedly dedicated to generation of bitcoins. The Cambridge Centre of Alternative Finance conducted a 'Global Cryptocurrency Benchmarking Study'. 'What is undeniable', said the report, is that 'the mining sector has evolved in a short time from hobby activity performed on personal computers into a professional and capital-intensive industry with its own value chain.'[12] Specialist studies estimate that the total energy consumed globally on this account is about 35 terawatt-hours and puts it on the level of energy consumption of countries like Denmark. Each transaction is said to consume roughly 100 kWh, which is the equivalent of electricity consumed by a light bulb burning continuously for three months. Julian Oliver, a New Zealander who uses wind energy to mine Zcash strongly feels that 'it's a huge use of energy, whatever the profit margins [and is not] remotely sustainable'.[13] There are environmentally astute cryptographers who are looking for mining methods that will use less energy or not use 'dirty' energy. So, mining pools are being set up in cold countries like Iceland where hydroelectric energy is being used for mining of bitcoins. There are proposals to use the waste heat generated in bitcoin mining to power alternate energy grids. But the progress is at a snail's pace and shows little possibility of fructifying in the near future.

Wrestling with large-scale acceptance, another problem that is eroding the credibility of cryptocurrencies like bitcoins or Ether is that several copycat currencies are being spawned online. Dogecoin is a case in point. Dogecoin is an alternative cryptocurrency (altcoin) that uses the iconic Shiba Inu dog from the 'Doge' meme as a mascot. Similar to bitcoin and its derivatives, Dogecoin can be mined and exchanged for goods and services, though it is programmed to level out at a threshold of 100 billion coins. This coin was launched on 6 December 2013 by an Adobe marketing professional Jackson Palmer and a software developer at IBM, Billy Marcus. On 17 December 2013, a Dogecoin YouTube channel uploaded a video called 'you can be a Dogecoin millionaire' featuring a sketch of Shiba Inu dog Kabuso becoming a millionaire. On Christmas Day, the same year, 30 million Dogecoins valued at $12,000 were hacked and stolen. Despite such roadblocks, this satirical currency eclipsed transactions of bitcoins and other altcoins on 14 January 2014. It made ripples when it funded the Jamaican bobsled team and Indian skiers Himanshu Thakur and Nadeem Iqbal for the Sochi Winter Olympics of 2014. After this, nothing of note happened to Dogecoin except that its 'Dogetipbot' (to pay tips in Dogecoins) endeavour sank into ignominious bankruptcy in May 2017. Notwithstanding the travails, in January 2018, Dogecoins is still growing strong with a market capitalisation of more than $1 billion. This is despite the fact that there were no new initiatives or updates in its underlying code in the last two years. This is a matter of concern to stalwarts of the crypto community who believe that a complacent acceptance of any form of digital currency is a worrying trend. CoinDesk published an interview with Dogecoin founder Jackson Palmer, who felt that Dogecoin's success could be a troubling sign for the market:

> It says a lot about the state of the cryptocurrency space in general that a currency with a dog on it which hasn't released a software update in over 2 years has a $1b+ market cap.[14]

We have many other copycat coins like Potcoin for the cannabis industry, celebrity coins like Trumpcoin, Putincoin, etc. But the less said about them the better.

More than anything else, that which has earned cryptocurrencies notoriety and a bad name is the unwanted association with the Deep Web. So, what is the Deep Web? The Deep Web does not need much of an introduction. The internet as we know it has two parts. One is called the 'Surface Web' and includes the net available to netizens. There is, however, a part of the net that is not accessible to search engines like Google and is called the 'Deep Web'. Accessing the Deep Web requires a specialised software programme such as Tor which allows anonymous online communication. The Deep Web is used for illegal transactions and other nefarious purposes through websites set up for this purpose like the 'Black Market Reloaded', 'Farmer's Market', 'Project Black Flag' and 'Silk Road'. Bitcoins, with their USP of anonymity were tailor-made for purchase of illicit drugs and arms on the 'Deep Web'. So, when a self-proclaimed libertarian set up Silk Road for purchase and sale of drugs and other contraband items, the currency of choice naturally was bitcoin.

Ross Ulbricht, a graduate in Physics from University of Texas and a masters in engineering from Pennsylvania State University founded Silk Road in February 2011 under the pseudonym 'Dread Pirate Roberts'. Silk Road was designed as a free market (read beyond government control), essentially for drugs. Ulbricht's ideology was simple, if somewhat skewed. He claimed that Silk Road gave its users freedom to decide what substances they wanted to put in their bodies, without having to resort to dealing with dangerous drug lords and sticky government laws on drugs. Its function was similar to eBay in that it matched buyers and sellers and delivered listed products to the customers through an unsuspecting postal service. As it worked on Tor, communications were entirely anonymous. Andrew Norry in his article 'The History of Silk Road: A Tale of Drugs, Extortion & Bitcoin' says:

> According to Ulbricht's outlook when setting up the site, listings on Silk Road were to be restricted to products that resulted in 'victimless crimes'. On that basis, listings related to child pornography, stolen credit cards, assassinations and weapons of mass destruction were banned.[15]

So, to start with, the products on offer on Silk Road were drugs like cannabis, ecstasy, psychedelics and a variety of stimulants and opiates. There was also drug-making equipment ready for purchase. Other than drug-related paraphernalia, there was the usual array of apparel, jewellery, computer equipment and the like. However, with increased firearm regulations and a consequential increase in demand of illegal guns, Ulbricht's site eased its ban on weapons of mass destruction. Slowly, more and more contraband products found their way into the product basket of Silk Road.

It is believed that the US authorities were aware of the existence of Silk Road from the day it was launched but were unable to track down Ulbricht. It took them almost two years of dedicated perseverance to track down the founder. The FBI managed to wriggle their way into the Silk Road network by bringing many of Ulbricht's closest associates on board. Using their identities, they moved in on Ulbricht. The final piece of the Ulbricht jigsaw puzzle fell into place when a connection was established between Silk Road and its founder. A Google search connected Dread Pirate Roberts with an alias named 'altoid'. This alias was traced to a bitcoin forum where Ulbricht had posted his email address. One eventful October afternoon saw Ulbricht sitting in a San Francisco library logged on as the administrator of Silk Road. He was using his Dread Pirate Roberts alias to communicate with an undercover FBI agent. A confident FBI contingent caught him red-handed. Andrew Norry writes:

> Agents found that Ulbricht's laptop had tens of millions of dollars of bitcoin on it, with millions more stored on USB drives found

> in his apartment. The computer also contained Ulbricht's private journal, which contained damning evidence against him.[16]

All this evidence was enough for a strong indictment. Ross Ulbricht was hoisted by his own petard. That was the end of Ross's libertarian dreams and the end of Silk Road with its hamper of contraband goods. Inspired by the initial success of Silk Road, several versions of Silk Road did pop up from time to time but died quick and uneventful deaths. Ulbricht's life sentence, without parole, continues.

The Asian saga is no different. It may not have the thrill and adventure of a Hollywood flick but it does have the makings of a manga or a Bollywood blockbuster. On 31 January 2018, the Korea Customs Service (KCS) issued a statement that a total of $600 million in foreign currencies has been exchanged illegally including unrecorded capital outflow using cryptocurrencies. In one case, which also accounts for majority of the alleged amount, the KCS said unregistered currency exchanges remitted 472.3 billion Korean Won ($443,962,000) for customers between South Korea and Australia from March to December 2017. All these money laundering transactions were facilitated by cryptocurrencies.

Figure 5.1: Seizure of Silk Road

Source: https://commons.wikimedia.org/wiki/File:Silk_Road_Seized.jpg

India has a similar story to narrate. Bitcoins and others of the ilk were being used to launder black money as was seen in the aftermath of demonetisation. Bitcoin exchanges like ZebPay, Coinsecure, Unocoin, etc. were doing brisk business until RBI's April 2018 notification. On 12 December 2017, the Income Tax Department conducted surveys on various bitcoin exchanges in Delhi, Gurugram, Mumbai, Pune, Hyderabad and Bengaluru to ensure there is no suppression in gains made from trading in bitcoins and also to ascertain that investment in bitcoins is being made from known sources of income. China, in the latter half of 2017, closed down several bitcoin exchanges like OKcoin, BTCC, Yunbi, etc. fearing that allowing them to function would perpetuate and leave open another mode of laundering black money. China also banned ICOs as they were associated with illegal fundraising.

This sure makes for a tawdry story with an unhappy ending. The bitcoin protagonist is caught up in the tentacles of security breach, fraud, hacks and thefts. That is not all. Silk Road and other global scams have revealed its nefarious underbelly. Like I said before, caveat emptor. Let the buyer beware.

Chapter 6

The Bitcoin Juggernaut

> *Bitcoin critics are underestimating [it]...it's like a reserve form of money, it's like gold and it's just a store of value.*
>
> —Peter Thiel, Co-Founder of PayPal

The bitcoin juggernaut has been on a roll. The years 2016 and 2017 saw a meteoric rise in the value of this cryptocurrency which rose from $439 in January 2016 to about $20,000 in December 2017. The libertarians, the privacy adherents and the bitcoin enthusiasts are popping celebratory bottles of champagne to felicitate this amazing rise. The last few years have seen a mainstream acceptance of bitcoins. Websites like Reddit, WordPress, Overstock, Amazon, etc. accept bitcoins as payment for purchases made. Bitcoins also trade on exchanges specifically set up for this purpose like Bitstamp, Coinbase, Bitfinex, Cryptsy, etc. ATMs that exchange bitcoins for dollars have also been set up in cities like San Diego and Vancouver. This digital currency, with a current circulation of 16.8 million, hit the four-digit mark in December 2017 and is straining at the leash to hit greater heights. So, what is it about this virtual currency that seems to have caught the fancy of the common investing public as well as the crypto geeks?

The bitcoin charisma is largely on account of its blend of transparency and anonymity. Each bitcoin blockchain has three parts: an identifying address called the 'public key', a 'ledger' that lists the history of all those who have transacted in bitcoins and a 'private key' which is a sophisticated digital signature that captures and confirms each transaction in a bitcoin file. The digital signature is unique to each individual user and his/her personal bitcoin wallet. The signature key tracks, tags and publicly discloses every transaction. So, while every bitcoin records the digital address of the bitcoin wallet it touches, the bitcoin system does not record the names of the individuals who own wallets. It is no wonder then that it has become exceedingly attractive to privacy advocates, security adherents and libertarians.

The fact that bitcoins are regulated by a free market economy and not the whims of a government or central bank adds to its charm. People strongly believe that using bitcoins will grant them immunity from global and domestic policy changes which is undoubtedly the cherry on the cake. Bitcoins are also being used as a hedge against inflation. The citizens of Zimbabwe made good use of bitcoins to cope with the problems of hyperinflation and economic woes. In 2008, Zimbabwe adopted the US dollar (among a mixed bag of other currencies) as its own. This, however, led to a debilitating liquidity crunch and acute cash shortage as the government could not print dollars but had to import them. So, the dollar came at a huge premium and the cost of the dollar far exceeded the bonds issued by the government. If reports are to be believed, in November 2017, $1 was equal to 35 quadrillion Zimbabwean dollars.[1] Adopting a cryptocurrency was a natural corollary to this economic catastrophe. Bitcoins began to be used to buy groceries, pay salaries, buy goods like cars and also finance the studies of children in Zimbabwe and abroad. It is not surprising then that the value of a bitcoin on the Harare bitcoin exchanges like Golix and SpectroCoin was much higher than other bitcoin exchanges.

China had similar reasons to jump onto the bitcoin bandwagon. The 2008 recession hit the common man in China hard. The devaluation of the renminbi in 2015 set alarm bells clanging again. A currency that was beyond the control of the Central government was considered as a godsend. So, China took to bitcoins like the proverbial duck to water. Another obvious reason was the fact that all other avenues of investment had lost their shine. The financial markets as well as the property market in China was put in a straight-jacket by a government eager to curb speculation. Martin Chorzempa, a research fellow specialising in internet finance at the Peterson Institute for International Economics in Washington DC points out:

> The Chinese were some of the most enthusiastic adopters of bitcoin, which has allowed them to easily skirt capital controls and transfer money outside the watchful eye of the government.[2]

Eric Zhao, who runs the popular Twitter account CN Ledger, observes:

> There are not many good investment choices for common people in China. Many people worry about inflation and lots of people feel insecure about their financial status. They buy it [bitcoin] simply because they believe it will appreciate in value.[3]

Despite the crackdown on initial coin offerings (ICOs) by the Chinese authorities and also the shutdown of bitcoin exchanges like BTCC, the bitcoin patina has not worn off and the common man in China continues to invest in bitcoins.

The Indian tale is no different. Until a few years back, the average Indian was not interested in virtual currencies. A few computer nerds, especially those with some offshore exposure, may have invested in the cryptocurrency. However, in the last few years, remunerative investment opportunities reduced considerably. The property market has been dead as a doornail and demand for gold has also seen a plunge. The stock market continued to go from strength to strength but it is dubbed as a 'Ferrari without brakes'[4]. The Dalal Street players spent sleepless night wondering when the bears would trounce the bulls. This was obviously an uncomfortable situation for an investor with piles of unused cash. So, the natural alternative was to make investments in bitcoins which were returning unprecedented and unheard-of yields. The Indian bitcoin exchange, ZebPay reported 2,500 Indians investing in bitcoins daily[5] despite the warnings issued by the central bank, RBI and the Indian Government.

November and December 2017 saw bitcoin scaling unprecedented heights. Several global events triggered the switch on the bitcoin powerhouse. The recent trend of selling cryptocurrency through ICOs to source start-ups showed bitcoins in an extremely attractive light. The global bitcoin fraternity was also upbeat that the US Securities and Exchange Commission would relent and approve the Winklevoss Bitcoin Trust ETF. The currency received a further shot in the arm with the Japanese cabinet passing bills that elevated digital currencies to similar status as fiat currencies. On 1 April 2017, the Japanese Parliament went a step further when it passed a law that accepted bitcoin as a legal method of payment. The Bitcoin Gold Fork of 25 October that allowed a free Bitcoin Gold to every user holding bitcoins added to the bitcoin sales pitch.

What added a fresh shine to this non-fiat currency was the news that CBOE (Chicago Board of Options Exchange) would begin trading in bitcoin futures on 10 December 2017. CME (Chicago Mercantile Exchange), the world's largest exchange in derivatives, also revealed its plans to begin trading in bitcoin futures by the last week of December. NASDAQ announced a similar trading schedule from January 2018. Not to be left behind, Goldman Sachs divulged that it would trade in bitcoin futures on behalf of its clients. No wonder bitcoin hit stratospheric heights even as 2017 headed for a close.

Chapter 7

The Brave New World: A Socio-Economic Revolution

> *The blockchain cannot be described just as a revolution. It is a tsunami-like phenomenon, slowly advancing and gradually enveloping everything along the way by force of its progression.*
>
> —William Mougayar, Author of Business Blockchain

A lot of people from different walks of life have described bitcoins and the technology underlying it in many varied and ineresting ways. Jordan Belfort, the Wolf of Wall Street, started by describing bitcoins as a 'Ponzi scheme' but then changed his mind and called it a 'social experiment'. A TED Talk featuring Bettina Warburg[1] talked about bitcoins as a way of reducing 'uncertainties' in the economic sphere. A Netflix film, 'Banking on Bitcoins',[2] dubbed it as a socio-economic experiment. My research in the subject has led me to strongly believe that the technology underlying bitcoins (not so much bitcoin itself) is all that and more. It is, in fact a socio-economic revolution, nay a tsunami, that will bring about far-reaching changes and impact the future of the entire human race.

Let me explain why I would call it a tsunami-like revolution rather than an experiment or an innovation. An experiment is considered a scientific procedure used to make a discovery, or test a hypothesis or demonstrate a known fact. The bitcoin protocol of 'peer-to-peer transaction', as proposed and implemented by Satoshi Nakamoto is not about making a discovery or testing a hypothesis or even demonstrating a known fact, it is about changing an established socio-economic order, which is what a revolution is all about.

The bitcoin technology and its tenets draw strength from the field of cryptography as well as finance and behavioural economics. Let us start by looking at how bitcoin technology has affected our understanding of the value of currency and consequently our transactions in currency. Historically speaking, the established way of managing transactions and finances in work-a-day world is through exchange of currency. A peek into the history of currency reveals that the concept of currency was first instituted by the Tang dynasty and Song dynasty of China in the seventh century. It was introduced in Europe by Marco Polo in the thirteenth century. It was only much later, in 1694, that Bank of England initiated the issue of permanent banknotes for funding the war against France. The Federal Government of the United States began printing banknotes in 1862. Initially, the paper currency was backed by gold and silver coins but slowly it evolved into simply a fiat currency or an acceptable legal tender. In fact, the modern-day banknote rests on the assumption that money is established by social and legal consensus.

So, paper currency does not have any intrinsic value except the value given to it by the central bank, as backed by the government. The characteristic feature of the currency today is that it is minted and issued by the government. Also, our currency moves through intermediaries like banks or other financial institutions. The banking system has evolved over decades and has in the contemporary world become the trusted custodian of our money. The interest we receive on our money is in consonance with the government diktat or the changing and evolving policies of the central bank. The government or the bank uses our money to generate income for the government by investing the money of its account holders in a range of investments. But the account holder does not have any quarrel with such investments or use of his money as he is sanguine in the belief that the money is backed by the sovereign and is therefore safe from harm like a theft or a fraud.

We were, of course, naive and wrong to think so. The subprime crisis with the collapse of banks like Lehman Brothers showed us that these third-party institutions cannot be trusted blindly. To prevent such a collapse, the regulatory frameworks were strengthened and stringent checks and balances introduced. However, a group of revolutionary thinkers decided, in their wisdom, to establish a new financial system that did away with the intermediaries and the 'trusted third party'. Satoshi Nakamoto implemented an open-source code that allowed participants of the network to not only generate their own currency called 'bitcoin' but also to affect transactions based on bitcoins with their peers. The transactions did not move through a central node or intermediary that kept a record of the transactions. It was a peer-to-peer transaction which was recorded in a common ledger that was publicly broadcast and recorded by every participant in the network. Such transactions were verified through a method of verification and consensus within the network itself. The code resisted double-spend as it was based on the concept of timestamp that allowed only the first transaction (in time) to come through. It also had an inbuilt security protocol that resisted fraud and any attempt at reversing the transaction as the transaction was recorded in a common public ledger and replicated by every participant at his end. The code also had an inbuilt cap of 21 million bitcoins by 2140 which prevented an infinite spawning of bitcoins. We have already discussed this at length in previous chapters, so suffice it to say that the peer-to-peer protocol of bitcoins was a revolutionary method that did away with the rigid parameters in place for financial transactions. Here was a system that did away with mints, banks and financial regulatory authorities. It was self-generating, self-governing and self-regulating. To a certain extent it also did away with the need for government as an active participant in economic activity. So here was a freshly-minted concept that was not only distributed and trust-less but also based on consensus. The cherry on the cake was that it was not beholden to an intermediary or a government.

This concept not only created ripples in the economic and financial spheres but also drove home and implemented an important tenet of behavioural psychology. Inherent in Satoshi's code is encouragement and incentivisation of desired behaviour among its participants. Incentives are the crux of game theory and economics in shaping human behaviour towards the common good. The bitcoin network incentivises miners who are rewarded with bitcoins on solving a complex algorithm. The participants of the network are given incentives in the form of a cache of bitcoin or transaction fee on the verification of transactions. This incentivises honest behaviour within the network and chances of a participant turning rogue become almost negligible.

To understand how this works, we first need to get a handle on the 'Byzantine Generals' Problem'. Need some imagination here folks. Let us ask the fairy godmother to blow some magic dust our way. Imagine that the majestic Byzantine army has laid siege of a castle. The army is divided into units headed by different generals. The only way to wrest victory from the hands of the enemy is to ensure a coordinated attack by all units of the army. The only problem is that a coordinated attack is not possible as some of the traitorous generals are likely to sabotage the attack by sending wrong or dubious messages to connected units. So how can the generals circumvent the traitors and reach a consensus about a unanimous time for attack? A similar consensus is required in the blockchain protocol underpinning the bitcoin. So how does the bitcoin technology achieve this consensus? How do the 'good guys' (honest nodes) ride roughshod over the 'bad guys' (rogue nodes)? How does good triumph over evil? In other words, how does blockchain technology overcome the Byzantine fault tolerance problem?

In computer science, the capability of a system to resist failure from faulty components that prevent other critical components from reaching a necessary consensus is termed as Byzantine fault tolerance (BFT). Blockchain technology addresses the Byzantine Generals' Problem by using a two-pronged firewall protocol. First, it uses proof-of-work protocol (PoW) that we have discussed in the chapter on the Ps and Qs of bitcoins. The PoW makes it impossible for a rogue node to manipulate or reverse a message as it requires significant expenditure of resources like processing power, time and electricity. The chain of work not only creates an ironclad history of transactions but also makes it prohibitively expensive and time consuming for external hackers or internal rogue nodes to make or reverse changes. Second, the protocol has an inbuilt concept of incentives that encourage participants to maintain and sustain the protocol i.e. broadcasting of blocks filled with transactions validated and verified through consensus.

Figure 7.1: The Byzantine Generals' Problem

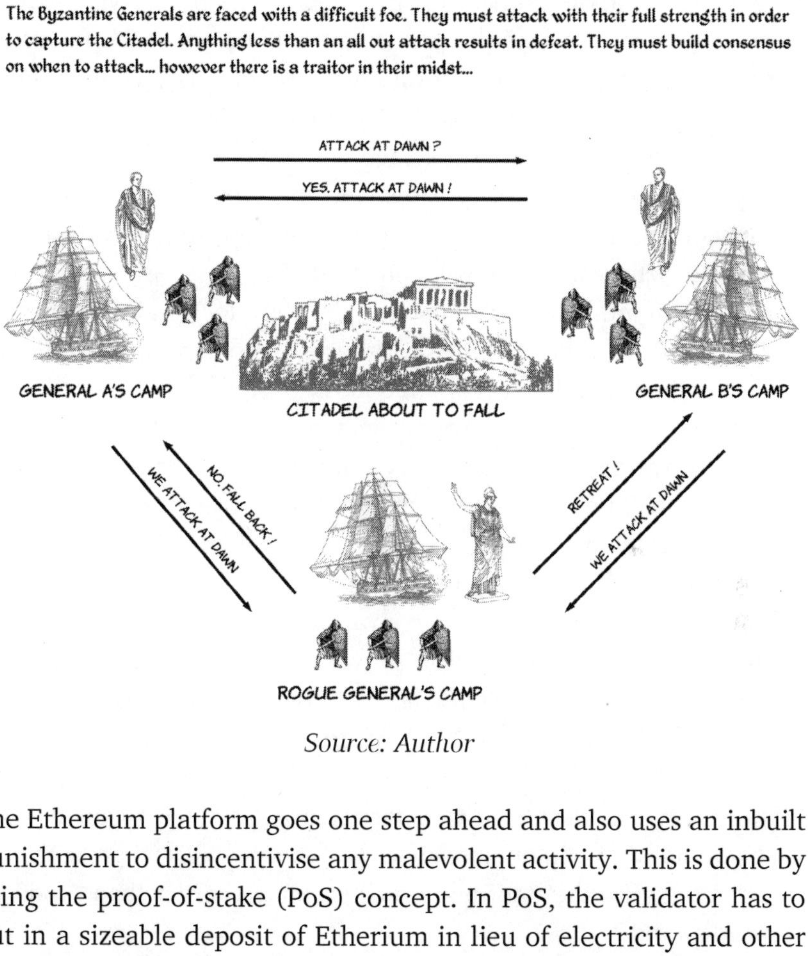

Source: Author

The Ethereum platform goes one step ahead and also uses an inbuilt punishment to disincentivise any malevolent activity. This is done by using the proof-of-stake (PoS) concept. In PoS, the validator has to put in a sizeable deposit of Etherium in lieu of electricity and other resources expended. If a situation arises where the validator attempts to defraud the system, he will lose the entire stake or deposit. This is referred to as the 'Casper Update' to Ethereum. This is explained precisely and simply by Kyle Wang in his article 'Cryptoeconomics: Paving the Future of Blockchain Technology':

> Casper forces participants to enter a SchellingCoin game where they are forced to bet their security deposits on what the majority will be...the majority of participants will accurately vote on which transactions are valid because each participant expects everyone else to reach the same conclusion.[3]

So, the Casper model envisages a situation where a participant will vote truthfully in the expectation that other participants will also vote truthfully. In such a case the participant will be rewarded for voting with the majority instead of voting with the minority. Such a model can defang a P + epsilon attack. The logic is simple. A P + epsilon attack entails the creation of a huge volume of accounts that would vote with the rogue minority. However, this would entail prohibitive cost. Also, the threat of losing all the deposits/stakes would loom large and act as an effective deterrent. So, the Nash equilibrium would be maintained. To put it simply, the blockchain system will maintain a state of harmonious consensus as no participant node will benefit from any unilateral change in the system.

There are some cryptographers who do not concur with the incentive-disincentive theory and strongly believe that the blockchain technology should appeal to the altruistic streak in man. One such detractor is Professor Silvio Micali of MIT. Professor Micali has proposed an incentive-less public blockchain that attacks the Byzantine Generals' Problem by swapping out the generals in each round through a randomisation process. This idea was put forth by Professor Micali at the 'Financial Cryptography and Data Security' conference in Malta in May 2017 where he stated that:

> We must use incentives as a last resort. I believe I can make Algorand work without incentives but I have no formal proof that I can, because these formal proofs are much harder than proofs of Algorand.[4]

Proponents of Micali rely on altruistic seeders like BitTorrent to reinforce this incentive-less theory. BitTorrent, as we know, allows for free download of music and movies from the net. Not so long ago, it was extremely popular with 'GenNext' but the advent of Netflix and

Spotify has caused a waning of its popularity. Charles Hoskinson, CEO of blockchain technology firm IOHK, refers to another such philanthropic initiative, folding@home, where thousands donate idle processing power for disease research. His balanced comment strikes the right note in the midst of academic discord:

> It is an open question of whether you need incentives or not and I don't think it can be determined in an academic model. It is actually going to be determined by evidence. You launch something and you see what happens.[5]

Be that as it may, the bitcoin protocol has spawned various views on game theory, specific to incentivisation of good behaviour in the blockchain environment.

The bitcoin protocol also throws up the issue of self-governance and self-regulation that is mandatory study for a student of political science. The technology underpinning blockchain works on autopilot and does not require external governance or regulation. However, when it comes to making changes in the code and the basic protocol that governs bitcoin, consensus completely eludes the developer fraternity. This has resulted in internal strife which has resulted in a soft fork that led to the genesis of Bitcoin Cash and several other failed attempts at forking. The internal squabbles are continuing and have escalated into an all-out fratricidal war but I'll leave that discussion for the next chapter.

Chapter 8

The Hubris: Crypto Fratricide

> *The nature of bitcoin is such that once version 0.1 was released, the core design was set in stone…So much of the design depends on all nodes getting exactly identical results in lockstep that a second implementation would be a menace to the network.*
>
> —Satoshi Nakamoto, Founder of Bitcoin

Bitcoin, right from its inception, was touted to be a decentralised consensus that did away with the mediation and approval of a third party. It was intended to be self-governing and self-regulating. The founding father, Satoshi Nakamoto, described the core design as being 'set in stone'. Yet, of late bitcoin has hit its own version of 'splitsville'. August 2017 saw the emergence of a bitcoin clone with one different characteristic—an 8 MB block size in the blockchain. It was called Bitcoin Cash (BCH) and each BCH was equivalent to a bitcoin. Another such split called the 'Bitcoin Gold fork' was planned for October 2017 but for reasons unknown was withdrawn before implementation. Jim Harper, of the Cato Institute, has summed up this phenomenon:

> Specifically, groups with differing visions are competing to win the favour of bitcoin miners and nodes, so that their vision prevails and can carry the bitcoin project forward.[1]

In the last two years, bitcoin has seen a turf war that attempted to undermine its dominance and its 'early bird' advantage. Let us look at the whys and wherefores of this ignominious split. Or should we say fork?

Bitcoin, as we know it, has some different versions that most of us are not even aware of. There is the standard bitcoin (BTC) which is maintained by the Bitcoin Core developers. Bitcoin Core evolved from bitcoin's original implementation by the bitcoin wizard, Satoshi Nakamoto. The Bitcoin Core developers are developers who for the most part have adhered to the original code implemented by Satoshi. These developers are risk averse and any modifications in the original protocol are pushed through only after an extensive peer review and consensus under the aegis of Bitcoin Improvement Proposals (BIPs). These Satoshi followers have resisted proposals to increase the size of the block which would necessitate a hard fork or a split into a new blockchain that forces all users to update. They have been, however, less resistant to a soft fork proposal called SegWit (Segregated Witness).

SegWit envisages allowing more transactions in the 1 MB block by separating and filtering some data from each transaction. There are detractors to this proposal as well. Kyle Wang, in his article, 'Governance in Blockchain Part I: The Bitcoin Experiment' says:

> SegWit works to increase the efficiency of the PoW system by eliminating something known as transaction malleability while better utilising the space within each block. In other words, the solution allows slightly more transactions to be crammed into each 1 MB block by separating out certain data from each transaction...[2]

SegWit proponents believed in the accuracy and validity of the SegWit proposal. They hold that SegWit would allow more transactions per second to be registered on the blockchain and thus increase scalability. Also, it would remove transaction malleability which is the result of a cryptographic trick to change a signature without changing what it stands for. Although SegWit was released on 24 August 2017, there were several detractors who had strong reservations about this fork. For one, a significant part of the developer community believed that it did not solve the problem of scaling and was also too complex a solution to the problem of block size. Others correctly pointed out that it was incompatible with ASICs (Application Specific Integrated Circuit Chips), a kind of bitcoin mining hardware to solve bitcoin blocks.

Then came SegWit2x which combined the SegWit protocol with an increase in block size to 2 MB. This proposal gathered pace in May 2017 and emerged from an agreement called the New York Agreement, signed by 50 leading bitcoin companies. The fork was slated for November 2017. However, the fork was shelved because of the strongly negative response of the developer community. This snowballed into a movement against SegWit2x called #no2x. The fork was accordingly cancelled. The movement was revived by a different group of developers in December 2017. The fate of the movement is still uncertain and does not appear to have coalesced into another hard fork. A Bitcoin Classic proposal projecting increase in block size to 2 MB also saw the light of the day and then sank without a trace.

In fact, the debate about increasing the block size has been going on for a while. In August 2015, a hard fork proposal called Bitcoin XT, that pushed for an increase in block size from 1 MB to 8 MB, was considered and discarded. There was then a lot of talk about Bitcoin Unlimited which was said to allow miners to set their own block size through what is called an 'emergent consensus' algorithm. Some in the developer community believe that this proposed fork was more of a political move by interested parties who wanted to shift the attention of the developer community away from the powerful Bitcoin Core developers. So naturally, this proposal received a very limited developer community acceptance. However, despite resistance from several quarters, especially from the Bitcoin Core community, the Bitcoin Cash hard fork did happen.

The thing about Bitcoin Cash is that it is a clone of the original bitcoin. Not only the code base but also the blockchain of Bitcoin Cash is the same as that of bitcoin. This meant that all those who had bitcoins, after the fork were also saddled with Bitcoin Cash. It also meant that bitcoin exchanges and wallets were forced to support the cloned Bitcoin Cash. Naysayers like Samson Mow, Chief Strategy

Officer at Blockstream are brutal in their assessment of the Bitcoin fork and genesis of Bitcoin Cash:

> Whatever happens though, Bitcoin Cash's rebirth has shown that markets can be manipulated with just a bit of computing power, a participating exchange and a healthy dose of greed. If you are running a digital exchange or wallet, beware the attack of clone coins.[3]

There are some who believe that bitcoin forks are not a bad thing and in fact only reflect the increasing maturity of the cryptocurrency ecosystem. Charles Hoskinson, CEO of Input Output, Hong Kong admits that bitcoin is going through an existential crisis and has spawned different roadmaps for the future. This naturally causes friction within the bitcoin ecosystem and resultant splits as different philosophies and protocols duel for domination. He, however, strongly holds that such splits are a sign of maturity and not chaos. This assertion comes with a rider. Care should be taken to ensure that such splits do not translate into the loss of underlying accumulated values and knowledge. Hoskinson makes this clear:

> No ecosystem can keep everyone happy nor can it satisfy divergent visions. So they have to find a way to split like so many open-source projects before them without destroying the value already accumulated and the underlying communities.[4]

Hoskinson further believes that Bitcoin Cash will not be a threat to the credibility of bitcoin. The cryptocurrency market is large enough and deep enough to allow both bitcoin as well as Bitcoin Cash to exist without sounding the knell of doom for either. He believed that Bitcoin Cash was a productive split with its existence neither threatening bitcoins nor requiring support from bitcoin's remaining adherents.

It is perhaps too early to get into the 'to-be-or-not-to-be' twist and stake your money on the yays and nays of cryptocurrency forks. Whether such forks will snowball into a royal battle that will end in the annihilation of one or the other, only time can tell. For the moment, we can only sit back and watch the 'Play of Clones'.

Chapter 9

The Burgeoning Bitcoin Bubble

> *Bitcoin is the best example of a speculative bubble...The bitcoin price is like a thermometer measuring the intensity of the epidemic.*
>
> —Robert J. Shiller, Nobel Prize-Winning Economist

Nostradamus-like prophecies of bitcoin boom and doom are making headlines. The slump in bitcoin price from an unheard of $20,000 in December 2017 to $8,000 in the first week of February 2018 has been grist to the bitcoin-bubble-burst mill. Several credible voices have joined the frenzy and blithely announced that bitcoin was showing definite bearish tendencies. James Faucette of Morgan Stanley announced that bitcoin's 'real value could be zero'.[1] Nouriel Roubini, often referred to by the pseudonym Dr Doom on account of his pessimistic economic outlook, announced on Twitter that the value of bitcoin would crash to zero. He also expressed his belief that the bitcoin price was kept afloat through the practice of 'Wash trades',[2] where people owning cryptocurrencies buy and sell the virtual currency to manipulate the price of bitcoins. Stephen S. Roach, Senior Fellow, Institute for Global Affairs, Yale University, has called bitcoin a 'dangerous speculative bubble by any shadow or stretch of the imagination'.[3] As the voices, both calm and hysterical, point to a burgeoning bitcoin bubble that will collapse, it would be best to understand what a financial bubble is and if bitcoin has the makings of one.

A bubble, financial bubble, a market bubble or an asset bubble, by whatever name it may be called, refers to a situation where the value of an asset or a commodity increases at a frenetic rate that has nothing whatsoever to do with its actual or intrinsic value. In fact, if truth be told, the value increase has a somewhat irrational, bordering-on-hysterical edge to it that is beyond the oft-applied parameters of valuation of the asset. Does this mean that just because an asset increases in value without a sound basis, it is dubbed as a bubble? Methinks not. To see if an asset value increase shows bubble-like proclivity, we need to understand the anatomy of a bubble. The anatomy of a bubble? I can almost hear a disbelieving snort there. Hear me out. The concept of a bubble does involve 'suspension of disbelief', so let us look at what a not-so-well-known economist has to say about the anatomical connotations of a bubble.

Hyman P. Minsky, in his book, *Stabilizing an Unstable Economy* (1986),[4] propounded the theory of financial instability which attracted a great deal of attention after the subprime crisis of 2008. Minsky has categorised five stages in a credit bubble namely: displacement, boom, euphoria, profit-making and panic. So, what characterises these stages? Minsky explains that displacement occurs when investors are besotted by a new paradigm. It happened in 1630s in Amsterdam when people were enamoured by tulips and the price of tulips rocketed to 20 times its original value. It has been recorded that tulip bulbs in 1636 fetched a price that was more than certain luxury homes in Amsterdam. Something similar happened in the 1990s during the dot-com bubble, when the NASDAQ composite went up from under 500 in 1990 to a never heard of 5,000 in March 2000, when dot-com companies achieved multi-billion dollar valuations as soon as they went public. When the NASDAQ bubble burst, the harried investor started to look around for a safer asset class for investment. Thus, began the love-affair with the housing sector in the United States which ballooned into the subprime crisis of 2008. The 2.5 percentage points decline in the interest rate of 30-year fixed-rate mortgages added to the attraction quotient of the housing sector.

The next stage in the credit cycle is categorised by Minsky as the 'boom' phase. In this phase the prices rise, first slowly and then with an accelerated momentum as more and more participants join the asset bandwagon. During this phase, Minsky believes that the asset in question attracts widespread media coverage. Fear of missing the bus takes hold of most investors, spurring more and more investors or participants to join the melee. In 1720, investment in the South Sea Company caught the fancy of investors. The South Sea Company was formed in 1711 to trade with Spanish colonies in South Sea (which is South America of today). Expecting a flourishing trade along the lines of the East India Company, investors snapped up the shares, which went up from £128 in January 1720 to £1,050 in June 1720.

Next comes the stage of 'euphoria'. This is when caution is thrown to the wind and the price of the asset touches new highs. This is an appropriate example of the 'greater fool' theory coming into play. The greater fool theory states that the price of an object is determined not by its intrinsic value but rather by irrational beliefs and expectations of market participants. A price can be justified by a rational buyer in the delusional belief that another party is willing to pay an even higher price. In other words, one is ready to pay a price for an asset that seems foolishly high, in the expectation that the asset can be resold at a higher price to a 'greater fool' later. This was what happened during the oft-quoted housing sector bubble of the United States. It also happened during the Japanese real estate bubble in 1989. Land in Tokyo sold for $139,000 per square foot, which was 350-times the value of Manhattan property. Similarly, during the dot-com bubble, the combined value of technology stocks on NASDAQ was higher than the GDP (Gross Domestic Product) of most nations. During this stage, the value increase of the asset is justified through new valuation techniques and metrics.

Then comes the 'profit-making' stage, when investors realise that asset value has peaked and is likely to plummet. So, they start to sell assets in an attempt to beat the bears waiting in the wings. Ascertaining the exact time of the 'fall' is, of course, hardly an exact science and the probability of a mismatch is pretty high. The warning bell, for the most part is ignored, caught as it is between the 'value spikes' of the asset. The first hint of the subprime crisis came in August 2007 when the French Bank BNP Paribas stopped withdrawal from investment funds that had substantial exposure to subprime mortgages because it was unable to value their holdings. Unfortunately, this red flag was regarded as just a tiny blip in the building crescendo and was ignored. Hence, the subprime crisis.

The final stage of the bubble is the stage of 'panic'. Investors are suddenly hit by the unpalatable truth that the value of their holdings is declining at a fast rate. They react by selling the asset to cut their losses. This results in a supply glut and a sudden fall in the value of the asset. This is what happened during the subprime crisis. The shock of the bankruptcy declaration by Lehman Brothers and the collapse of Freddie Mac and Fannie Mae sent S&P 500 into a tailspin. The markets lost $9.3 trillion in market capitalisation in October 2008 alone. This, then is the physiology of a bubble, examples and all.

Now that we have a detailed anatomy of a bubble, let's see if the bitcoin cycle falls within the ambit of a 'bubble' as enumerated by Minsky. After the subprime crisis, investors were looking for an investment opportunity that was beyond the pale of banking institutions and government intervention. And voila! Bitcoin arrived. A freshly minted paradigm. It was initially embraced only by computer geeks but slowly it started gaining widespread acceptance. Transactions in bitcoin began to be accepted by well-known e-commerce sites. ATMs to exchange bitcoins for fiat currencies were set up. Certain countries like Japan accepted bitcoin as legal tender. The European Union and the United States gave it a modicum of credibility by accepting it as an 'asset' and VAT/GST was applied to transactions in bitcoins. The CBOE gave the go-ahead for trading in bitcoin futures and Goldman Sachs agreed to deal in bitcoin derivatives for their clients. So, the value of bitcoin started to increase steadily. By mid-2017, bitcoins had not only gained public acceptance but also became a profitable investment with quick returns. This led to bitcoin euphoria in November and December 2017 when the value of bitcoin hit hitherto unheard-of heights. This was despite the fact that Chinese and South Korean governments had shut down bitcoin exchanges and the United States had pulled the rug from under ICOs. The bitcoin mania was so strong that even a hint of the term 'blockchain' (the technology that powers bitcoins) by a company meant that its valuation would go through the roof.

The shares of Long Island Iced Tea Corp. Rose as much as 289 per cent after the unprofitable Hicksville, New York-based company rebranded itself Long Blockchain Corp. This started a trend whereby obscure microcap companies reoriented to focus on some aspect of the mania sparked by bitcoin's 1,500 per cent rally in 2017.

Speculations are on about the causes of formation of this crypto bubble. Some attribute it to the irrational exuberance of the crypto community, others to herdism and cognitive dissonance. Commenting on the psychological basis of a bubble, Robert Shiller, the Yale economist in his Nobel Prize lecture on 8 December 2013 said:

> Irrational exuberance is the psychological basis of a speculative bubble. I will define a speculative bubble as a situation in which news of price increases spurs investor enthusiasm which spreads by psychological contagion from person to person.[5]

Experts may hold academic discourses on the run-up to the bitcoin bubble till they are blue in the face but the fact remains that the modern-day financial community is caught in a crypto bubble of its own making. That the bitcoin bubble is teetering on the edge of Minsky's euphoria-profit making stage is also clear as day. The possibility of an imminent crypto crash has definitely raised its ugly head. Whether this is the panic stage of the crypto bubble or just a correction is however hard to ascertain. Only time can tell. Or history.

SECTION IV

JUDICIAL JARGON

Chapter 10

Legal Laminate

> *We need better cross-border payments because it is good for development, it's good for financial inclusion. So, bitcoin can help us, it can pay us a service by forcing us to upgrade our systems. That's a positive lesson.*
>
> —Benoit Coeure, ECB Executive Board Member

Bitcoins have been in the eye of the storm ever since their inception. In the earlier years of the bitcoin fairy tale, wrangling was limited to the yays and nays of the programming community who good-naturedly bickered about the blockchain technology instituted by the mysterious Satoshi Nakamoto. After the Winklevoss twins made millions on this virtual currency, people other than techies, looking for a quick buck, joined the bitcoin bandwagon. During the initial phase of its popularity curve, governments of the world shrugged off the sudden lionisation of this digital currency as just another temporary trend. There were no guidance notes, no regulations, no warnings and no legislation. Some governments watched the meteoric rise of cryptocurrencies, sanguine in the belief that the trend would fade. There were others who wholeheartedly embraced the new technology and actively aided its accelerated momentum. There were some countries, however, that were openly antagonistic to the concept but these were few and far between.

Japan was perhaps the only country that unabashedly hailed the concept of digital currency. If truth be told, Tokyo was overrun with signages proclaiming 'bitcoin accepted as payment here'. So, whether it was the grocery mart or the salon, bitcoin had attained credibility as a means of payment for purchase of goods. To meet the rising demand of the tech-savvy cryptocurrency enthusiasts, bitcoin exchanges sprung up everywhere. The Japan-based Mt Gox heist muddied the waters a bit, but soon, the bitcoin mania reasserted itself. In April 2017, the Parliament of Japan passed a bill accepting bitcoin as legal tender. Virtual currency legislation was also passed to ensure that the users and digital currency investors were kept safe from charlatans and fraudsters. So today, Japan has 16 bitcoin exchanges registered with the FSA.[1] Other cryptocurrency operators, who were in the cryptocurrency business before the advent of the new regulations, have been allowed to continue with their operations while their registration applications are pending with the FSA. A company called Remixpoint, an energy company that generates and sells energy to customers all over Japan, is offering bitcoin as a payment method. Not only that, it's actually offering a discount to any customer who pays in bitcoin. The company has a subsidiary called BITPoint, which is a cryptocurrency exchange and payment service provider and any payments in bitcoin are processed by BITPoint on receipt. Utility bill payments in bitcoin aren't something totally new, but that a company the size of Remixpoint is attempting to incentivise its customers to pay in bitcoin is exactly the sort of initiative that will lead to a long-term acceptance and adoption of virtual currencies as a popular mode of payment. Then there is Yahoo! Japan that has hinted that it would buy a 40 per cent stake in BitARG, a registered Japanese exchange based in Tokyo. Nikkei Asian Review recently reported the 'Japanese trading platforms are expanding overseas in an effort to grow trading volume and enhance liquidity'.[2]

Japan has also seen a steep increase in the number of merchants accepting bitcoins. News.bitcoin.com[3] reported that a leading used-car automotive group and dealership had recently embraced cryptocurrency as a means of payment. Smaller merchants in Japan are also accepting bitcoins. Housing and facility construction specialist Hiroden Co. Ltd., located in Hirosaki (a small town in rural

Aomori prefecture), began accepting bitcoins on a trial basis from February 2018 onwards, with a limit of one million yen including tax. A Tokyo-based stress care specialist, Stylefulness accepts bitcoin payments. Similarly, Tokyo CRC, Tokyo Campervan Rental Center Group, started accepting bitcoins at its different locations. As an incentive to use bitcoins, Tokyo CRC offered a 20 per cent discount on rental fees between 4 January 2018 to 31 March 2018 for customers paying in bitcoins. During the summer of 2017, Recruit Lifestyle, the retail support arm of a Japan-based human resources conglomerate Recruit Holdings, allowed virtual currency as a payment option at shops that would adopt its point-of-sale app.[4]

The Japanese Government is doing its bit to encourage the use of digital currency. On 1 July 2017, the Japanese regulators instituted a tax reform which removed a consumption tax that dissuaded foreign investors from purchasing bitcoins in Japan's market. This opened up Japan's markets to international investors. The largest interbank clearing network in Japan has selected bitFlyer to demonstrate a proof-of-concept, utilising miyabi[5] (blockchain with a top speed of over 4,000 transactions per second, that guarantees immutability, finality, Byzantine fault tolerance, low latency and has no single point of failure) to show how blockchain can be used to revolutionise the banking industry and create a much faster settlement platform. If adopted, the largest banks in Japan will be connected through blockchain and demonstrate to the world that blockchain can be implemented securely, creating a better and more united financial world. Japan is, thus, in the forefront of the cryptocurrency revolution.

The legislators of Japan are not blind to the fact that the bitcoin ecosystem is a paradise for hoodwinkers and tricksters who happily use it for purposes like tax evasion, money laundering and other illicit activities. So, Japan has instituted regulations to restrict such illegal activity. Japan's Financial Services Agency (FSA) analysed the blockchain technology and developed clear and fair laws to regulate the virtual currency exchanges. Way to go, Japan. However, if truth be told, most countries have reacted with panic-generated aggression in the face of a deluge of reported unlawful activities in the digital space. Most countries like China and South Korea reacted with a hard clampdown on bitcoin exchanges and shut down the bitcoin shop.

Not only did South Korea come down with a heavy hand on the bitcoin trading exchanges, it also issued a document entitled 'Virtual currency holdings and transaction-related information for civil servants' wherein a notification, of sorts, was issued barring all civil servants from 'holding and trading virtual currency'. The publication quoted the personnel affairs department, explaining that if employees trade in digital currencies for their personal benefit, they 'are in violation of the prohibition of forbearance obligations under the civil servants' law'[6] especially if trading is done during work hours. 'Even if there is no job relevance', the officials 'could be subject to discipline'.[7] The Korean Anti-Corruption and Civil Rights Commission issued the 'Code of Conduct Guide to Cryptocurrency' to all government departments and public agencies. This document adds cryptocurrency to Article 12 of the Civil Servant Code of Conduct, prohibiting public officials from using 'the information learned during their duties to assist in trading or investing'[8] in cryptocurrency. Earlier this year, a bill was introduced requiring public officials to declare their cryptocurrency investments. It followed accusations that some government employees were involved in insider trading, using undisclosed knowledge of future regulations as well as market manipulation. So, the bitcoin scenario in South Korea appears pretty grim, which is surprising considering that in the initial years of cryptocurrency evolution, South Korea had been one of the first countries to enthusiastically embrace virtual currency as an investment manna.

For obvious reasons, bitcoins have now become associated with tax evasion and money laundering. Amidst the rising hullabaloo about the legal sanctity, or should I say lack of it, the somewhat-staid UK and EU governments are also planning on a crackdown on bitcoin. The UK Treasury is planning to regulate bitcoin and other cryptocurrencies in order to bring them in line with anti-money laundering and counter-terrorism financial legislation. Under the aegis of such legislation, traders will be required to disclose their identities, ending the anonymity that has made the currency attractive for drug dealing and other illegal activities. Under the EU-wide plan, online platforms where bitcoins are traded, will be required to carry out due diligence on customers and report suspicious transactions.

The UK Government is negotiating amendments to the anti-money laundering directive to ensure firms' activities are overseen by national authorities. The UK Treasury said:

> We are working to address concerns about the use of cryptocurrencies by negotiating to bring virtual currency exchange platforms and some wallet providers within anti-money laundering and counter-terrorist financing regulation.[9]

Although the powers-that-be in Goldman Sachs and JP Morgan have openly denounced bitcoins, Sir Jon Cunliffe, a deputy governor of the Bank of England, hit a balanced note when he put the bitcoin turbulence in the right perspective by reasonably observing that digital currency was too small to pose a systemic threat to the global economy. He also cautioned that bitcoin investors needed 'to do their homework'.[10] The Labour MP John Mann, a member of the House of Commons Treasury, pointed this bitcoin brouhaha in the right direction with his comment that 'these new forms of exchange are expanding rapidly and we've got to make sure we don't get left behind—that's particularly important in terms of money laundering, terrorism or pure theft'.[11] He rightly advised against a 'regulatory lag'. The United Kingdom's legal stance was summed up by Stephen Barclay, the economic secretary to the UK Treasury, who set out the government's plans in a written parliamentary answer in November 2017:

> The UK Government is currently negotiating amendments to the anti-money laundering directive that will bring virtual currency exchange platforms and custodian wallet providers into anti-money laundering and counter-terrorist financing regulation.[12]

Most countries across the globe have accepted bitcoins and altcoins as the future, albeit with a sense of resignation. However, there are a few countries that have expressed open hostility and resistance to cryptocurrencies. They have, in fact, banned use of bitcoins and have not budged from their stand. The founding fathers of the bitcoin-ban have been Bolivia, Ecuador, Kyrgyzstan, Nepal,

Colombia and Bangladesh. The Central Bank of Bolivia issued a resolution, banning bitcoin and any other currency not regulated by the country or economic zone in 2014. The National Assembly of Ecuador banned bitcoins and other digital currencies due to the establishment of a new state-run electronic money system. The newly minted electronic money system would be controlled by the government and tied directly to the local currency, the dollar. 'Electronic money is designed to operate and support the monetary scheme of dollarisation,'[13] stated economist Diego Martinez, a delegate of the President of the Republic to the Board of Regulation and Monetary and Financial Policy. Similarly, in July 2014, statement of the National Bank of the Kyrgyz Republic made clear that 'the use of virtual currency, bitcoins, in particular, as a means of payment in the Kyrgyz Republic will be a violation of the law of our state'. In September 2014, Bangladesh Bank held that 'anybody caught using the virtual currency could be jailed under the country's strict anti-money laundering laws'.[14] There are some countries who had a more open-minded stance towards virtual currencies but of late decided to change their generous stance. So, in Algiers, bitcoin was legal up to 2017. But Algeria is now envisaging the passing of a new finance law that will ban bitcoins. According to the 'Journal Officiel' (28 December 2017):

> Article 117- The purchase, sale, use and holding of so-called virtual currency is prohibited. Virtual currency is that used by internet users via the web. It is characterised by absence of physical support such as coins, notes, payments by cheques or credit card. Any breach of this provision is punishable in accordance with laws and regulations in force.[15]

The global map shows large areas where bitcoin is legal but there are pockets that indicate it is contentious and some grey areas that indicate fence-sitters. The openly hostile pockets are few and far between.

Be that as it may, the question that needs an answer is—how legal is legal? Apparently not a lot. Despite the sound and fury regarding regulations and legality of cryptocurrency, the world has a long way

Figure 10.1: Legal Status of Bitcoin

Source: Based on information gathered from https://en.wikipedia.org/wiki/Legality_of_bitcoin_by_country_or_territory

to go before they can come to grips with the far-reaching impact of a nascent technology and its made-in-heaven marriage with finance. This becomes pretty clear when we look at facts and figures thrown up by a Benchmark Study of Cambridge University.[16] This research reveals that 52 per cent of small cryptocurrency exchanges have a formal government licence or authorisation while only 35 per cent of large exchanges hold an approved licence. If we see an area-wise break-up, we will find that 85 per cent of all exchanges based in the Asia-Pacific region do not have a licence. Also, only 47 per cent and 43 per cent of European and Latin American-based exchanges, respectively, hold a licence. This means that on an average 48 per cent of bitcoin/altcoin exchanges are functioning outside the government purview and to that extent may be considered either illegal or at least tethering on the brink of illegality. This study also flags an important concern about cryptocurrency wallets. In contrast with exchanges and firms designated as money transfer operators, the compliance requirements for the cryptocurrency storage function performed by wallets are less clear. The fact that wallet providers are often operating globally and therefore falling within the ambit of different jurisdictions muddies the wallet compliance waters. For example, if cryptocurrencies are legally considered to be 'money', does that require companies providing basic cryptocurrency storage services to be compliant with existing banking regulation, or does this only apply to wallet providers that take custody of user funds and/or provide integrated currency exchange services? Twenty-four per cent of incorporated wallets have a formal licence from a regulatory authority and all of them are wallet providers that offer national-to-cryptocurrency exchange services. However, what is shocking is that 25 per cent of wallets providing centralised national-to-cryptocurrency exchange services do not have a government licence. The study reveals that only 54 per cent of payment service providers surveyed have a formal government licence or authorisation. While 86 per cent of payment services providers are based in North America, only 40 per cent of Latin American payment companies have a licence. The proportion of companies based in the Asia-Pacific region and Europe that have a licence is approximately similar at 42 per cent and 46 per cent respectively. The unpalatable reality that emerges is that a large chunk of the global exchanges and wallet providers are functioning outside the pale of law. The trek down the regulatory path promises to be a long haul. So, let us see what the governments of the world are doing about framing new regulations or amending old regulations to monitor cryptocurrency transactions.

Chapter 11

Regulatory Reckoning

> *There ought to be a hard look at the policy of anonymous currencies, because the ability to track information of money flowing is one we use seriously against terrorism and as a [a tool] against improper, illegal behaviour.*
>
> —Brian Moynihan, CEO, Bank of America

A fledgling currency that circumvents third party institutions like banks. A digital currency that by its very nature self-regulates. An electronic coin that thumbs its nose at all current monetary policies and regulations. Yes, the bitcoin is all that and more. For the legal arm of the governments of the world, it is proving to be a square peg in a round hole. Most of the countries are walking the tightrope between legally embracing bitcoins and publicly discrediting them as illegal balderdash. It is no wonder then that most governments of the world have an ambivalent stance to this new kid on the block. A look at both sides of the coin, metaphorically speaking, would make for a better understanding.

Regulations for 'Money Transmitters' in the United States

The United States has given a certain level of credibility to bitcoins by accepting and treating them as MSBs (Money Service Businesses). An MSB is a legal term used by financial regulators to describe a 'money transmitter', business that transmits or converts money. The Bank Secrecy Act (1970)[1] defines the term 'money transmitter' to include a person that provides money transmission services, or any other person engaged in the transfer of funds. The term 'money transmission services' means the acceptance of currency, funds, or other value that substitutes for currency from one person for transfer to another person through established channels. The term 'money transmitter' defined in the somewhat antiquated Bank Secrecy Act, however, came a cropper when it was faced with the new-age virtual currency transactions that were in the nature of transmissions.

The existing FinCEN (Financial Crimes Enforcement Network)[2] regulations were also of no help in the digital currency ecosystem as they only defined 'real' currency. Real currency was defined as—

The coin and paper money of the United States or of any other country that:

1. is designated as legal tender and that
2. circulates and
3. is customarily used and accepted as a medium of exchange in the country of issuance.

Such a definition clearly did not include within its ambit 'virtual currency' that may operate like a currency in some environments, but does not have all the attributes of real currency. In particular, virtual currency did not have legal tender status in any jurisdiction. So, to regulate such virtual currency transactions, FinCEN issued a guidance note on 18 March 2013.[3] Thankfully, the guidance note did not seek to enlarge the scope of the definition of 'real' currency. Instead, it introduced a fresh nomenclature—'convertible' virtual currency. Convertible virtual currency was defined as a currency having an equivalent value in real currency, or a currency that acts as a substitute for real currency. FinCEN categorised three participants in generic virtual currency arrangements, namely 'exchanger', 'administrator' and 'user'. Within this limited context, an 'exchanger' is a person engaged in the business of exchange of virtual currency for real currency, funds, or other virtual currency. An 'administrator' is a person engaged in the business of issuing (putting into circulation) a virtual currency, with the authority to redeem (to withdraw from circulation) such virtual currency. A 'user' is a person that obtains virtual currency to purchase goods or services on the user's own behalf.

The guidance makes clear that an administrator or exchanger of convertible virtual currencies that—

1. accepts and transmits a convertible virtual currency or
2. buys or sells convertible virtual currency in exchange for currency of legal tender or another convertible virtual currency for any reason (including when intermediating between a user and a seller of goods or services the user is purchasing on the user's behalf)

—is a money transmitter under FinCEN's regulations.

The guidance also clarifies that 'a user who obtains convertible virtual currency and uses it to purchase real or virtual goods or services is not an MSB under FinCEN's regulations'. Here the term 'obtains' is further elaborated. A 'user' may obtain a virtual currency by the processes as varied as 'earning', 'harvesting', 'mining', 'creating', 'auto-generating', 'manufacturing', or 'purchasing', depending on the details of the specific virtual currency model involved. However, the process of 'obtaining' the digital currency has little or no relevance to its legal treatment. What is material to the conclusion is the use or application of the convertible virtual currency.

Going by this logic, a person is not considered a 'money transmitter' and consequently an MSB under certain circumstances. For instance, when a user mines bitcoin and uses the bitcoin solely for his own purpose and not for the benefit of another, he can take refuge in the 'exempt' clause. This is because here the activity of the 'miner-user' does not involve either 'acceptance' or 'transmission' of the convertible virtual currency. These two parameters are essential for an MSB categorisation. This would be equally applicable to both an individual as well as a corporation. The legal intent is clear. Activities that, in and of themselves, do not constitute accepting and transmitting currency, funds or the value of funds, are activities that do not fit within the definition of 'money transmission services' and therefore are not subject to FinCEN's registration, reporting and record-keeping regulations for MSBs. At times, it may become necessary for a user to convert bitcoin (that he has mined) into a real currency simply because the seller of goods and services in the market refuses to accept payment in a virtual currency. A pragmatic user may also wish to diversify his currency portfolio or invest in an asset that requires conversion of a cryptocurrency into a fiat currency. In undertaking such a conversion, although the user is accepting a real currency and transmitting a bitcoin, the conversion and transmission is for his own use. A user's conversion of bitcoin into a real currency or another convertible virtual currency, therefore, does not in and of itself make the user a money transmitter. So, a bitcoin user using bitcoins it has mined to pay for the purchase of goods or services, pay debts it has previously incurred or to purchase real currency or another convertible virtual currency, so long as the real currency or other convertible virtual currency is used solely in order to make payments or for own investment purposes is not treated as an MSB. However, a user engaging in such a transaction, which pays bitcoin to a third party at the direction of the counter party, may be engaged in money transmission.

There are stringent regulations in place for MSBs in the United States. Every MSB has to register with FinCEN by electronically filing FinCEN Form 107. The MSB's owner or controlling person is required to register within 180 days of establishing the MSB. The law stipulates a renewal of MSB registration by the end of a 180-day period. Renewal of MSB registration after the lapse of two calendar years is also mandated. All MSBs are required to develop and implement an anti-money laundering (AML) compliance programme. This is a firewall to prevent individuals from using the MSB to facilitate money laundering or to finance terrorist activities. MSBs are also required to electronically file a Currency Transaction Report in FinCEN Form 112 detailing cash-in or cash-out currency transaction, or multiple transactions, totalling more than $10,000 during one business day for any one person, or on behalf of any one person. The MSBs are also obliged to report transactions and patterns of transactions that are suspicious and involve $2,000 or more in the Suspicious Activity Report.[4]

New York State's Call to Arms

Given the large-scale hacks and scams involving virtual currencies, the New York State regulators have put in place a wide variety of stringent regulatory practices to monitor and regulate bitcoins and other altcoins. Benjamin Lawsky, Superintendent of the New York State Regulator makes the rationale for such a regulatory framework clear in a post on Reddit's discussion board, a forum for virtual currency advocates:

> In developing this regulatory framework, we have sought to strike an appropriate balance that helps protect consumers and root out illegal activity—without stifling beneficial innovation.[5]

Against a backdrop of clear regulatory intent, the State of New York allows exchanges to trade cryptocurrencies only when they have obtained a charter or a licence, known as BitLicense, from the New York State Department of Financial Services (NYSDFS). In accordance with the New York State Administrative Procedure Act (SAPA), the final DFS (Department of Financial Services) rules for virtual currency business activity were published in the New York State Register's 24 June 2015 edition[6]. To start with, only 6 firms were able to meet the rigorous eligibility criterion of NYSDFS. Circle Internet Financial, XRP II, Coinbase Inc. and Bitflyer USA were issued BitLicenses, while charters were granted to Gemini Trust Company and Itbit Trust Company.

The BitLicense regulation emanates from and draws strength from the clear-cut definition of virtual currency as well as virtual currency business activity. Virtual currency is defined as a digital unit that is used as a medium of exchange or a form of digitally stored value. The regulatory document describes 'virtual currency' as a digital unit of exchange that:

(i) *has a centralized repository or administrator;*

(ii) *is decentralized and has no centralized repository or administrator; or*

(iii) *may be created or obtained by computing or manufacturing effort.*

The exceptions are also detailed clearly to avoid any misinterpretation in a legal no man's land. The regulation lays down that virtual currency shall not be construed to include any of the following:

(1) digital units that are used solely within online gaming platforms and have no market or application outside of those gaming platforms, or can be redeemed for real-world goods, services, discounts, or purchases, but cannot be converted into, or redeemed for, Fiat Currency or Virtual Currency as defined herein;

(2) digital units that can be redeemed for goods, services, discounts, or purchases with the issuer and/or other designated merchants or can be redeemed for digital units in another customer affinity or rewards program, but cannot be converted into, or redeemed for, Fiat Currency or Virtual Currency as defined herein; or

(3) digital units used as part of Gift Cards;

'Virtual currency business activity' is also specified to mean the conduct of any one of the following types of activities involving New York or a New York resident:

(1) receiving Virtual Currency for Transmission or Transmitting Virtual Currency, except where the transaction is undertaken for non-financial purposes and does not involve the transfer of more than a nominal amount of Virtual Currency;

(2) storing, holding, or maintaining custody or control of Virtual Currency on behalf of others;

(3) buying and selling Virtual Currency as a customer business;

(4) performing Exchange Services as a customer business; or

(5) controlling, administering, or issuing a Virtual Currency. The development and dissemination of software in and of itself does not constitute Virtual Currency Business Activity.

The prerequisites required for issuing of licence are clearly demarcated. The rules require each Licensee to maintain at all times such capital in an amount and form as the superintendent (New York Regulator) determines is sufficient to ensure the financial integrity of the Licensee and its ongoing operations based on an assessment of the specific risks applicable to each Licensee. In determining the minimum amount of capital that must be maintained by a Licensee, the superintendent may consider a variety of factors, including but not limited to:

(1) *the composition of the Licensee's total assets, including the position, size, liquidity, risk exposure and price volatility of each type of asset;*
(2) *the composition of the Licensee's total liabilities, including the size and repayment timing of each type of liability;*
(3) *the actual and expected volume of the Licensee's Virtual Currency Business Activity;*
(4) *whether the Licensee is already licensed or regulated by the superintendent under the Financial Services Law, Banking Law, or Insurance Law, or otherwise subject to such laws as a provider of a financial product or service and whether the Licensee is in good standing in such capacity;*
(5) *the amount of leverage employed by the Licensee;*
(6) *the liquidity position of the Licensee;*
(7) *the financial protection that the Licensee provides for its customers through its trust account or bond;*
(8) *the types of entities to be serviced by the Licensee; and*
(9) *the types of products or services to be offered by the Licensee.*

Looks like a never-ending list but ensures that in case of a hack or a heist, the Licensee would have enough capital to cover for all liabilities and also ensure the customers do not lose their money. So, each Licensee shall hold capital required to be maintained in accordance with this section in the form of cash, virtual currency, or high-quality, highly liquid, investment-grade assets, in such proportions as stipulated. That's not all. There are some more safeguards for the customers. Each Licensee is mandated with maintaining a surety bond or trust account in US dollars for the benefit of its customers in such form and amount as is acceptable to the superintendent for the protection of the Licensee's customers. The section lays down that:

(a) *To the extent a Licensee maintains a trust account in accordance with this section, such trust account must be maintained with a Qualified Custodian.*

(b) *To the extent a Licensee stores, holds, or maintains custody or control of Virtual Currency on behalf of another Person, such Licensee shall hold Virtual Currency of the same type and amount as that which is owed or obligated to such other Person.*

(c) *Each Licensee is prohibited from selling, transferring, assigning, lending, hypothecating, pledging, or otherwise using or encumbering assets, including Virtual Currency, stored, held, or maintained by, or under the custody or control of, such Licensee on behalf of another Person except for the sale, transfer, or assignment of such assets at the direction of such other Person.*

Apart from the initial risk assessment, the New York Code stipulates a regular examination of the books and capital of the Licensee. The balance of rights and obligations is maintained by a provision in the Code whereby each Licensee, as part of its anti-money laundering programme, shall maintain records and make reports in the manner prescribed in the Code.

The Code mandates that each Licensee shall maintain certain information for all virtual currency transactions including details pertaining to payment, receipt, exchange or conversion, purchase, sale, transfer, or transmission of virtual currency. This information includes:

i) *the identity and physical addresses of the party or parties to the transaction that are customers or account holders of the Licensee and, to the extent practicable, any other parties to the transaction;*

ii) *the amount or value of the transaction, including in what denomination purchased, sold, or transferred;*

iii) *the method of payment;*

iv) *the date or dates on which the transaction was initiated and completed; and*

v) *a description of the transaction.*

The Licensee is also bound to report all transactions in the nature of receipt, exchange, conversion, purchase, sale, transfer, or transmission of virtual currency, where the aggregate amount exceeds the US dollar value of $10,000 in one day, by one person. In such cases, the Licensee is bound to notify the DFS within 24 hours.

Each Licensee is also required to adhere to a customer identification programme, under the aegis of the anti-money laundering scheme. This entails verification of the customer's identity, to the extent reasonable and practicable, maintaining records of the information used to verify such identity, including name, physical address and other identifying information and check customers against the Specially Designated Nationals (SDNs) list maintained by the Office of Foreign Asset Control (OFAC), a part of the US Treasury Department. Enhanced due diligence may be required based on additional factors, such as for high risk customers, high-volume accounts, or accounts on which a suspicious activity report has been filed. Licensees that maintain accounts for non-US Persons and non-US Licensees need to ensure strict compliance with enhanced due diligence policies, procedures and controls to detect money laundering, including assessing the risk presented by such accounts based on the nature of the foreign business, the type and purpose of the activity and the anti-money laundering and supervisory regime of the foreign jurisdiction. Each Licensee is also required to flag customers that have initiated a transaction exceeding $3,000. A prohibitory clause forbids a Licensee from maintaining relationships of any type in connection with their virtual currency business activity with entities that do not have a physical presence in any country. This was an attempt to filter out shell companies set up as conduits for laundering activities offshore.

There are lots of other provisions but I'm sure by now you would be losing patience with this never-ending list of provisions so I'll call a halt to this regulatory litany. Suffice it to say, the New York Code is more detailed and balanced than the Federal Tax Code. The Federal Code would do well to take a leaf out of the New York regulation to make it more secure and with the right balance of rights and obligations to and for the government as well as the customer.

Canada Takes Bitcoin Bull by Its Horns

Canada is another country that has taken the bitcoin bull by its horns. Like the United States, it has set the regulatory ball rolling.

On 19 June 2014, the Parliament of Canada approved a national law on treatment of digital currency financial transactions with a generous dollop of anti-money laundering mandate thrown in. This was the much-feted Bill C-31 that amended Canada's 'Proceeds Of Crime (Money Laundering) and Terrorist Financing Act' (PCMLTFA)[7] to legislate over digital currency financial transactions as a matter of anti-money laundering law. Division 19 of Part 6 amends the Proceeds of Crime (Money Laundering) and Terrorist Financing Act to, among other things, enhance the client identification, record-keeping and registration requirements for financial institutions and intermediaries and extend the application of the Act to persons and entities that deal in virtual currencies and foreign money services businesses. Furthermore, it makes modifications with regard to the information that the Financial Transactions and Reports Analysis Centre of Canada may receive, collect or disclose and expands the circumstances in which the Centre or the Canada Border Services Agency can disclose information received or collected under the Act. This amendment extended to not only persons and entities that have a place of business in Canada but also persons and entities that do not have a place of business in Canada.

256 (2) Paragraph 5(h) of the Act is replaced by the following:

(h) persons and entities that have a place of business in Canada and that are engaged in the business of providing at least one of the following services:

- *(i) foreign exchange dealing,*
- *(ii) remitting funds or transmitting funds by any means or through any person, entity or electronic funds transfer network,*
- *(iii) issuing or redeeming money orders, traveller's cheques or other similar negotiable instruments except for cheques payable to a named person or entity,*
- *(iv) dealing in virtual currencies, or*
- *(v) any prescribed service;*

(h.1) persons and entities that do not have a place of business in Canada, that are engaged in the business of providing at least one

of the following services that is directed at persons or entities in Canada and that provide those services to their clients in Canada:
- *(i) foreign exchange dealing,*
- *(ii) remitting funds or transmitting funds by any means or through any person, entity or electronic funds transfer network,*
- *(iii) issuing or redeeming money orders, traveller's cheques or other similar negotiable instruments except for cheques payable to a named person or entity,*
- *(iv) dealing in virtual currencies, or*
- *(v) any prescribed service;*

With this amendment, any dealing in virtual currencies was to be treated as an MSB and subject to the record-keeping, verification procedures, suspicious transaction reporting and registration requirements under the PCMLTFA as a money services business. As in the United States, digital currency MSBs were to be registered with the financial intelligence unit of Canada called The Financial Transactions and Reports Analysis Centre of Canada (FINTRAC) and were required to implement the complete anti-money laundering compliance regime. This Bill also prohibited banks from opening and maintaining correspondent banking relationships with digital currency MSBs that are not registered with FINTRAC.

Pursuant to the amended PCMLTFA, digital currency MSBs will be required to undertake the following obligations:

Report Suspicious Transactions

Digital currency MSBs will be required to report to FINTRAC every suspicious financial transaction and attempted suspicious financial transaction. There is no monetary threshold (i.e. dollar amount) that triggers the requirement to report a suspicious transaction.

Report Terrorist Property Transactions

Digital currency MSBs will have to file with FINTRAC, a terrorist property report when it has property in its possession or control that it knows is owned or controlled by or on behalf of a terrorist or terrorist group; and when it has property in its possession or control that it has reason to believe is owned or controlled by or on behalf of a listed person.

Report Cash Transactions of $10,000 or more

Digital currency MSBs will be required to report to FINTRAC when they receive an amount of $10,000 or more in cash in the course of a single transaction, unless the funds are received by a public body or a financial entity.

Electronic Funds Transfers

The digital currency MSBs will be required to report to FINTRAC when it sends out of Canada at the request of a person, an electronic funds transfer of $10,000 or more in a single transaction or receives from outside Canada at the request of a person, an electronic funds transfer of $10,000 or more in a single transaction.

Politically Exposed Persons

When a digital currency MSB sends or receives an international money transfer of $100,000 or more, it must determine if it involves a politically exposed person (PEP) inside or outside of Canada and if it determines that the funds involve a PEP, it must confirm the source of funds. Determining PEPs is a difficult part of anti-money laundering compliance because the obligation is a worldwide one.

Ascertaining ID

Digital currency MSBs will have to undertake obligations to ascertain the identity of persons and companies using their services to complete certain financial transactions.

Records Retention

Digital currency MSBs will be subject to fairly onerous record-keeping obligations under the PCMLTFA. They must keep large cash transaction records, records regarding third parties when certain transactions are conducted for third parties.

Risk Assessments

Digital currency MSBs will have to undertake a risk assessment to evaluate and identify, in the course of its activities, the risk of the commission of money laundering offences and terrorist activity financing offenses.

This is a tall order for practitioners of business dealing in bitcoins and other virtual currencies in Canada. Views have been aired in the public realm that these regulations are restrictive enough to throttle the mainline artery that is fed on decentralisation and deregulation. I think not. Such a regulation would ensure that scams are not perpetrated against unwary citizens and any unlawful activity associated with cryptocurrency transaction is nipped in the bud. Unfortunately, virtual currency regulations are not a result of regulatory foresight but have invariably gathered force in the aftermath of unsavoury financial scandals.

Fear Factor Sets Regulatory Ball Rolling in Australia

This fear factor played a pivotal role in the regulatory drive in the otherwise laid-back regulatory environment of the land down under. In August 2017, the Commonwealth Bank of Australia (CBA) was caught in an unbecoming scandal. The Australian Transaction Reports and Analysis Centre (AUSTRAC) filed a claim in the Federal Court alleging that CBA failed to report terrorism financing suspicions within 24 hours, was either slow or negligent in reporting 54 suspicious matters relating to accounts or people under law enforcement investigation and in 38 instances did not appropriately monitor risk, even after becoming aware of suspicious activity.[8] This scandal set the alarm belling clanging and made the Government of Australia sit up in consternation. Without much ado, the Australian Government set into motion the process of regulating of cryptocurrencies like bitcoins. On 13 December 2017, the Parliament of Australia enacted the AntiMoney Laundering and CounterTerrorism Financing Amendment Act 2017.[9] The amended Act commenced from 3 April 2018.

Section 4 of the said Act makes registration of digital exchange currency providers mandatory. Section 4 stipulates:

> *Providers of registrable digital currency exchange services must be registered with the AUSTRAC CEO.*

Section 5 of the Act provides for a comprehensive definition of digital currency.

digital currency means

(a) a digital representation of value that:
  - *(i) functions as a medium of exchange, a store of economic value, or a unit of account; and*
  - *(ii) is not issued by or under the authority of a government body; and*
  - *(iii) is interchangeable with money (including through the crediting of an account) and may be used as consideration for the supply of goods or services; and*
  - *(iv) is generally available to members of the public without any restriction on its use as consideration; or*

(b) a means of exchange or digital process or crediting declared to be digital currency by the AML/CTF Rules; but does not include any right or thing that, under the AML/CTF Rules, is taken not to be digital currency for the purposes of this Act.

Division 1 of the Regulation provides for a system of registration for providers of digital currency exchange services. Division 2 sets out offences and civil penalties in relation to the provision of registrable digital currency exchange services by persons who are not registered. Division 3 requires the AUSTRAC CEO to maintain the Digital Currency Exchange Register and sets out the process of applying for registration. Infraction of the law attracts a penalty that ranges from an imprisonment of 2 years and penalty of 500 units to imprisonment of 7 years and 2,000 penalty units. The AUSTRAC CEO must decide to register the person in accordance with the application if the AUSTRAC CEO is satisfied that it is appropriate to do so, having regard to:

(a) whether registering the person would involve a significant money laundering, financing of terrorism or other serious crime risk; and

(b) *such other matters (if any) as are specified in the AML/CTF Rules under this paragraph.*

The new Bill mandates that digital currency exchange providers identify and verify the identities of customers using their services; report suspicious matters, international transactions and any transactions involving physical currency that exceeds AUD $10,000 (for a foreign currency equivalent) to AUSTRAC; have an anti-money laundering and counter-terrorism financing programme in place to monitor, mitigate and manage money laundering risks; and maintain records of certain transactions and customer identification for a period of seven years.

Following registration with AUSTRAC, cryptocurrency exchange service providers are placed on AUSTRAC's new Digital Currency Exchange Register. Failure to register with AUSTRAC constitutes a criminal offence, with a first offence carrying a penalty of up to 2 years' imprisonment and/or a fine of $105,000 and higher penalties are applicable for repeated offences. Digital currency exchange service providers in breach of the laws may alternatively be pursued under the civil penalty provisions and be subject to penalties of up to $21 million for corporations and $4.2 million for individuals.

Thankfully, the legislation effectively targets the 'entry' and 'exit' points of the digital currency system—i.e. when a person uses regular money to buy digital currency or convert digital currency back into regular money. As a result, the laws will not affect how digital currency can be transferred between users nor the privacy of such transactions. An extremely good start to monitor the underbelly of cryptocurrencies without placing too many restrictions on the use/transaction of the newbie virtual currencies.

As is obvious from the analysis of regulatory mechanisms adopted by developed countries like the United States, Canada and Australia, the bitcoin regulations are nothing but a polite substitute, a euphemism for anti-money laundering. The legal framework is hinged around the belief that bitcoins and others of its ilk are a conduit for money laundering and terrorism. These regulations are aimed at the underbelly of cryptocurrencies. They, however, do not encourage a responsible use of the digital currency. Japan is, perhaps, one of the few countries that have legislated a somewhat more crypto-friendly act.

Japanese Virtual Currency Legislation: A Balancing Act

The Japanese regulators stepped in after the sound and fury of the Mt Gox heist. The Financial Action Task Force (FATF) guidance note of 2015[10] recommended that all virtual currency (VC) exchangers be registered or licensed and be subject to scrutiny like other financial institutions. The 2015 guidance became the preface to the Virtual Currency Act[11] passed by the parliament of Japan in April 2017. The Guidance Note on the Virtual Currency Legislation gives a short and pithy account of the law on virtual currencies. The VC Act, at first glance, appears to be another anti-money laundering legislation, seemingly no different from the West's penchant of coming down with a heavy statutory hand on virtual currency transactions.

The VC Act classifies virtual currencies as Type I VC and Type II VC. Type I VCs refer to the financial value (recorded by way of electronic means in the electronic devices etc., excluding any fiat currency/currencies of Japan or otherwise) and assets denominated in any such fiat currency which may be used to pay the price for the goods purchased or services received or may be received in lieu of goods sold and services rendered from/to a specified person or persons. These include bitcoins, Litecoins and other virtual currencies that are used for payment purposes. Type II VC refers to financial value (recorded by way of electronic means in the electronic devices etc., excluding any fiat currency/currencies of Japan or otherwise) and assets denominated in any such fiat currency which may be exchanged, as against unspecified person/persons, with any such financial value of Type I VC and which may be transferred via electronic data processing system. These refer to virtual currencies that cannot be used directly for purpose of payment of goods and service but can be exchanged with other cryptocurrencies. These include Ether which cannot be used for payment but can be exchanged with bitcoins, Litecoins, etc.

This legislation describes a virtual currency exchange clearly. Under the VC Act, the virtual currency exchange business (the VC

Exchange Business) means any of the following acts carried out as a business:

(i) *Sale and purchase of VC (i.e. exchange between VC and a fiat currency), or exchange a VC to another VC;*

(ii) *an intermediary, brokerage or agency service for the acts described in above (i); and*

(iii) *management (custody) of a fiat currency or VC on behalf of the users/recipient in relation to the acts described in above (1) and (2).*

So, a virtual exchange business would entail and include:

1. An exchange in which its users can sell and/or purchase VC from other users
2. Shop which sells and/or purchases VC
3. Operator of bitcoin ATM
4. Operator of ICO (initial coin offering) and
5. A brokerage firm which intermediates sales or purchase of VC.

The VC Act, however, clearly enunciates that it does not include a person who trades VC for its own investment purpose, mining firm, software developer and wallet service provider which is not relevant to VC sales/purchase. This is very similar to the Federal Regulation of MSBs in the United States and Canada. Like other legislations on the subject, this Act requires a mandatory registration of all virtual currency exchanges with the Japanese Financial Services Agency (JFSA). Pursuant to this Act, the VC Exchange Business operators are under a duty to ensure customer identity verification, accountability to the customers, segregation of customers' assets from the proprietary assets, bookkeeping, compliance, internal audit and so on. Although, the KYC norms appear to be identical, the Japanese regulators have stolen the march over other developed countries in that they have put into place a statute that respects and maintains the privacy and security of bitcoin users. Bitcoins, as we know, were an attempt to overcome the third-party trust crisis through a private and self-regulated currency that was not subject to the caprices of the government. The regulations instituted by the West, if not implemented with caution, are likely to strangulate the basic tenets of self-regulation of the virtual currency revolution. The Japanese Government, on the other hand has ensured that even while it is sounding the death-knell for illicit activities spawned by the beyond-the-stronghold-of-enforcement privacy of digital currencies, it will actively encourage a responsible use of virtual currencies.

So, the VC Act ensures accountability of virtual currency exchanges to its users. The Act clearly articulates the requirement of a VC exchange to provide adequate explanation to its users for user protection. All users must be fully informed of their transactions, the handling fees charged and where it can file complaints. The VC Act stipulates that the users be provided with receipts for deposit of virtual currency. An important clause in the Act is the statutory need of VC exchanges to securely control their electronic information system so that their VC and records are protected against cyber-attack. Another such clause is regarding protection of personal information of users obtained by the exchanges. The VC exchanges must ensure the protection of personal information they obtain. So, while the VC exchanges have a duty to the government to ensure that illegal activities are not conducted under their umbrella, they also have a duty to safeguard the information of its users. So, the message going out is that responsible bitcoin users are welcome. But those who are found wanting will not be spared. The reason for this balanced approach is not far to find. Japan is an extremely techno-savvy nation with a battery of regulators well versed in the art of the technology that underpins virtual currencies. This makes for a clarity of thought in legislation that is missing in other similar statutes.

Winter of Crypto Discontent

A clutch of countries that have banned bitcoins outright are Morocco, Bolivia, Ecuador, Nepal and Bangladesh. Most other countries are either dithering on the regulations or playing a confusing game of passing the buck. India, unfortunately, is one such country along with a host of other nations of the European Union, Africa and the Asian subcontinent. China and South Korea, until recently were the countries with the highest volume of bitcoin mining and a huge turnover on bitcoin exchanges set up for bitcoin trading and investment.

However, the summer of 2017 saw a government clampdown on bitcoin exchanges in China. It was winter of discontent for the bitcoin fans in South Korea as well. The government bludgeoned a thriving bitcoin market into nothingness, claiming that bitcoins were solely responsible for an outflow of capital from the country. Whether such fears had a valid basis or were unfounded is anybody's guess but the fact remains that despite public posturing about soon-to-arrive virtual currency legislation, there appears to be nothing in the offing.

India: Legislation on the Anvil

India's regulators also seem to be dragging their feet on a legislation to monitor bitcoins and altcoins. There have been sporadic press releases cautioning against use of virtual currencies by the Reserve Bank of India (RBI). The 24 December 2013 press release cautioned 'users, holders and traders of virtual currencies (VCs) including bitcoins regarding the potential economic, financial, operational, legal, customer protection and security related risks associated in dealing with such VCs'. A press release dated 1 February 2017 further clarified that RBI had not given 'any licence/authorisation to any entity/company to operate such schemes or deal with bitcoin or any VC'. The Blockchain and Cryptocurrency Committee (BACC), which was set up under the aegis of the Internet and Mobile Association of India (IAMAI), has been attempting to lobby the government for clear-cut regulations around the use of bitcoin. The industry has tried to self-regulate with the use of e-KYCs to authenticate users. However, much to the disappointment of bitcoin players no regulatory legislation was announced as a part of the 2018 Budget. The finance minister, while presenting the Budget in the Parliament, said, 'The government does not consider cryptocurrencies as legal tender or coin and will take all measures to eliminate the use of crypto assets in financing illegitimate activities or as part of the payment system.' This studied but non-committal statement did not appease the lobbyists who complained that it was simply a reiteration of the government's earlier stand. In fact, the minister's remark talking about a clampdown on 'crypto assets financing illegitimate activities' spooked the cryptocurrency market leading to a significant slide in bitcoin trading and investing volumes. The Public Interest Litigation (PIL) in the Supreme Court calling for a ban or strict regulation of bitcoins has added fuel to the fire. December 2017 saw a spate of surveys conducted on bitcoin exchanges. Almost 100,000 notices were issued by the Income Tax Department to bitcoin investors, consequent upon the surveys so conducted. The Finance Ministry constituted a panel in the same month to follow bitcoin investing/ trading patterns, volumes and also to expedite a regulatory enactment. Representatives from Enforcement Directorate (ED), Reserve Bank of India (RBI) and Income Tax Department have been nominated to this panel. So, 'wait and watch' seems to be the epitaph for the regulatory tombstone.

Regulatory Way Forward: Addressing the Elephant in the Room

Most countries of the world are shying away from regulating virtual currencies. This reticence, for the most part, stems from their inability to make sense of the complexities of the new-age currency. The head-in-the-sand approach to bitcoins or the wait-and-watch approach will be the Waterloo for regulators. Virtual currency and the technology underpinning it is an idea whose time has come. Governments can ignore it at their own peril. Turning a blind eye to this peer-to-peer, self-regulating electronic coin will do nothing but fan the flames of illicit embers or create a Frankenstein's monster that will be difficult to rein in. The need of the hour is to evaluate the digital ecosystem in a country and regulate it in a manner so as to ensure that it does not become a handy tool for money laundering, tax evasion or terrorism financing. At the same time, the regulations cannot be allowed to strangle this new laissez-faire technology that has taken root. The Virtual Currency Act of Japan is a step in the right direction and regulators could model their regulatory framework on the Japan model with minor changes necessitated by domestic factors. I agree that putting together regulations for a fledgling currency cannot be easy and will certainly require a great deal of time and effort. The obvious fix would be to issue a guidance note as a prelude to comprehensive regulations. The second fix would be to accept that the regulations would need to evolve slowly and keep pace with the growth of the digital environment. This means regulations in keeping with the current crypto environment and amendments can be introduced as and when loopholes are ascertained or new issues need to be addressed.

The governments of the world also need to remember that the term virtual currency is not a pejorative term that is synonymous with illegal activity. Christine Lagarde, the IMF boss struck the right note on the IMF blog when she stated that 'a judicious look at crypto assets should lead us to neither crypto-condemnation nor crypto-euphoria'. Lagarde believes that the world needs a 'clear-eyed approach' that 'can help us harness the gains and avoid the pitfalls of the new crypto-assets landscape'.[12] That, my friends, is the only way forward. *Ordo ab chao*. The only way to make order out of chaos.

Chapter 12

Taxing Matters

> *If we could get regulation right, to make sure the bad stuff we didn't want to see happening in the ecosystem was avoided and at the same time not have regulation be too overbearing, then we had a real chance of helping a very powerful technology make serious improvements to our system.*
>
> —Benjamin Lawsky,
> Former Superintendent Financial Services
> for the State of New York

Sri, a techie working for an MNC in Bangalore (India) sold some bitcoins (that he had purchased while studying in Berkeley in 2011) in December 2017, making a hefty profit. The amount was credited in his bank account and he instructed his CA to file his return and pay the necessary taxes. The CA admitted in all honesty that there was no provision in the current Income Tax Act for taxability of profits generated from a bitcoin transaction. Sri was caught in a bind. He wanted to pay his taxes but how?

Taxability of bitcoins is a big grey mass akin to a black hole that raises more questions than it answers. The tax experts find it difficult to put a label on cryptocurrency. Is it a currency? Well, we all know it is not a fiat currency. Does that mean it is a foreign currency? Not sure if it could be reckoned as such. After all, it transcends borders and cannot be pinned to any country. So, let's not get into the currency imbroglio. Then how do we treat income generated from cryptocurrency transactions? Not a clue. It would, perhaps, be better to treat it as an asset or a security like shares. After all, it is traded and invested through bitcoin exchanges. An asset without physical contours? An asset that has no intrinsic value? An asset that is mined through complex algorithmic computations? There is that. No wonder tax legislators and revenue services the world over are grappling with the provisions that would make bitcoins taxable. The interpretation of the statutes vis-à-vis cryptocurrencies is different in different countries. Let us take a look at how some of the developed and developing nations are writing their bitcoin tax stories.

The United States Writes its Bitcoin Tax Story

The Internal Revenue Service (IRS) of the United States issued a notice in 2014[1] describing how existing general tax principles would apply to transactions using virtual currency. The notice provided guidance in the form of answers to frequently asked questions. The notice acknowledged that in some environments, cryptocurrencies operate like 'real' currency (coin and paper money) and are customarily used and accepted as a medium of exchange. The notice made it clear that although such currencies do not have legal tender status, the sale or exchange of convertible virtual currency, or the use of convertible virtual currency to pay for goods or services in a real-world economy, has tax consequences that may result in a tax liability. This notice, of course, addresses only the US federal tax consequences of transactions in, or transactions that use, convertible virtual currency.

For federal tax purposes, virtual currency is treated as property. General tax principles applicable to property transactions apply to transactions using virtual currency. However, the notice of 2014 makes it clear that a taxpayer who receives virtual currency as payment for goods or services must, in computing gross income, include the fair market value of the virtual currency, measured in US dollars, as on the date of receipt of such virtual currency. So, taxpayers are required to determine the fair market value of virtual currency in US dollars on the date of payment or receipt. If a virtual currency is listed on an exchange and the exchange rate is established by market supply and demand, the fair market value of the virtual currency is determined by converting the virtual currency into US dollars (or into another real currency which in turn can be converted into US dollars) at the exchange rate. Logically, therefrom, it emerges that if the fair market value of property received in exchange for virtual currency exceeds the taxpayer's adjusted basis of the virtual currency, the taxpayer has a taxable gain. The taxpayer has a loss if the fair market value of the property received is less than the adjusted basis of the virtual currency. The character of the gain or loss generally depends on whether the virtual currency is a capital asset in the hands of the taxpayer. A taxpayer generally realises capital gain or loss on the sale or exchange of virtual currency that is a capital asset in the hands of the taxpayer. For example, stocks, bonds and other investment property are generally capital assets. This means profit from sale of bitcoins held as investment will be treated as a capital gain. However, it would do well to remember that inventory and other property held mainly for sale to customers in a trade or business are examples of property that is not a capital asset.

The federal law also stipulates that, when a taxpayer successfully mines' virtual currency, the fair market value of the virtual currency as on the date of receipt is to be included in gross income. So, if a taxpayer is in the business of 'mining' of virtual currency and the mining activity is not undertaken by the taxpayer as an employee, the net earnings from self-employment (generally, gross income derived from carrying on a trade or business less allowable deductions) resulting from those activities will constitute self-employment income and would be subject to self-employment tax. Even the services performed by an independent contractor would fall within the ambit of this self-employment tax.

There are some obvious contradictions that have crept into this legislative framework. Although, virtual currency is not treated as currency (a term used in common parlance for money here), virtual currency paid by an employer as remuneration for services constitutes wages for employment and is subject to federal income tax withholding. This framework stipulates that a payment made using virtual currency is subject to information reporting to the same extent as any other payment made in property. For example, a person who in the course of a trade or business makes a payment of fixed and determinable income using virtual currency with a value of $600 or more to a US non-exempt recipient in a taxable year, he is required to report the payment to the IRS and to the payee. Examples of payments of fixed and determinable income include rent, salaries, wages, premiums, annuities and compensation. Payments made using virtual currency are subject to backup withholding to the same extent as other payments made in property. Therefore, payers making reportable payments using virtual currency must solicit a taxpayer identification number (TIN) from the payee. The payer must backup withhold from the payment if a TIN is not obtained prior to payment or if the payer receives notification from the IRS that backup withholding is required.

The provisions are somewhat different for a third party that contracts with a substantial number of unrelated merchants to settle payments between the merchants and their customers. Such a third-party settlement organisation (TPSO) is required to report payments made to a merchant in Form 1099-K, if, for the calendar year, both

1. the number of transactions settled for the merchant exceeds 200 and
2. the gross amount of payments made to the merchant exceeds $20,000.

This amount will be calculated by aggregating transactions where the TPSO settles payments made with virtual currency and where the TPSO settles payments made with real currency. When determining whether the transactions are reportable the value of the virtual currency is the fair market value of the virtual currency in US dollars on the date of payment. A penal clause has also been inserted for failure to comply with tax laws so enunciated. For example, underpayments attributable to virtual currency transactions may be subject to penalties. In addition, failure to report virtual currency transactions when required to do so may be subject to information reporting penalties. However, penalty relief may be available to taxpayers who can show 'sufficient cause' for any such violation. The provisions are, however, silent about the treatment of cryptocurrencies generated through a soft or hard fork. So, when the bitcoin fork happened, generating Bitcoin Cash (BCH), would the sister coin be considered as 'mined' and hence, taxable in the hands of the investor. Any thoughts on that?

In the latter part of 2016, the IRS made it clear that it was searching for cryptocurrency tax evaders. The agency sent a broad request to Coinbase, the largest bitcoin exchange in the United States, requesting records of all customers who bought digital currency from the company from 2013 to 2015. Coinbase balked, but a court ruled that it must provide the records of roughly 14,000 customers, fewer than 1 per cent of its patrons, who made transactions involving more than $20,000 of virtual currencies. The current tax burden on account of cryptocurrency transactions appears pretty steep in the United States. So, the tax-rate on short-term transactions (less than one year) would be as high as 39.6 per cent and this is without considering state taxes that may range from 3–13 per cent. Long-term gains would be lower and range from 0–20 per cent. The bitcoin enthusiasts are a perturbed lot on account of such a heavy tax burden but it appears that there is a silver lining here, or should I say a sliver of silver lining. It transpires that that digital assets like bitcoin and Ethereum are great for non-cash charitable contributions. So as William Brock, an accountant explains: if a person bought $1,000 worth of Ether and it appreciated to $10,000, he can wriggle out of the tax-net by gifting the cryptocurrency directly to a charity. This would make him eligible for deduction of $10,000 as well as exemption of tax on capital gains of $9,000. So, it would be a good idea to find the closest cat-shelter or soup kitchen and indulge in a virtual currency philanthropic streak.

Definitely amusing, if you come to think of it. People tried to find another way out of this Scylla and Charybdis taxation problem. Under the old rules, some cryptocurrency investors applied a legal manoeuvre often used with real estate investments to defer their capital gains. Under what is called a 1031 exchange, taxpayers can sell one property and defer taxes as long as the proceeds were reinvested in a similar, or 'like-kind' property. The tax guys wised up to this strategy pretty quickly. Now the tax legislation limits the use of 1031 exchanges to real estate. So, cryptocurrency investors in the

United States are left holding the wrong end of the cryptocurrency-taxation stick.

Canada's Taxing Tale

Canada Revenue Agency (CRA) began its bitcoin narrative in 2013. An interpretation letter[2] was issued which clearly stated that bitcoin was not a currency within the meaning of the term as defined by the central bank, the Bank of Canada. Instead, the bitcoin was a commodity, like gold or oil. The 2013 interpretation reads as under:

> Virtual currencies, such as bitcoins, are not considered to be a currency issued by a government of a country, such as American dollars. As such, they are generally treated as a commodity for purposes of the Income Tax Act. Therefore, using bitcoins to purchase goods or services would be treated as a form of barter transaction.

So, if you are a taxpayer in Canada, you need to remember that a virtual currency is a commodity and also that any purchase or sale of goods and services using bitcoins would be considered a 'barter transaction'. When I came across the barter clause for the first time in the context of tax implications for bitcoins, I was somewhat nonplussed. Study of ancient civilisations shows that the Mesopotamian tribes used the barter system in 6,000 BCE. So, how does this ancient tool of commerce tie in with twenty-first century tax implications for cryptocurrencies? I decided to find out. As we all know, a barter transaction can be described as one where 'two persons agree to a reciprocal exchange of goods or services and carry out that exchange usually without using money'. The CRA takes the view that barter transactions fall within sections 3 and 9 of the Income Tax Act for the purposes of determining whether an amount has been paid as consideration for goods or services. There are two prerequisites for making this determination. One is a consensus among the parties to the barter transactions about the value of the bartered commodity. The second is to ensure that the value is at arm's length and is stated in Canadian dollars. Thus, if a Canadian business sells its goods or services in exchange for bitcoins, that business has to report its income from such a transaction in Canadian dollars. So, if Harry is a sole proprietor who owns and operates a bookstore in Ontario and Rachy buys a book from the bookstore using bitcoins with a value of $20 in Canadian dollars, the transaction, for the purpose of taxation, would be valued at $20. This means that whenever a transaction is effected, where a taxable supply of goods or services is made and the consideration for that supply is bitcoins, the consideration for the supply is deemed to be equal to the fair market value of the bitcoins at the time of the supply. Barter transaction rules also apply when one type of virtual currency is exchanged for another type of virtual currency. Interpretation Bulletin IT-490, 'Barter Transactions', provides that in the case of goods bartered by a taxpayer for other goods or services, the value of those goods must be brought into the taxpayer's income if they are business-related. As such, an exchange of one type of virtual currency for another in such circumstances would trigger a disposition for income tax purposes. However, it is not the act of buying or receiving a bitcoin that in itself would be taxable, it is the act of using the said bitcoin that will make it taxable.

The next step would be to ascertain if the resulting gain is to be treated as income or capital gain, as only such a categorisation can decide the taxation provisions that would be applicable. Determining whether such a transaction is on account of income or capital can only be made following an assessment of all the facts relating to the particular taxpayer's circumstances. These CRA notifications, however, lack clarity of approach on several issues. Whether a bitcoin transaction is trading, investing or speculative is a question of fact but the dividing line between these activities is so fine that it may straddle the line between income and capital. No wonder the Canadian courts have churned out a large body of case laws wrestling with the ambiguity between investing, which produces a capital gain or loss and trading, which results in business income or expenses. The courts have ascertained certain essential factors for making such a determination. The list is more indicative than comprehensive and includes factors like frequency of transactions, period of ownership, knowledge and experience of bitcoin markets, relationship of the transaction to taxpayer's regular business, time spent in studying the bitcoin market and investigating potential purchases and most importantly—source of funds for purchase of virtual currencies. So, if Harry purchases a bitcoin on 1 June 2013 for $100 and sold it for $500 on 1 December 2013, his gains would be $400. As the frequency of transactions was limited and had nothing to do with Harry's regular business, the profits would be taxable as capital gains.

As the bitcoin ecosystem threw up different taxation puzzles, the revenue authorities of Canada grappled with them and came out with the income tax implications for different situations. So, what is the treatment of bitcoin mining by the CRA? This has been clarified in a notification (or interpretation as the CRA is wont to call it) dated 28 March 2014.[3] Where a taxpayer mines bitcoin in a commercial manner, in computing the taxpayer's income from the business for a taxation year, the value of property described in the inventory at the end of the year must be determined. Section 10 of the Act and Part XVIII of the Income Tax Regulations set out the rules pertaining to the valuation of a taxpayer's inventory for this purpose. The rules allow for a valuation by the following methods:

1. *Valuation of each item in the inventory at the cost at which it was acquired or its fair market value at the end of the year, whichever is lower.*
2. *Valuation of the entire inventory at its fair market value at the end of the year.*

As in the case of a bitcoin transaction, the activity of mining may also result in taxable income or capital gain. If it is treated as a capital property, the miner's adjusted cost base would be the bitcoin's fair market value at the time of acquisition. Also, since bitcoin mining demands considerable computing resources, a bitcoin's adjusted cost base would presumably include the cost of generating the computing power necessary to acquire the coin. The miner thus incurs a capital gain or loss depending on the bitcoin's value upon disposal. Alternatively, if thought of as earning business income, the miner's income is the bitcoin's fair market value at the time that the miner uncovered the unit. If the miner later sells the uncovered bitcoin for an amount greater than its value on discovery, the excess is also included in business income. Bitcoin mining, as we all know, requires one to devote extensive computing resources to the endeavour. Presumably, these costs should constitute deductible business expenses.

Where virtual currencies are acquired as gifts, interpretation bulletin 'Miscellaneous Receipts' provides that an amount received as a gift is not subject to income tax in the hands of the recipient. However, where an individual receives a 'voluntary payment' or other valuable transfer or benefit from the individual's employer, or from some other person in connection with that employment, the amount of the payment or the value of the transfer or benefit must generally be included in the individual's income pursuant to subsection 5(1) or paragraph 6(1)(a) of the Act. Similarly, 'voluntary payments' or other transfers or benefits received by a taxpayer in respect of, or in connection with, a business carried on by the taxpayer, must be included in the taxpayer's income from that business. As with any business income, taxpayers must report all taxable amounts received in a year on that year's income tax and benefit return.

Several vital questions on the GST/HST implications of bitcoin transactions still remain unanswered. For instance, neither the Canadian Parliament, the Canada Revenue Agency, nor a Canadian court has any answers to the following pertinent questions:

1. Is bitcoin mining a 'taxable supply' for the purpose of subsection 165(1) or 123(1) of the Excise Tax Act?
2. Are bitcoin traders required to collect and remit Goods and Services Tax/Harmonized Sales Tax?
3. What method should we use to value bitcoins for the purpose of subsection 165(1) of the Excise Tax Act?
4. Are fees relating to bitcoin transactions a part of 'the value of the consideration' for a taxable supply under subsection 165(1) of the Excise Tax Act?

The CRA would need to address these issues before it can sit back and give itself a pat on the back for executing a tax regime that is comprehensive and takes cognizance of the all various triggers for taxability of virtual currencies.

The German Taxing Drill

The cryptocurrency stance of the German Federal Ministry of Finance, Bundesministerium der Finanzen, is at odds with the approach of the US and Canadian governments. The German Government has clarified that cryptocurrencies such as bitcoin will not be taxed when they are used in payments.

According to the guidance document of 27 February 2018[4], when used for purchases, cryptocurrencies will receive the same tax treatment as legal tender. The ministry cited a 2015 European Union Court of Justice judgement pertaining to value-added taxes (VAT) as the basis for the decision. The relevant extract of the judgement reads as under:

> Referring to a 2012 report by the European Central Bank on virtual currencies, the referring court states that a virtual currency can be defined as a type of unregulated, digital money, which is issued and controlled by its developers and accepted by members of a specific virtual community. The 'bitcoin' virtual currency is one of the virtual currency schemes with 'bidirectional flow', which users can purchase and sell on the basis of an exchange rate. Such virtual currencies are analogous to other convertible currencies as regards their use in the real world. They allow both real and virtual goods and services to be purchased. Virtual currencies differ from electronic money, as defined in Directive 2009/110/EC of the European Parliament and the Council of 16 September 2009 on the taking up, pursuit and prudential supervision of the business of electronic money institutions amending Directives 2005/60/EC and 2006/48/EC and repealing Directive 2000/46/EC (OJ 2009 L 267, p. 7), in so far as, unlike that money, for virtual currencies the funds are not expressed in traditional accounting units, such as in euro, but in virtual accounting units, such as the 'bitcoin'.
>
> According to the Revenue Law Commission, the 'bitcoin' virtual currency is a means of payment used in a similar way to legal means of payment. Furthermore, the term 'legal tender' referred to in Article 135(1)(e) of the VAT Directive is used in

order to restrict the scope of the exemption as regards banknotes and coins. It follows, according to the Revenue Law Commission, that that term must be taken to mean that it relates only to banknotes and coins and not to currencies. That interpretation is also consistent with the objective of the exemptions laid down in Article 135(1)(b) to (g) of the VAT Directive, namely to avoid the difficulties involved in making financial services subject to VAT.

It must be held, first, that the 'bitcoin' virtual currency with bidirectional flow, which will be exchanged for traditional currencies in the context of exchange transactions, cannot be characterised as 'tangible property' within the meaning of Article 14 of the VAT Directive, given that, as the Advocate General has observed in point 17 of her Opinion, that virtual currency has no purpose other than to be a means of payment.

Consequently, the transactions at issue in the main proceedings, which consist of the exchange of different means of payment, do not fall within the concept of the 'supply of goods', laid down in Article 14 of the directive. In those circumstances, those transactions constitute the supply of services, within the meaning of Article 24 of the VAT Directive.

Article 135(1)(e) of the VAT Directive must be interpreted as meaning that the supply of services such as those at issue in the main proceedings, which consist of the exchange of traditional currencies for units of the 'bitcoin' virtual currency and vice versa, performed in return for payment of a sum equal to the difference between, on the one hand, the price paid by the operator to purchase the currency and, on the other hand, the price at which he sells that currency to his clients, are transactions exempt from VAT, within the meaning of that provision;

A translated excerpt from the ministry's recently issued document affirms the legality of cryptocurrencies as a payment method:

Virtual currencies (cryptocurrencies, e.g., bitcoin) become the equivalent to legal means of payment, insofar as these so-called virtual currencies of those involved in the transaction as an alternative contractual and immediate means of payment have been accepted and no other purpose serve as a means of payment.

For purchases, tax is calculated (in accordance with the EU's VAT Directive) based on the converted value of the cryptocurrency-fiat pair value at the point of sale, which is reported by the vendor. In addition, taxes may also be applied to fees collected by providers of digital wallets and other types of services relating to cryptocurrencies. No Tax is, however, applicable to block rewards sent to miners. The ministry says the transaction fee, which miners can receive from other users of the system, is paid on a voluntary basis and is not directly related to the miners' services. Digital wallets that incorporate a fee, however, do incur a taxable event.

Likewise, intermediaries who facilitate cryptocurrency conversions to or from fiat currency would not be considered liable for taxes. The European Union ruling considers such conversions a 'supply of services' that are tax exempt. Intermediary operators of exchanges that purchase or sell cryptocurrencies will also be exempt, but that won't be the case for exchanges that facilitate a marketplace. Thus, the German taxation of bitcoins is more reasonable and fair to the virtual currency holders and users.

Japan's Tax Narrative

Singed by the Mt Gox heist, Japan has made a wise move to stave off potential financial disasters within its borders by passing legislation on 1 April 2017 to accept bitcoins and other altcoins as a legal tender. This will not only make for better digital money management but also give the right push to digital and financial innovation and add to the revenue coffers. In Japan, digital currencies will now be recognised as asset-like values that can be used to make payments as well as be transferred digitally. In efforts to prevent money laundering, digital currency exchanges will need to register within Japan and report to the Financial Services Agency (FSA) as their governmental regulator.

In February 2016, the FSA, the country's financial regulator, looked into proposals to consider legislative revisions that would recognise bitcoin and digital currencies as equivalents to conventional currencies. References were made to the Paris-based international body, Financial Action Task Force (FATF) Guidance Note, for a risk-based approach to virtual currency.[5] The revision, if approved, would see bitcoin as 'fulfilling the functions of a currency'. Under the FSA's proposed definition, virtual currencies would serve as a medium of exchange. So, they can be used to purchase goods and services. It also clarifies that such-like currencies could be exchanged for legal tender through purchases or trades with an unspecified partner.

By March, the Japanese cabinet passed a set of bills, recognising virtual currencies like bitcoin to contain asset-like values that can be used to make payments and be transferred digitally. Fundamentally, bitcoin and digital currencies are to be officially recognised alongside fiat currencies, fulfilling a similar purpose. Japan amended the Payment Services Act to include digital currencies as payments. A separate bill passed in May 2016 mandated regulation of digital currency exchanges by the FSA in Japan.[6]

It was only by April 2017 that accounting guidelines[7] were mandated whereby virtual currency holders could include bitcoins and other sister coins as inventory while issuers could deem it as a liability. That's the closest a company or an individual can get to considering digital currencies on a balance sheet. The accounting model is set upon reward point programmes, commonly offered by the likes of airlines. The accounting of rewards points sees them recognised when they're redeemed while their entire value is booked as a liability, under International Financial Reporting Standards. What is causing perturbation to bitcoin users is that such an accounting model will adversely affect companies' operating profits, particularly those that richly reward customers. Experts quote the example of Tokyo-based e-commerce giant Rakuten whose net profit fell in the fiscal year 2016 due to costs of a promotional campaign with aggressively high reward points. Chikako Suzuki, a partner at PwC pointed out that the risk is for 'companies that hold virtual currency could turn out to have distorted valuations or that huge losses surface suddenly'.[8] This has caused many bitcoin adopters to leave their digital currency holdings off their books entirely.

Let us look at the tax legislation as it stands. The following 'persons' are mandated to pay tax on cryptocurrency investment gains:

1. People who receive annual remuneration in excess of ¥200,000 per year.

2. People who receive a salary from one place, but receive other miscellaneous income throughout the year that exceeds ¥200,000 per year.
3. People who receive a salary from more than one place, with other miscellaneous income totalling in excess of ¥200,000 per year after allowable deductions.
4. Those receiving any remuneration from a family corporation, shop, interest on a loan made, rental income from real estate or machinery, etc.
5. Anyone postponing tax on remuneration received via the disaster exemption clause.
6. Anyone receiving income which is not subject to withholding tax at the source.

In summary, if you receive no income in a taxable year and the profits realised on your cryptocurrency investment are less than ¥200,000, then you are not subject to tax (other than ordinary municipal taxes). If you are one of the people required to file an annual income tax return (e.g. business owners and sole proprietors) then you must continue to do so, irrespective of whether or not your investments are ultimately taxable or not.

However, Japan has demarcated tax treatment of bitcoins from treatment of stocks and futures. While gains from transactions in stock are taxed at a fixed rate of 20.315 per cent, crypto gains are treated as 'miscellaneous income'. The problem with such a dispensation is that no set off of losses from 'other business' is allowed against profits from bitcoins. The opposite is also true—money lost in cryptocurrency investments cannot be used to offset income and profits gained from other sources. Further, the above tax rates do not include municipal taxes which total 10 per cent and will be added at every income level. Because of this, cryptocurrency owners in Japan, who also happen to be higher-rate taxpayers, will be paying 55 per cent in taxes on their profits. This is in stark contrast to the tax deduction strategies that can be employed by a stock-market investor who is able to 'harvest losses', or a real estate investor who is able to claim all manner of expenses to reduce his taxable profits.

So, although the Japanese regulatory framework for virtual currencies is progressive and encompasses all manner of incentives for bitcoin players, the same cannot be said for its taxation provisions. The provisions protect and exempt taxpayers earning less than ¥200,000, inclusive of profits from crypto transactions. But, for those above the capped limit, a heavy tax burden is imposed. The fact that set off of losses or gains from crypto business is not allowed against loss or gain of other business, makes for a daunting tax scenario for the big crypto players. Such a regime may encourage the big players to shift base to countries with less stringent tax laws.

The Ozzie Tax Connection

The Government of Australia has taken a leaf out of the taxation manual of the United States and Canada. As in the United States, Ozzies have mandated that bitcoin is neither money nor Australian or foreign currency. Rather, it is property and is an asset for capital gains tax (CGT) purposes. The government has decreed that other cryptocurrencies that have the same characteristics as bitcoin are also to be treated as assets for CGT purposes. So what transaction of virtual currency would attract tax in Australia?[9] For taxation purposes, a CGT event occurs when an individual disposes of his cryptocurrency. This means, if you sell, trade or exchange your cryptocurrency, convert it to a fiat currency like Australian dollars, or use it to obtain goods or services, a CGT event is triggered. If you make a capital gain on the disposal of a cryptocurrency, some or all of the gain may be taxed.

Capital gains or losses that arise from the disposal of cryptocurrency that is a personal use asset will, however, be disregarded. Cryptocurrency may be a personal use asset if it is acquired and kept or used mainly to purchase items for personal use or consumption. Cryptocurrency is not a personal use asset if it is acquired, kept or used:

1. as an investment
2. in a profit-making scheme
3. in the course of carrying on a business.

However, there is a cap on this exemption. Only capital gains from personal use assets acquired for less than $10,000 are disregarded for CGT purposes. Also, if a person holds the cryptocurrency as an investment for more than 12 months before selling it, he would be eligible to a discount on the CGT. As per this legislation, a capital loss can be used to reduce capital gains made in the same year or a later year. However, net capital losses cannot be offset against other income. There is a rider here. If the disposal is part of a business you carry on, the profits you make on disposal will be assessable as ordinary income and not as a capital gain.

The Australian Taxation Office (ATO) has made some semblance of record-keeping a must for all users/investors/traders of cryptocurrencies. The ATO directed the following necessary records to be maintained—

1. the date of the transactions
2. the value of the cryptocurrency in Australian dollars at the time of the transaction (which can be taken from a reputable online exchange)
3. what the transaction was for and who the other party was (even if it's just their cryptocurrency address).

As there are some grey areas in such taxation standards set out, the ATO has started a consultation with industry and other interested stakeholders to seek feedback on two contentious issues pertaining to bitcoins. These issues and the questions for consultation are as under:

1. Record-keeping
    - Are there any practical issues that arise in relation to the CGT record-keeping rules, so far as cryptocurrency transactions are concerned?
    - Are there any specific factors that you think we should consider when developing further public advice and guidance about CGT record-keeping for cryptocurrency?

2. Exchanging one cryptocurrency for another
    - Are there any practical issues in relation to complying with the taxation obligations that arise for each cryptocurrency to cryptocurrency transaction?
    - Are there any specific factors that you think we should consider when developing further public advice and guidance about cryptocurrency to cryptocurrency transactions?

So, the law on taxability of cryptocurrencies is still at a fledgling stage and is slowly but steadily evolving as it goes along even in the developed countries.

The Indian Story

What about developing nations like India? As is to be expected we are lagging behind the developed nations in tax legislation on cryptocurrencies like bitcoins. From 2013 to 2017, all we have heard from the government are the statutory 'injurious to health' warnings that have been issued by the Reserve Bank of India. The legality of bitcoins and other altcoins has been glossed over and the only categorical statements heard are that 'bitcoins are not legal tender'. But then that is true for most countries all over the world, except Japan of course. However, the fact remains that even if bitcoins are not regarded as legal tender, Indians are investing, trading and making purchases in bitcoins. The volume of such transactions was small from 2012 to 2016. But with more than 1,500 per cent increase in value of bitcoins in 2017, there was a quantum jump in this volume. The various bitcoin exchanges admitted to a trebling of transaction volumes in India in 2017 alone. The revenue authorities were caught in a bind. There were no regulations for monitoring bitcoins, nor were there any tax provisions for taxation of cryptocurrencies. Even so the potential revenue generation on such taxation could not be overlooked. So, the Indian Income Tax Department took upon itself the task of examining such investments and trades especially if they were being used as a means of money laundering or for illicit activities within the country. Surveys were conducted in December

2017 at several bitcoin exchanges in Bengaluru, Gurugram, Pune, Delhi, Bombay, Hyderabad, etc. to get data about individuals who were transacting in bitcoins. Subsequently, 100,000 notices were issued to High Net Worth Individuals (HNIs) which for purposes of the Indian subcontinent refer to individuals with portfolio of more than ₹25 lakhs. That is all well and good. The issue that is hanging fire is the nature of taxability of cryptocurrency transactions. Since there is no specific legislation on taxation of bitcoins and altcoins, taxability would have to be ascertained on the basis of the existing provisions. A tall order. So, let's give it a shot.

The first question we need to answer is whether a bitcoin is a currency or an asset. The RBI Act does not include definition of a currency.[10] It simply says in Section 2(bix) which is the 'definition' section that:

> *'foreign currency' and 'foreign exchange' have the meanings respectively assigned to them in the Foreign Exchange Regulation Act, 1973;*

The Foreign Exchange Management (FEMA) Act 1999[11] defines currency as:

1. *'currency' includes all currency notes, postal notes, postal orders, money orders, cheques, drafts, travelers cheques, letters of credit, bills of exchange and promissory notes, credit cards or such other similar instruments, as may be notified by the Reserve Bank;*
2. *'currency notes' means and includes cash in the form of coins and banknotes;*

Bitcoins do not fall under any of the heads detailed above. It could be treated as currency under the head 'similar instruments'. But, the RBI has not issued any notification clarifying that virtual currencies fall within the ambit of 'similar instruments'.

The Coinage Act of 2011[12] defines the term 'coin' in Section 2 (a):

> *as a coin which is made up of any metal or any other material stamped by the Government or any other authority empowered*

by the government in this behalf and which is a legal tender including a commemorative coin and the Government of India rupee note.

Bitcoin, clearly does not fall within the meaning of 'coin' as defined under the Coinage Act. This means that despite the fact that bitcoins are used to purchase goods/services, it cannot be treated as currency within the existing legislative framework. So by default does it fall into the category of an asset?

Let us look at the definition of an asset under the Income Tax Act[13] as it exists today. Section 2(14) of the Income Tax Act defines a capital asset as under:

(14) 'capital asset' means property of any kind held by an assessee, whether or not connected with his business or profession, but does not include-

(i) any stock-in-trade, consumable stores or raw materials held for the purposes of his business or profession;

(ii) personal effects, that is to say, movable property (including wearing apparel and furniture, but excluding jewellery) held for personal use by the assessee or any member of his family dependent on him.

Explanation- For the purposes of this sub-clause, 'jewellery' includes-

(a) ornaments made of gold, silver, platinum or any other precious metal or any alloy containing one or more of such precious metals, whether or not containing any precious or semiprecious stone and whether or not worked or sewn into any wearing apparel;

(b) precious or semi- precious stones, whether or not set in any furniture, utensil or other article or worked or sewn into any wearing apparel;]

(iii) agricultural land in India, not being land situate-

Will the term 'property' apply to a bitcoin? The term 'property' has not been defined under any Indian statute. So, let us take a look at the dictionary meaning of property. Property means 'a thing or things' belonging to someone or a 'possession'. By this general meaning alone, bitcoins and other virtual currencies would be categorised as property and by another hop, skip and jump would also deem to fall in the 'capital asset' nomenclature. This means that if bitcoins are held for purposes of investment, they would be liable to capital gains tax on sale at a profit. Whether this would be a short-term capital asset or a long-term capital asset would depend on the period of holding of the bitcoins. If it is a short-term capital gain (held for less than 36 months) it would be taxable according to the slab rates applicable to the taxpayer. If the period of holding is for more than 36 months, long-term capital gains would kick in and the profits would be taxable at a flat rate of 20 per cent with indexation benefits (inflation-adjusted). However, if the transactions in bitcoins are substantial and frequent, it could be held that the taxpayer is trading in bitcoins and the income would be taxable as business income. On the other hand, if bitcoin trading is treated as a current account transaction under the FEMA, we have a completely different take. A current account transaction, by its very categorisation includes all those transactions that are not capital in nature. This includes remittance for import of goods or services, or remittance for personal purposes, etc. The question whether dealing in bitcoins is a current account transaction or not depends wholly on whether bitcoins are categorised as 'goods' or as 'assets'.

Another pertinent query that comes to mind is whether bitcoins earned through mining would be taxable? If profits earned from bitcoins are taxable as business income, then the bitcoins earned in the 'mining' process would be taxable as business profits. Bitcoins generated during the mining process are classifiable as self-generated capital assets. Since the cost of acquisition of such bitcoins is not available, the taxpayer can take the benefit of judgement of the Supreme Court in the case of B.C. Srinivasa Setty (1981).[14] The court held that if the cost of acquisition of an asset cannot be ascertained, the machinery provision for computation of capital gains will fail. Therefore, no capital gains can be levied on transfer of such assets. This would mean that bitcoins generated through mining may be exempt from tax. A more sensible approach would be to consider the value of bitcoin (in Indian rupees) on the day of generation of the bitcoin as the cost of acquisition. So, the profits on the day of sale of the bitcoin would be taxable under the capital gains tax provision.

However, if the generation of cryptocurrency is a frequent occurrence and 'mining' is in the nature of a business, the profits could be taxed as business income. Here, expenses on account of energy consumed would then have to be allowed as business expenses.

Another corollary to this discussion would be whether bitcoin transactions would fall within the ambit of goods or services? The ambivalence here is more obvious. If bitcoin gets classified as a currency, it will be considered as 'money' in the CGST Act and no GST can be charged on its trading. However, exchanging bitcoin to rupees might be considered a service for the purpose of levy of GST under the category of 'financial services'. Here, if the supplier charges any commission for providing exchange services, then GST shall be payable at 18 per cent on the commission. There is a conflicting view also. If bitcoin is not considered as currency, any trading in bitcoin would be considered a service. Therefore, the supplier (who is selling the bitcoin) may be required to pay 18 per cent GST on the total value charged by him from the buyer. In the bitcoin mining process, individuals process the transactions and secure the network by using specialised hardware. In exchange, they are awarded new bitcoins. In other words, the bitcoin is a consideration awarded to individuals in lieu of their services to secure the network. Therefore, bitcoin miners may be required to pay GST on the fair market value of the bitcoin at 18 per cent.

Like I said, confusion reigns supreme. The government will need to hurry up and clarify such matters through amendments of the existing provisions of Income Tax, GST, RBI, FEMA and FERA or by issuing a separate 'Virtual Currency Legislation' as done by Japan. First and foremost, the government needs to specify if bitcoin is an asset or a currency and then define transactions in virtual currency that may fall within the ambit of GST and those that would be excluded from the scope. Until then, litigation would be the byword as the current taxing provisions would be subject to interpretation that would be more subjective than objective.

Chapter 13

Minting Mores

> *Regulators of all countries agree that it's time to develop national cryptocurrencies, this is the future.*
>
> —Olga Skorobogatova, Deputy Governor of the Central Bank of The Russian Federation

Some speculation has been rife about countries minting their own digital currencies to fight the onslaught of cryptocurrencies like bitcoins. It is not implausible of course but would the proponents of the bitcoins be happy about a fiat cryptocurrency? Methinks not. After all, the idea of bitcoin generation was born from a mistrust of the fiat currency and third-party institutions like banks. So, to bring decentralised cryptocurrencies within the ambit of the banking channels and government regulations would be the biggest irony ever. Satoshi Nakamoto, wherever he is, whoever he is, would undoubtedly be grinding his teeth in horror and anger at this new development. A government backed digital currency would principally mean the demolition of the basic tenets of modern day cryptocurrency that upholds the right of the individual to make financial transactions privately, through a decentralised and self-regulated electronic system that is beyond the whims and caprices of the government in power. Be that as it may, this new minting mores cannot be wished away. A fiat cryptocurrency is, as Victor Hugo put it succinctly, an idea whose time has come.

Canada's Experiment with a Fiat Digital Currency

The Bank of Canada has released a document on the relevance of minting a fiat virtual currency appropriately called 'Central Bank Digital Currency (CBDC): Motivations and Implications'.[1] This document, authored by Walter Engert and Ben S.C. Fung, examines the impact of cryptocurrencies like bitcoins on the financial system and the wider economy of Canada. This document envisages a virtual currency that will add to the existing basket of financial instruments and is not intended to replace or shake down the existing system of a traditional financial institution. The document clearly states:

> CBDC in this paper is designed to conform as much as possible to a familiar environment and mimic bank notes...The benchmark CBDC here is designed to minimise disruption by having properties similar to its physical analogue, cash.

Some of the features of this new currency are:

1. The benchmark CBDC is denominated in the sovereign currency; for Canada, the Canadian dollar.
2. The benchmark CBDC would be available 24/7, like cash and other electronic payment methods.
3. The benchmark CBDC is anonymous or pseudonymous, depending on the technology used. As a result, transactions using CBDC would be impossible to trace.
4. The CBDC is subject to the risk of theft and loss, including through technological impairment. The latter could occur, for example if CBDC were stored on a hard drive that was reformatted or destroyed, or if a user lost the password/private key.
5. Transactions are non-reversible, unless both transacting parties agree and engage in a reversing transaction.
6. The central bank supplies as much digital currency as the public is willing to hold. As a result, supply is demand-determined and perfectly elastic.
7. Similar to current banknote distribution in Canada, households and firms would purchase the benchmark CBDC at a regulated

financial institution (e.g. a bank) with their deposits at those institutions or with bank notes.

8. Bank customers could also withdraw CBDC from their bank accounts, which is conceptually similar to the withdrawal of cash.
9. These regulated financial institutions would have accounts at the central bank, or have accounts at clearing banks that have accounts at the central bank, where they could purchase the benchmark CBDC for customers directly or indirectly with their deposits or bank notes.
10. Banks would have to comply with KYC and anti-money laundering (AML)/combating the financing of terrorists (CFT) requirements for their CBDC operations, similar to bank notes today. However, once the benchmark CBDC is withdrawn from a bank, it would be anonymous to the issuer and the counterparty in a transaction. There would be no direct access to the central bank for households and firms to obtain, store or return the benchmark CBDC.
11. To be used for payments, benchmark CBDC transactions need to be confirmed nearly instantaneously and the underlying transactions need to be settled irrevocably as quickly as possible.
12. The timing of finality and irrevocability of benchmark CBDC transactions depends on the technological solution underpinning the CBDC.
13. The choice of this distribution channel for the benchmark CBDC follows from the decision for this CBDC to mimic cash. This is reinforced by a concern that a central bank may not have the expertise (or interest) to open digital currency accounts for any (and all) interested parties and manage the range of related transactions.

The payment network for the benchmark CBDC is distributed and bilateral and not tiered. The specific features and feasibility of these elements depend on the design of the digital wallet and ledger. Let us just cut to the chase. What all this jargon means is that the validity and usefulness of a CBDC would be intricately connected to the digital wallet in which it is stored and the network over which it is transferred.

The implications of such a digital legal tender would be widespread and would affect not only seigniorage but also the monetary policy of the country. The Bank of Canada envisages that overall, there would probably be some substitution of the benchmark CBDC for bank notes and some substitution of CBDC for competing electronic payment methods, particularly in certain contexts where personal security and privacy are especially valued. As a result of the latter, the sum of the value of bank notes in circulation and CBDC would likely be larger than the value of bank notes in circulation currently. Other things being equal, this would increase seigniorage revenue somewhat. But this assessment does not include the production costs (fixed and variable) of CBDC. Further, if a central bank provides both banknotes and CBDC, total cost to the central bank could increase, in part because there would be smaller gains from 'economies of scale'. This would, in fact, reduce the seigniorage and thus reduce the benefit to the government.

On the monetary policy front, the paper is optimistic that the benchmark CBDC (which does not pay interest) is supplied in the same way as bank notes, so it would not have material implications for the implementation of monetary policy. More fundamentally, the central bank is sanguine that it would remain the ultimate (monopoly) supplier of reserves, bank notes and CBDC, so it could continue to set related terms and conditions of these instruments and therefore control monetary policy. Also, since the benchmark CBDC does not pay interest, a significant shift to CBDC from conventional financial instruments seems unlikely. The fact that the benchmark CBDC is subject to risk of theft and loss, would discourage significant holdings of CBDC, other things being equal. What if such a currency impacts the deposits significantly? The paper has an ace up its sleeve to control such a negative shift. The banks could respond by increasing interest rates on their liabilities or bundling superior services on such accounts relative to CBDC to maintain their funding. As a result, the steady-state impact of the benchmark CBDC on bank deposits and other claims would likely be small. The paper, however, acknowledges that the balances of convenience could shift (more readily) toward CBDC in stress periods, with attendant volatility and potentially significant disruptions of the financial system.

The paper argues that digital currency would benefit retail payment efficiency in two ways, which would also apply to the benchmark CBDC. First, CBDC would have lower user costs than cash, which could prompt substitution from cash to CBDC for retail and person-to-person payments. Second, CBDC would facilitate transactions that are currently foregone because of frictions that inhibit some types of transactions. For example, some consumers avoid online purchases because of security and privacy concerns when providing their credit card information. The benchmark CBDC would facilitate such online transactions because it is anonymous and because potential losses from fraud to the consumer would be limited to only the amount of the single, specific transaction. Also, smaller merchants often avoid selling online because of card fees, especially for small-value transactions. The paper promises that CBDC would facilitate small-value online transactions given a relatively low (or no) associated fees. As a result of these considerations, the benchmark CBDC would provide competition to other electronic payment methods, possibly in terms of reduced costs and, in particular, in terms of enhanced privacy. The impact on larger transactions would, of course, be different but that is a thesis in itself and would make for some heavy-duty financial acrobatics that I will refrain from at this point of time.

Essentially the paper focuses on the economics of CBDC. So, technological considerations, associated costs and risks to the central bank are not considered in this paper. The irony of using CBDC is, however, not lost even to the authors of the paper. That CBDC may facilitate criminal activity, which cannot be overlooked as it would offer anonymity in the manner of any other cryptocurrency. Additional restrictions could be instituted to circumvent such an eventuality. Perhaps a cap could be imposed limiting the amount of CBDC held in each digital wallet. An enterprising charlatan could of course outwit regulatory agencies by setting up multiple wallets. Alternatively, CBDC transactions in excess of a threshold value could be required to satisfy user identification requirements; this would eliminate anonymity for such transactions. These kinds of restrictions, however, would be self-defeating in that they would reduce the demand for CBDC, decrease seigniorage (other things being equal) and increase the cost of using CBDC for making payments. Finally, the benchmark CBDC could promote financial inclusion, although this would require access to and use of the underlying technology, which could be a constraint for some individuals. However, financial inclusion is not a concern in most advanced economies, including Canada. Interest bearing CBDC is also being considered. Adopting some of the existing private cryptocurrencies is also on the anvil. Undoubtedly, institution of a fiat digital currency is being examined with seriousness. But the research is at an extremely preliminary stage and a decision on adopting CBDC appears to be in the realm of an uncertain future.

The Dutch Mint

Let's see how other countries are faring on this platform. Netherlands has been hard at work on the adoption of their own virtual currency since 2015. Several experiments were conducted to ascertain the factors that would impact the implementation of such a currency as legal tender. The experiments by De Nederlandsche Bank (DNB) sought to simulate bitcoin both in its early days and in the year 2140, when the final bitcoins are expected to be mined. The bank presented the results at the third-annual Dutch Blockchain Conference held just outside Amsterdam in 2016. The tests, conducted in 2015, utilised an experimental digital currency called DNBcoin. The head of the central bank's market infrastructures policy department, Ron Berndsen, explained that researchers within the institution wanted to get a hands-on experience working with the technology. During the conference, Berndsen told attendees:

> The general idea was that by adapting the bitcoin software ourselves, we could learn deeper how an actual implementation of the blockchain really works than if we could only perform desk research.[2]

To create the simulation environment, the DNB put together a working group of in-house experts who would act as fictional participants in a digital currency system. To do so, the bank 'bootstrapped' a team of 'intrinsically motivated' members of the bank. The group then adapted the open-source bitcoin software to replicate what its members believed the bitcoin ecosystem might have looked like in the first two months of the digital currency's existence. Using five networked laptops, the DNB team mined their first DNBcoin block—known as the genesis block—and quickly generated thousands of blocks. Along the way, they sent coins to one another, testing the ins and outs of the process like setting transaction fees. The bank's network created new blocks, along with freshly minted DNBcoins, about every three minutes, compared to the roughly 10 minutes expected in the bitcoin network. Though the end of bitcoin's lifecycle is more than a century from now, the DNB wanted to simulate what those conditions might look like as well. 'The second DNBcoin prototype takes the other extreme of bitcoin by jumping to the year 2140, when the last fraction of the 21 million bitcoins will be issued,'[3] Berndsen said in his speech. For this experiment, the central bank team needed to mine all of the DNBcoins in advance. To do so, they were created using a single laptop before opening the network to other computers.

To cut back on the amount of power needed to mine the DNBcoins, the team began with an initial block reward of one billion DNBcoins, then programmed the system to quickly lower the number of coins rewarded per block. Berndsen explained:

> In doing so we were able to generate 3 billion DNBcoins in 30 seconds. In addition, we observed that after all DNBcoins had been generated, blocks could still be mined and added to the blockchain. The reward was reduced to zero but transaction fees were still collected by the miner who finds the next block.[4]

While the first two prototypes were built with the specific aim of learning more about how central banks might use virtual currency, a third experiment is currently being developed to explore other aspects of blockchain. This third foray will target listed digital assets, trust, network resilience and the 'intelligence to initiate or trigger transactions'. These experiments are essentially aimed at three primary tasks of banks i.e. promoting smooth functioning of the payment system, providing supervision and oversight and establishing the framework for an informed monetary policy. The barriers identified during the course of the experiments are interoperability, industry fragmentation and self-interest among financial incumbents. As Berndsen concluded:

> The blockchain technology offers a number of advantages over existing technologies. But there are also some drawbacks and barriers to overcome.[5]

Other Forays

Central banks around the world seem to have stepped up their efforts towards developing digital versions of their fiat currency to leverage the benefits of the underlying technology of blockchain technology. Canada and Netherlands are already in the fray. The Bank of Montreal, the Royal Bank of Canada and the Bank of England are also making headway in this regard. Russian Government-controlled Sberbank runs an electronic payment service called 'Yandex.Money' and a digital currency of the same name. Deputy Governor of the Central Bank of The Russian Federation, Olga Skorobogatova, opined that:

> Regulators of all countries agree that it's time to develop national cryptocurrencies, this is the future. Every country will decide on specific time frames. After our pilot projects, we will understand what system we could use in our case for our national currency.[6]

Some governments are adopting bitcoins as a substitute for a national cryptocurrency. Swiss Government in 2016 began to accept digital currency as a means of payment for city fees. Swiss Federal Services, a government-owned railway company of Switzerland, sells bitcoins at its ticket machines. Sweden's central bank, Riksbank, is reportedly looking into introducing a digital currency to the country, called the eKrona. It makes sense as Sweden is projected to be one of the first countries in the world to go completely cashless after seeing dramatic falls in the usage of cash. However, if it does decide to introduce the e-currency, it won't be until the fag end of 2018. It appears that the central bank still has a lot it needs to work out. Cecilia Skingsley, Deputy Governor at Riksbank, told a national daily:

> This is as revolutionary as the paper note 300 years ago. What does it mean for monetary policy and financial stability? How do we design this: a rechargeable card, an app or another way?[7]

Surprisingly, two African countries have boarded the fast train on fiat cryptocurrencies. In 2015, Tunisia made the decision to boost its eDinar digital currency using the blockchain, with the help of universal contracting platform, Monetas. According to an interview with Monetas's chief executive, Johann Gevers, the eDinar can be used to make money transfers, pay for goods and services like bills and manage official government identification documents.

Gevers informed the media that:

> We are delighted to be working in partnership with the Tunisian Government, National Post and DigitUS to increase financial inclusion with an open mobile money platform that is able to operate across mobile networks. This is an important first step towards a freer and more prosperous world.[8]

Senegal followed the Tunisian example and launched its version of a national digital currency. It has the same value as the country's currency, the CFA franc and can be stored in all mobile money and e-money wallets. This currency is based on the blockchain and has been designed to be compatible with other digital currencies in Africa. The Senegalese bank, Banque Regionale de Marches (BRM) and eCurrency Mint are the two institutions behind the currency. A joint statement from BRM and eCurrency Mint stated that:

> The eCFA is a high-security digital instrument that can be held in all mobile money and e-money wallets. It will secure universal

> liquidity, enable interoperability and provide transparency to the entire digital ecosystem in WAEMU (West African Economy and Money Union).[9]

The Estonian Government has positioned Estonia as one of the most tech-friendly countries in the world. It was one of the first governments to store its data on the blockchain, as part of its 'e-Residency programme'. Thanks to the success of this, it is looking to launch its own digital currency, named 'estcoin'. According to a blog post by the managing director at e-Residency, Kaspar Korjus:

> No other country has come close to developing both the technology and the legal frameworks that would enable them to introduce and securely manage tradable crypto assets globally.[10]

Korjus also said that the Ethereum founder, Vitalik Buterin, has been supporting the Estonian Government with its plans. The country is inviting its citizens and e-residents to give their feedback on how they think a digital currency could work in Estonia. LHV Pank, the largest independent Estonian bank in the world, began its experiment with programmable money when it issued € 100,000 worth of cryptographically protected certificates of deposits. CUBER (Cryptographic Universal Blockchain Entered Receivable) Technology, a subsidiary of LHV Pank, is focussing mainly on bitcoin-based digital securities. CUBER encompasses both CUBER securities and CUBER wallet.

Venezuela is currently in the midst of an economic crisis, facing chronic food shortages and high inflation. To combat this, President Nicolas Maduro has decided to create a new digital currency, the 'petro'. At the announcement of the currency, Maduro said the petro would allow Venezuela to 'advance in issues of monetary sovereignty, to make financial transactions and overcome the financial blockade'.[11] The new currency would be backed by Venezuela's oil, gas, gold and diamond wealth. There are sceptics who are opposing such a move but such opposition is political posturing rather than an objective response to a progressive move.

India has also shown an academic interest in minting its very own cryptocurrency. Institute for Development and Research in Banking Technology (IDRBT), a research arm of the Reserve Bank of India has issued a white paper on 'Applications of Blockchain Technology to Banking and Financial Sector in India'.[12] The white paper issued is a concerted effort by all the stakeholders i.e. academicians, bankers, regulators and technology partners and delineates the technology, concerns, global experiences and possible areas of adoption of blockchain technology within the financial sector in India. The objective of the paper was to evaluate the applicability of blockchain technology to the contemporary financial ecosystem. As Mr R. Gandhi, Deputy Governor, RBI says:

> The Institute has also attempted a proof-of-concept (PoC) on the applicability of BCT to a trade finance application with active participation of NPCI, banks and solution provider, the details of which are presented in the white paper.[13]

The white paper acknowledges the efforts made by Canada and Netherlands to mint their own cryptocurrency. So, there is a likelihood that this acknowledgement may transmute into an effort to issue a national cryptocurrency sometime in the future. For the moment, the white paper restricts itself to a roadmap for adoption of blockchain technology for the banking sector with special emphasis on centralised KYC, cross-border payments, syndication of loans, trade finance and capital markets.

The attempts at issuing fiat cryptocurrencies by governments of the world reflect the widespread impact of virtual currencies as well as blockchain technology with its disruptive concept of immutability. However, the experiments with a state-sponsored virtual currency are not without an inherent irony. Bitcoin and its technology work on a decentralised distributed public network that does not acknowledge demarcations of government and state. By its very nature, the technology and its network are global. This means, anyone from any country can be a part of the distributed ledger without requiring any government approvals or sanctions. Given its global ambit, it would perhaps be more appropriate to consider a unified global cryptocurrency with international regulations to monitor it and a consistent taxing mandate to chart its taxing narrative. It is certainly a better idea for government heads and economic experts to mull over. Adopting an existing cryptocurrency by the global community as a cryptocurrency of choice may not be such a bad idea either. Anybody listening?

SECTION V

A MOTLEY MIX

Chapter 14

Others of The Ilk

> *The governments of the world have spent hundreds and hundreds of trillions of dollars bailing out a decaying, Dickensian, outmoded system called banking, when the solution to the future of finance is peer-to-peer.*
>
> —Patrick Young, Financial Analyst

The year 2009 saw the birth of the first cryptocurrency, the bitcoin. The creation of this 'digital gold' set the stage for the debut of more cryptocurrencies. The year 2011 ushered in the 'Namecoin'. By the time a beleaguered net-browser could wrap his head around the concept of a decentralised self-regulated currency (or is it an asset?), he was inundated with a slew of virtual currencies that have been tagged as 'altcoins' or 'alternative coins'. Litecoin, Peercoin, Dogecoin, Zetacoin, Novacoin, Ether, the list is endless. At the last count, there were 1564 altcoins listed as on 10 April 2018[1], much to the amazed consternation of both users and observers.

So, what are altcoins? Altcoins are a misnomer for virtual coins that came after and attempted to substitute the 'big daddy' of digital currencies, the bitcoin. The majority of altcoins are a variant (fork) of the bitcoin and are built using bitcoin's open-source, peer-to-peer (P2P), original protocol with some tweaking of the underlying code. Altcoins can differ from bitcoin in a range of ways. Some have a different economic model or a different coin-distribution method. Others employ different proof-of-work mining algorithms. Several altcoins offer a more versatile programming language to build an application, while yet others offer more privacy compared to bitcoin. Some altcoins were the result of a hard fork while others were spawned by a soft fork. We have already discussed this in the chapter 'The Hubris: Crypto Fratricide'.

The bitcoin blockchain has been subject to several forks during the course of its short existence. The thing about forks, we need to remember, is that forks have to be consensus-based. This means that the majority of network participants have to agree to the changes in the base code and the programming protocol. So, if the fork is essentially consensus-based and where the miners, programmers, wallet providers and exchanges work in tandem to change their software, it is said to be a soft fork. Forks without consensus would result in the network splitting into two different blockchains with two different networks, distributed ledgers and coins in circulation. Such a split is a hard fork. On 1 August 2017, a hard fork in the bitcoins blockchain resulted in the birth of Bitcoin Cash (BCH). The BCH network produced a cryptocurrency with the same history as the legacy chain but also an 8 MB block size limit and the removal of SegWit (a proposed soft work that was implemented in the summer of 2017). The BCH traded around $200–300 per token in the first week of its existence while bitcoin traded at a much higher $2,700. When an altcoin forks at the blockchain level, an alternate system of consensus rules must be used and the coin will have an entirely different distributed ledger. So, when the 'network agreement' was not met in these two cases, two blockchains sharing the same history came into existence. Stands to reason that since there are two networks there are also two tokens. Translated simply it means that if you hold 10 BTC you also hold 10 BCH. Ethereum Classic was another instance of a hard fork. Ethereum Classic is an Ethereum fork that exists on a parallel Ethereum platform. The Ethereum community fractured when a disagreement occurred about how a theft of funds should be handled. The majority of users wished to change

Ethereum's code in order to get the lost funds back. A minority believed that Ethereum should not be tampered with or altered by third parties. Even in cases of users exploiting the smart-contract feature to trick others, the blockchain must remain 'immutable' or unchanged. Thus, the minority created the Classic version of Ethereum, which still survives and thrives.

Some altcoins have different monetary policy rules built into the currency to encourage different uses and treatment. Policies such as minimum spend, interest (positive or negative) on coins stored will vary. So will policies on coin mining. Some altcoins are made to discourage ASIC (application specific integrated circuit) or GPU (graphics processing unit) mining. This limitation is designed to reduce the advantage of specialised coin miners, as in the case of Litecoin, upon which half of all altcoins are based. An altcoin blockchain may also store different metadata about the coin's previous transactions or may allow the coin to be repurposed as an alternate asset. While some altcoins can be attempts to enrich founders and offer little new, many have found niches because of the way their differences encouraged new miners and uses.

Ethereum: A Worthy Contender

So, let us take a look at some of the popular altcoins that have established themselves. This will help us get a good idea about how the crypto turf war will pan out. The most promising dueller by far is Ethereum. This altcoin is the product of a creative collusion between Microsoft, Intel and JP Morgan Chase. After bitcoins, it is, perhaps, the strongest contender in the cryptocurrency battle. It was the first successful attempt to incorporate the now extremely popular smart-contract feature into the blockchain itself. Interestingly, Ethereum is more than a currency. It is a blockchain platform powered by Ether cryptocurrency. Unlike bitcoin, which was released in 2009 by the phantom of the bitcoin opera, Satoshi Nakamoto, Ethereum was created without playing out a game of hide-and-seek by a 21-year-old Russian-Canadian, Vitalik Buterin, after he dropped out of Waterloo University in Ontario.

The aim of Ethereum was not to substitute online payment platforms like PayPal or be used as a unit of currency. It went a step ahead and made it possible to programme binding agreements into the blockchain—the smart-contract concept. Two people, for instance, could programme a bet on a FIFA match, say Germany and South Korea, directly into the Ethereum blockchain. Once the final score came in from a mutually agreed upon source, say, the CNN broadcast of the match, the money would be automatically transferred to the winning party. Ether can be used as a currency in this system, but Ether is also necessary to pay for the network power needed to process the bet. No wonder, it is often dubbed as Bitcoin 2.0. Joseph Lubin, a co-founder of Ethereum confidently and publicly announced that:

> Bitcoin presented the broad strokes vision and Ethereum presented the crystallisation of how to deliver that vision.[2]

A team of seven co-founders helped Mr Buterin write-up the software after he released the initial description of the system. Mr Buterin's team raised $18 million in 2014 through a pre-sale of Ether, which helped fund the Ethereum Foundation, which supports the software's development. One of Mr Buterin's co-founders, Joseph Lubin, set up ConsenSys, a company based in Brooklyn that hired over 50 developers to build applications on the Ethereum system, including one that enables music distribution and another that allows for a new kind of financial auditing.

Like bitcoin, Ethereum has its own fan following and its smart-contract platform offers more to the commercial sector, be it industry or export or insurance, than its bitcoin daddy. Seems to me it will be the currency of the future. Unless, bitcoin also incorporates the concept of a smart contract. There's a thought.

Ripple: Old Wine in a New Bottle

Ripple is a Google-backed altcoin that attracted an impressive $90 million in total funding right at its inception. The Ripple USP is that it allows for transacting with any unit of value, from fiat currency to frequent flier miles. The Ripple website claims:

> Ripple provides one frictionless experience to send money globally using the power of blockchain. By joining Ripple's growing, global network, financial institutions can process their customers' payments anywhere in the world instantly, reliably and cost-effectively.[3]

Despite the tall claims, Ripple does not offer much in the way of new features. It appears to be a hybrid mix of other blockchain applications. It has a distributed ledger, a variety of wallet applications and a native asset, XRP. Where Ripple decided to differentiate itself from blockchains like bitcoin is in its use of gateways, issuance and trust lines. Sounds like Greek? Brian Schuster, developer, solution architect and writer in the blockchain industry, explains these terms in his article dated 7 December 2017 on Hacker Noon entitled 'The Ripple Currency Problem: Why Permissioned Blockchains Will Devalue XRP'.[4] Schuster explains the mechanics of Ripple technology which has created a blockchain gateway that allows transfer of non-native assets (blockchain or otherwise) onto a particular blockchain. This includes bank assets with its basket of currencies like dollar, yen, etc. or other blockchain assets like Bitcoin Cash (BTC) or Litecoin (LTC). Unlike most other blockchain technologies, the Ripple network allows transaction of non-native assets like currencies and commodities like gold. The transfer of such assets is made possible through an 'issuance methodology'. This methodology allows an individual account holder on the blockchain to 'lock' a particular asset (let's say gold) on the blockchain ledger. After the locking-through issuance is affected, the non-native asset can be sent to other accounts. The Ripple network also offers a 'trust line' facility. This facility is more of an 'old-wine-in-a new-bottle' feature and offers a way of securing issuance transactions between individual parties. As opposed to XRP, which can be sent to anyone, an issuance can only be sent to parties who both agree to open a line of communication. So, while

Harry can send and receive XRP from anyone in the world, he can only send the gold he claims to have to accounts that actually trust his word i.e. through trust lines.

The Ripple gateway, thus allows transaction of assets as varied as fiat currency, virtual currencies and gold on its network. This allows financial institutions like banks to ride piggyback on the Ripple network. This, as Schuster quips, is the secret sauce behind the Ripple success story.

Monero, Zcash and PIVX: Privacy Proponents

Monero and Zcash are the privacy proponents. All cryptocurrencies are geared towards privacy and anonymity but Monero and Zcash more so than most. Monero allows the transacting parties to send and receive funds without the transactions being publicly visible on the blockchain. The founders claim that the transactions are completely untraceable due to Monero's leveraging of ring signatures. Unfortunately, because of Monero's emphasis on privacy, it has become the currency of choice for darknet and other criminal organisations. Zcash also claims to offer greater privacy to users. Unlike Monero, transactions in Zcash are shielded rather than made completely private. This means that the details of the transaction itself, such as the users involved and the amount traded, are hidden. Zcash does this by using a 'zero-knowledge' proof that allows for parties to exchange funds without revealing each other's identity.

Another digital currency that boasts of heightened privacy is the PIVX (Private Instant Verified Transaction). The founders contend that:

> [W]e believe that you have the right to exchange privately and securely, without interference from corporatocracy pressures, governmental influences, prying eyes and nefarious individuals and movements.[5]

PIVX, formerly known as Darknet (DNET), offers a fork-based (it is a Dash fork) cryptocurrency with custom proof-of-stake (PoS) code and a community focused governance system (Community Designed Governance). The white paper on PIVX says:

> It (PIVX) utilises a custom proof-of-stake protocol for securing its network and uses an innovative variable seesaw reward mechanism that dynamically balances 90 per cent of its block reward size between masternodes and staking nodes and 10 per cent dedicated for budget proposals.[6]

The open-source cryptocurrency platform has replaced the previous proof-of-work consensus algorithm. It has also instituted a seesaw reward algorithm. It is a Dash fork, based on the Bitcoin Core. It has brought a new meaning to the concept of 'mining' which has been renamed 'staking'. Unlike the generation of a bitcoin, generating a PIVX does not require intensive hardware for mining. Community members can earn PIVX by holding on to some tokens in their wallet while keeping it connected to the internet. PIVX inherited all the features of Dash, including master nodes, instant transfers and private transfers. PIVX Core programmers are working on improving the Dash Core with enhanced features like IPv6 (Internet Protocol Version 6) support along with IPv4 (Internet Protocol Version 4) and Tor (software that enables anonymity on the internet) network support. Let me explain how this works. An IP address constitutes binary numbers but can be stored as text for human readers. For example, a 32-bit numeric address (IPv4) is written in decimal as four numbers separated by periods. An IPv6, on the other hand uses a 128-bit IP address that is written in hexadecimal and separated by colons. So, a Dash Core with IPv6 would be faster and more secure and Tor support would make transactions on this network more private and resistant to access. If you want a quick overview of the parallels between Dash Core and PIVX, a look at Table 14.1 would make things crystal clear.

Table 14.1: Parallels and Differences between Dash and PIVX

Coin Features	Dash	PIVX
Consensus Algorithm	Proof-of-work (PoW)	Proof-of-stake (PoS 3.0)
Hashing Algorithm	XII	Quark
Hardware Mineable	Yes	No (but multiple supported)
Block Time	150 seconds	60 seconds
Coins Supply	17.6 million (in 100 years)	312 million (in 100 years)
Masternodes	Yes	Yes
Instant Send	Yes	Yes
Private Send	Yes (Conjoint)	Yes (conjoint with untraceable zerocoin protocol)
Variable Masternode reward	No	Yes (seesaw algorithm)
Variable Mining/ Stalking reward	No	Yes (seesaw algorithm)
Decentralised Governance	Yes (masternode voting)	Yes (masternode voting)
IPv6	No	Yes (both wallet and masternode)
Budget Funding	Yes. 10 per cent of block reward	Yes. 10 per cent of block reward

The seesaw reward algorithm is an interesting change in the Dash Core protocol. It is a statement of differing intent. It announces to the world that PIVX protocol is different from protocols followed by other cryptocurrencies. The majority of cryptocurrencies that use masternodes, split their block reward equally between the mining and masternode distribution mechanisms. The intended fairness of this reward distribution can be overcome by the growth of masternodes held by a few large investors which will lead to centralisation of the budgeting system. This would be like having a majority shareholder in a company. The additional benefits of masternodes can lead to fewer users conducting proof-of-stake (PoS) mining activities and thus lowering the security of the PoS network.[7] To ensure an even ratio between staking nodes and masternodes in the network, the PIVX programmers developed a variable 'Seesaw Reward Balance System' that adjusts its block reward size between masternodes and staking nodes. Each PIVX PoS block reward is split with 10 per cent dedicated to the budgeting system and 90 per cent dedicated to both the masternodes and stake mining reward. The reward portion is further split between masternodes and staking nodes. The rationale is simple. The higher the masternode count, the smaller the reward portion of each PoS block that will be apportioned to the masternodes and the larger the reward portion for staking nodes. On the other hand, when the masternode count falls, the reward portion for masternode is increased and the reward portion for the staking node is decreased. It is also claimed that the Seesaw Reward Balance System is more profitable for users running masternodes than it would be to stake equal number of coins. The reason behind this is the extra cost, risk and time associated with maintaining the masternodes rather than staking alone.

The white paper (quirkily called the 'Purple Paper' by the founders) on PIVX claims that the Seesaw Reward Balance System provides more benefits than the reward split methods used by a majority of masternodes using proof-of-stake cryptocurrencies. The greatest benefit, without a doubt, is the inbuilt protocol that allows rewards to all coin holders. PIVX is a more centralised and fair system, that does not limit rewards to the masternodes but to all coin owners. Profitability of the masternodes is of course kept higher as long as the coin supply does not exceed the threshold limit of approximately 40 per cent of coin supply. Other benefits detailed in the white paper are:

1. It can indirectly affect the total count of masternodes in the network by varying its reward size to alter its profitability versus staking.

2. Promotes staking by increasing its reward payment portion when masternode count is high and thus maintaining a high level of network security.[8]

The PIVX team claims that it is the first to explore the implementation of zerocoin protocol with non-optional minting to the platform. A successful integration of the zerocoin protocol will further enhance the network privacy, making every end-to-end transaction untraceable. PIVX believes in having an inclusive governance by the community. If the internet news is to be believed, the team is currently involved in discussions to further improve the existing masternode voting system by including non-masternode PIVX holders in the decision-making process and utilisation of its block reward budget. These discussions are held as publicly viewable live meetings for increased transparency continuing until an ideal governance solution is devised and implemented.

NEM: New Kid on the Block

NEM (New Economy Movement) started out as a fork of NXT, another open-source cryptocurrency and payment network platform. The NEM team, however, decided to rebuild the system from the ground up. NEM.io Foundation is a non-profit organisation founded in Singapore and is the driving force behind the development of the NEM platform. The NEM team is led by Lon Wong. The NEM platform and its associated coin XEM, created a blockchain with certain distinguishing key elements.

On the bitcoin blockchain, bitcoins are mined, while PIVX currency is generated through 'staking'. On the NEM platform, XEMs (currency/asset of NEM) are produced by a process of 'harvesting'. An alternative to mining, harvesting is a system designed by NEM to generate XEM, in order to help maintain the integrity of the NEM blockchain. Every time someone carries out a transaction, the first computer to see and verify the transaction will notify nearby users of that transaction, creating a cascade of information. This process is called 'generating a block'. Whenever someone with more than 10,000 vested XEM generates a block in NEM, they receive the transaction fees on that block as payment.

Bitcoin and most other mining cryptocurrencies use a proof-of-work system where the computer works at cracking a complex computational problem for the blockchain and the user of the computer is rewarded with coins. When it comes to harvesting, NEM uses a proof-of-importance system instead. 'Importance' is a measure of how much you're invested into the NEM system. The XEM assets in your wallet become 'vested' after a fixed period of time. Once you have 10,000 XEM vested you will be able to generate new blocks and earn the transaction fees for all transactions on that block.

NEM is the 'new kid on the block' but some cryptocurrency observers are calling NEM 'the sleeping giant'. Built from scratch to avoid the same pitfalls as other bitcoin forks that become nothing more than 'just another altcoin', NEM's future may have promise. Its value rose from the start and new projects are coming to the platform that make full use of its ability to trade not only currency, but also assets. One of the most promising NEM projects is Landstead, a land and property registration system running entirely on the NEM platform and infrastructure. This online application allows governments to generate and store citizenship data, register properties, assign property to citizens and much more. The benefit, of course, is that it's all on the NEM blockchain which means other users of the blockchain will automatically look at and verify each transaction made. It would be impossible for someone to assign themselves a new property by hacking the database because the hacker would need to 'convince' at least 51 per cent of the blockchain, instead of hacking and tampering with the data directly. Sounds good. Japan has embraced this new kid with fervour. This augurs well for the future of blockchain technology.

Decred: Hybrid Consensus

Another crypto contender that deserves mention is a bitcoin fork called Decred. It is a virtual currency that offers additional features of governance and over-the-counter trades (OTC). It also utilises a mix of proof-of-work and proof-of-stake. The Table 14.2 features gives a quick overview of the similarities and differences between bitcoin and Decred.

Table 14.2: Features of bitcoin vis-à-vis Decred

Coin Features	bitcoin	Decred
Concept	Virtual currency	Virtual Currency + governance + over the counter (OTC) trades
Consensus Algorithm	PoW	PoW+ PoS
Market Cap	$93 billion	$160 billion
Release Date	January 2009	February 2016
Release of coins	Mining	8 pre-mined

The website describes Decred succinctly as:

1. An innovative hybrid proof-of-work (PoW) proof-of-stake (PoS) consensus voting system
2. A censorship-resistant blockchain-anchored public proposal platform
3. Smart contracts that work such as Lightning Network
4. Cross-chain atomic swaps between different digital currencies
5. Cross-platform wallets for ease of use[9]

Bitcoin mining is resource intensive and requires huge quantum of electricity and specialised hardware called Application Specific Integrated Circuit (ASIC) miners. The bitcoin blockchain is also created around a proof-of-work algorithm that allows a small group of miners to hold on to the power centre. The Decred proponents strive for a better balance of power. Linda Xie in an article, 'The Beginner's Guide to Decred' on Medium dated 17 October 2017 explains this paradigm shift:

> Decred attempts to create a better balance of power between miners and users by allowing users to participate directly in the network consensus and act as a check on miners. That involves a hybrid consensus mechanism of both PoW and PoS.[9]

So, in a Decred PoS token holders can validate transactions virtually to receive rewards as well as vote on network proposals. This allows token holders to have a direct say in the progression of the project which aligns incentives. Stakeholders lock up their Decred tokens in return for a ticket that, when randomly selected, allows the ticket holder to act as a block validator. In Decred, 60 per cent of newly generated tokens go to the PoW miners, 30 per cent to PoS voters and 10 per cent towards a development subsidy whereas for bitcoin, 100 per cent of the reward goes to the PoW miners. Through this differentiated set-up of funds set aside towards a development subsidy, Decred allows developers to get paid for their work on proposals if the community approves the payout.

Both bitcoin and Decred have a cap of 21 million coins. In Decred, 8 per cent was pre-mined with an even split between 4 per cent distributed in an airdrop and 4 per cent used for paying back costs for company and individual developers initially funding the project. The airdrop involved giving free tokens to selected individuals who had registered for the airdrop event in advance. This was done to create a wider distribution of tokens and encourage greater participation from the community. Recently, Decred crossed another milestone when Decred and Litecoin completed an on-chain atomic swap which directly enables peer-to-peer trading. While this doesn't substitute for some features that exchanges can offer such as high-frequency trading, it allows holders of Decred and Litecoin to do over-the-counter trades without needing to trust a third party.

If we discussed all the virtual currencies in the contemporary digital ecosystem, it would require several volumes to do justice to such a discussion. Suffice it to say that there are hordes of cryptocurrencies that are skirmishing and battling to attain some semblance of dominance in the strife-torn world of digital currencies. The rest of the world is still looking on askance at this crypto-wrestling wondering which platform or currency will be the victor. Only time can tell. One thing is, however, certain—there is a vast community of programmers and coders working to make money transactions more and more quick, secure and foolproof. Evolving protocols that make online transactions more user-friendly and utilitarian are adding to the quality base. So, whatever the result of the crypto fratricide, we can be assured of a system of financial transactions that is much more advanced than the current system riddled with security holes galore.

Chapter 15

Moribund Masala

> *You can't stop things like bitcoin. It will be everywhere and the world will have to readjust. World governments will have to readjust.*
>
> —John McAfee, Founder of McAfee

Bitcoins and others of its ilk have stormed the bastions of global fiat currency and offered a credible alternative to financial institutions that were hinged around the concept of third-party trust and the monetary policies of the government in power. This maverick 'currency' or 'property' (depending on the regulatory framework of the country in question) has raised more questions than it has answered. The half-baked opinions aired in the media and social media forums have added to the cauldron of seething cryptocurrency confusion. So, any study of digital currencies comes with a heavy baggage of myths and misconceptions that need to be debunked. This chapter is all about evaluating the truth or otherwise of such misconceptions.

The most widespread belief is that bitcoins have no intrinsic value. Perhaps that is true to a certain extent. Or should I say it is as true for bitcoins as for any fiat currency in the world. There was a time when currency in circulation was backed by sovereign gold but this is not true anymore. So, what gives bitcoin its intrinsic value? Is this intrinsic value at par with the value of other commodities?

For this, we need to look at how the blockchain is underpinning the bitcoin functions. We know for a fact that each bitcoin gives the holder the ability to embed a large number of transactions in a globally distributed and timestamped permanent data store, namely the bitcoin blockchain. There is, of course, a trade-off between the exact number of messages and how quickly they can be embedded. As per the latest calculations, a blockchain takes about 10 minutes to embed or push through a transaction. Each block in the blockchain would allow embedding messages amounting to 1 MB. We also know that a transaction fee of 0.001 BTC would have to be paid for a quick pass-through of such a transaction. This message embedding certainly has intrinsic value since it can be used to prove ownership of a transaction at a certain point in time. Considering that electronic notarisation services charge something like $10/document, this would give an intrinsic value of around $10,000 per bitcoin. This valuation may not appeal to the more academically inclined amongst us. For them, I would simply say that the value of the bitcoin has an apparent market orientation. The value of the bitcoin emerges from the acceptance and usage of the bitcoin as a mode of payment as well as an investment. This is why the value of bitcoin has skyrocketed from a miniscule 23 cents in its earlier days to as much as $19,000 sometime in December 2017. This value is indispensably associated with the value it trades at on the various trading platforms or bitcoin exchanges like CoinDesk. So, its value is ultimately determined by what it trades for within the precincts of a demand-supply chain. While some other tangible commodities do have intrinsic value, that value is generally much less than its trading price. Gold, for instance, if judged by only its industrial value as a metal, would have a value much below its traded value. In any event, while historically intrinsic value, as well as other attributes like divisibility, fungibility, scarcity, durability, etc. helped establish certain commodities as mediums of exchange, it is certainly not a prerequisite. While bitcoins are accused of lacking 'intrinsic value' in this sense, they make up for it in spades by possessing the other qualities necessary to make it a good medium of exchange, equal to or better than other tangible commodities. This is perhaps why bitcoins have been accepted in the traditional

F&O market with aplomb by investors as well as the CBOE (Chicago Board of Exchange) that allowed bitcoins into the tight circles of the derivatives market in the United States. So, the bitcoin has not only become an indispensable cog in a self-regulated, stand-alone market ecosystem but is also networked with other traditional financial instruments like the fiat currency, securities, etc. The fact is that the value of any currency or asset in the world is the value we give it. The value we give any asset or currency is based on a universal consensus. So, a dollar or euro or a rupee has value only because we accept it as a mode of payment. Otherwise it is just a piece of paper. Similarly, metals like gold, platinum and precious stones like diamonds, sapphires or emeralds have the value we give it. Otherwise they are nothing but shimmering metals and sparkling stones that we have dug out of rocks and dirt. Tulips were just flowers with no intrinsic value even at the peak of the tulip mania in 1632. So, bitcoins have value that we accord it like every currency of the world and every other tangible asset that we value.

The second part of the very same misconception is that bitcoins are not backed by any tangible asset or cash. My salvo for the naysayers would be—fiat currency is not backed by any tangible asset like gold either. The detractors might pipe in with a waggle and simply say that currency is backed by the government. But that does not help when the whirlpool of market forces sucks at and debilitates the fiat currency. We have seen this happen in Venezuela and recently in Zimbabwe. In Zimbabwe, the worst of the inflation occurred in 2008, leading to the abandonment of the currency. The peak month of hyperinflation occurred in mid-November 2008 with a rate estimated at a mind-boggling 79,600,000,000 per cent per month.

Another misconception that I have come across often, especially in government circles, is that bitcoin users can hide behind the veil of blockchain technology and are therefore beyond even the long arm of the enforcement agencies all over the world. This is perhaps the reason why most countries have come up with regulations that are targeted more at obliteration of digital currencies than monitoring to ensure that it is not used for illicit activities. But this premise has a skewed logic to it. Let us look at it this way. To use bitcoins as payment or for purpose of investment, a user has to start by setting up his bitcoin wallet. This can be done by the user himself but for the most part it is done through third-party agencies like wallet providers or through a trading exchange. In case of the latter, KYC guidelines kick in. This means that the identities of the bitcoin users and all high value transactions is available with the agencies as well as the trading exchanges. A survey conducted in metro cities of India on bitcoin trading exchanges yielded information of high-value transactions in more than 100,000 cases. In July 2017, US Department of Justice (DOJ) charged Alexander Vinnik of BTC-e on 19 counts of illegal money transmission and money laundering. According to the indictment, Vinnik and the bitcoin trading platform BTC-e helped launder over $4 billion in illicit funds since 2011. BTC-e's domain was subsequently seized by US Enforcement.[1] In November 2017, a federal judge in San Francisco ruled that Coinbase (a bitcoin trading exchange) must supply the IRS with identifying information on users who transacted more than $20,000 annually on its platform between 2013 and 2015. This was done when it was noticed that the number of tax returns claiming gains from virtual currency didn't line up with the emerging popularity of digital currencies like bitcoin as an investment vehicle. The US Securities and Exchange Commission recently began cracking down on initial coin offerings (ICOs), a new type of blockchain-based fundraising mechanism, to regulate securities. A similar clampdown was seen in China and South Korea.

Setting up your own wallet may make things a little more difficult for regulators and enforcers but not impossible. The early proponents of cryptocurrencies claimed that virtual currency offers privacy as it does not work on real-world identities but on pseudonyms. Users can create as many wallets and as many pseudonyms as they want to and transact anonymously. Joseph Bonneau and Steven Goldfeder in an article published on 15 December 2017[2] have rightly pointed out that the vast majority of bitcoin users don't get significantly more privacy than they would with traditional bank transfers and they probably get much less than they would by paying with cash. That's because it's possible to link a user's pseudonyms together by studying patterns in the blockchain. Their conclusion is based on a paper entitled 'A Fistful of Coins' published by research scholars of University of California and George Mason University.[3]

What's more, most users leave a paper trail when they buy or sell bitcoin in exchange for dollars or other fiat currencies, as reputable exchange services record identities to comply with 'know your customer' laws. The most technically savvy users can still hide their identities through coin-mixing protocols, in which users swap coins with each other to jumble ownership patterns, but these remain difficult and sparsely used. Several blockchain analysis firms like 'Elliptic' already offer their services to law enforcement to delve deep into such coin mixing protocols and to pierce the veil of pseudonyms. Mike Orcutt, in an article published on 11 September 2017, titled 'Criminals thought bitcoin was the perfect hiding place but they thought wrong'[4], pointed out that while bitcoin users can withhold their identities, they can't avoid revealing other information that can be useful to investigators. Every bitcoin transaction is recorded on its blockchain, a publicly accessible record of all transactions made using the currency. Blockchains 'provide a really useful source of truth', says Jonathan Levin, co-founder of 'Chainalysis'[5], which develops software tools for analysing blockchain data. Chainalysis combines its analysis with other publicly available information to identify users through the unique strings of numbers they use on the blockchain, called addresses and then map how they move funds around. Since 2015, the company has supported investigations by the US Internal Revenue Service, the Federal Bureau of Investigation, the Securities and Exchange Commission, the Drug Enforcement Administration, Immigration and Customs Enforcement and Europol.

So those who think their money laundering and other illicit activities are hidden—beware! Big Brother is watching and waiting to trip you up.

A number of media gurus and so-called experts have gone on record to claim that bitcoins are nothing but a Ponzi scheme and should therefore be banned. This 'Ponzi' chant was started by the Wolf of Wall Street and taken up by others. Even after Jordan Belfort retracted his statement, the converts decided to stick to this epithet. So, what exactly is a Ponzi scheme? A Ponzi scheme is a financial fraud wherein a schemer sells a fake investment scheme to investors showcasing its ability to earn a quick buck. In Ponzi schemes, the schemer basically says, I found a great way to make money fast. The more you give me, the more I can invest in that cause and the more I can earn for us all. But a Ponzi scheme doesn't actually 'earn money'. Once a Ponzi scheme gets too many investors, the system will always crash. This is because the investors all expect more money than they invested and they will get impatient. These schemes come to an end either because the schemer runs away with the money or the schemer runs out of money or authorities clampdown on the scheme. Bitcoin is not a Ponzi scheme for obvious reasons. Nakamoto cannot be compared with charlatan Charles Ponzi. Moreover, bitcoin does not have a central authority that floats the scheme. Nor does it make promises of a quick return. A Ponzi scheme always requires new investors to pay off earlier investors. This is not the case with bitcoin, as the system can work with practically any number of users. However, the network is stronger and more resilient when used by more people. If bitcoin is a Ponzi scheme, then all other forms of money were also initially developed as Ponzi schemes. So, bitcoin may be many things but it is definitely not a Ponzi scheme.

Another bitcoin bugbear is that it is an energy guzzler. 'Bitcoin mining uses as much energy as all of Denmark or Iceland' is a comment one comes across often enough. Mining of digital gold is undoubtedly an energy intensive process requiring hardware that is energy starved. There is no survey to indicate the exact amount of energy resources the bitcoin mining fraternity consumes but it probably would be several gigawatts at any given point in time, roughly equal to the output of a massive power plant such as Hoover Dam. No wonder the ecology experts are predicting a situation where bitcoins alone would use up all the electricity of the world in a few years. So are the predictions right? Let us put this in perspective. The world is using electricity at a faster rate than it can generate. Continuous urbanisation, construction activity, mining of metals like gold and other precious stones, railways, automobiles (Tesla cars), oil rigs are all using electricity. So, why target only bitcoins? Surprisingly, the bitcoin fraternity is more concerned about usage of huge quantities of electricity. They are looking for low-electricity solutions and alternatives. Bitcoin mining apparatuses are being set up in places like Iceland which have excess electricity but no way to transport it to electricity deficient regions.

Energy hungry cryptocurrency companies are planning to relocate to Iceland in search of huge volumes of cheap energy. Johann Snorri Sigurbergsson, a spokesman for Icelandic energy producer HS Orka, told *The Washington Post* that:

> There was a lot of talk about data centres in Iceland about five years ago, but it was a slow start. But six months ago, interest suddenly began to spike. And over the last three months, we have received about one call per day from foreign companies interested in setting up projects here.[6]

Located in the middle of the Atlantic Ocean and famous for its hot springs and mighty rivers, Iceland produces about 80 per cent of its energy in hydroelectric power stations, compared with about 6 per cent in the United States. That and the cold climate makes it a perfect location for new data-mining centres filled with servers in danger of overheating.

There are other solutions to this problem as well that are being seriously considered by those who believe in innovation. Mining always produces heat equivalent to the energy consumed, for example, 1,000 watts of mining equipment produces the same amount of heat as a 1,000-watt heating element used in an electric space heater, hot tub, water heater, or similar appliance. Someone already in a willing position to incur the cost of electricity for its heat value alone could run mining equipment specially designed to mine bitcoins while capturing and utilising the heat produced, without incurring any energy costs beyond what they already intended to spend on heating. If research on lower-energy methods pans out, bitcoin can change or be replaced by a greener competitor. Until then, we just grin and bear it as we do most other things in the contemporary era.

Another misconception we need to track is the belief that bitcoins are finite and hence will place inflationary pressure on the digital currency. It is no secret that bitcoins are capped at 21 million by 2140. But can we say that this status will not change? Not really. The programming community is one of the most innovative of all sectors. It may be change averse but not innovation averse. This is why in the nine years since the birth of bitcoins, many other currencies have appeared. Ethereum, Dogecoin, Dash…the list is endless. All of these currencies have their own special codes that allow different features, although the blockchain technology is essentially the same. There are rumbles of discontent within the community regarding size of the block and speed of transactions. These result in soft forks or hard forks. This throws up the possibility that the code may be tweaked to allow for generation of more bitcoins and other altcoins. So, amendment in the bitcoin protocol is not beyond the realm of imagination. So far, the bitcoin community has fiercely defended the bitcoin cap. But politics among users, not math, keeps things that way for now. Those politics may shift if bitcoin adherents move more in tandem with the belief of economists that the currency will hit a deflationary spiral as bitcoins are accidentally lost over time and the supply dwindles. Some in the programming community also believe that the protocol will become unstable as inflationary rewards for bitcoin miners (who secure the system using tremendous computing power) are phased out in favour of transaction fees. This is the reason why some of the more recent cryptocurrencies have eschewed the finite bitcoin supply framework. Instead, they follow a digital version of Milton Friedman's proposal for low but constant inflation.

The other day I came across a somewhat startling comment by a Silicon Valley investor, Tim Draper. He said, I assume in all seriousness, 'In five years, if you try to use fiat currency, they will laugh at you.'[7] Once I started to look around, I found many more comments in a similar vein. Kim Dotcom, creator of Megaupload, went on record to predict that bitcoin will overtake other payment schemes.[8] For the moment, the bitcoin protocol does not allow for a universal payment usage as it is not structured to handle the tens of thousands of transactions made in cash or through a bank account. The family of bitcoin coders is working on it but no consensus has been reached just yet. Another problem that needs to be addressed is that bitcoin transactions once free are now increasingly expensive, with fees averaging \$20 but with a peak rate as high as \$400 based on demand. Finally, bitcoin transactions do not take effect immediately because of the limitations of the blockchain. New transactions are added only every 10 minutes, on an average, and when users desire extra security, they can take more than an hour. Even with planned improvements, it's unclear if the technology can ever become a universal payment system. Bitcoin is more like a reserve store of value, akin to gold bullion or US Treasury notes, than a day-to-day tender.

There is also the belief that bitcoin is the clarion call of all that is illicit. The publicised Mt Gox heist, the publicly condemned Silk Road and the Dark Web, the instances of bitcoin-mounted tax evasion and money laundering has strengthened the conviction that bitcoin is synonymous with illegal activities. The clampdown on bitcoin exchanges and ICOs by governments and regulatory authorities all over the world has added fuel to the fire and convinced the man on the street that bitcoins are best left alone. It is true that some illicit activities have happened due to the anonymity offered by bitcoins but why blame cryptocurrencies for the human tendency to make a quick buck by turning a blind eye to the law of the land. All frauds up until now have involved the fiat currencies of the day. There have been Visa card frauds and PayPal frauds but the government has not banned these agencies because their benefits outweigh the costs. The Twin Towers of the World Trade Center were rammed in by terrorists in a plane. But establishments of the world did not ban air travel. They just put in more stringent measures to resist another such mishap. In fact, even banks are not secure anymore. India was recently rocked by the Nirav Modi scandal, where the owner of a well-known chain of diamond jewellery defrauded a public sector bank of more than ₹ 11,000 crore by using Letters of Undertaking (LoUs) sanctioned by the government. As far as money laundering and financial crimes are concerned, a recent report estimated that 98 per cent of an estimated $1.6 trillion of global money laundering goes through the nets of the traditional financial system i.e. banks and intermediaries.[9] Also, serious criminals looking to hide their tracks are more likely to choose a currency that is issued and managed centrally rather than a decentralised currency like bitcoin that is open-source, public, peer-to-peer and has a code that mandates that every transaction be recorded and the database of all such transactions be distributed over millions of computers on the bitcoin network.

As a matter of fact, as I have already discussed at length, blockchain technology will be able ensure that culprits are brought to book. Moreover, blockchain technology has given rise to the concept of triple entry. Accounting today works on a double entry system. So, in a transaction between two parties, an entry of the transaction is reflected in the accounts of both the parties. But here we have a system where the entry will be reflected in the accounts of the transacting parties as well as in the distributed ledger shared by all nodes or persons in the blockchain. If used responsibly, bitcoins would be a great financial enabler.

There are murmurs from some quarters that quantum computers would be the death knell for bitcoin security. Maybe. Maybe not. For one, quantum computers do not exist. Perhaps they will be a reality in the distant future. But we cannot be naive enough to believe that in the period of reckoning, the blockchain technology will not have made that quantum leap to plug security loopholes. So, let us not put the cart before the horse and jump to conclusions without any basis.

It is true that bitcoin and the blockchain technology have the potential to disrupt the current financial ecosystem. So, we have the founders and supporters of the current systems bad-mouthing bitcoin and its concomitant technology out of fear of dismemberment and obliteration. In such an environment of anxious unease, it is best to look at both sides of the metaphorical coin. This is what this book is all about.

Chapter 16

Future Fables

> *Bitcoin is a technological tour de force.*
>
> —Bill Gates, Microsoft Co-Founder

On one of my frequent travels, I was passing the time by desultorily searching the internet for articles on bitcoins. Looking over my shoulder, my co-traveller remarked, 'Won't quantum computing throw a wrench in the bitcoin works?' I was a bit nonplussed by the question. I had not thought so far ahead. But as I thought about it at leisure, I realised that to understand the significance of a new technology or trend, it is important to know first how that technology or trend will pan out in the next five to ten years. Easier said than done, of course. Attempts to evaluate such a future impact are prone to fall flat on their face or fall laughably short of the truth. Bitcoins, I believe, fall in the latter category. During the course of my information-gathering spree on bitcoins, I chanced upon an article by scholars of Ryerson University dated 17 October 2016 wherein on the basis of combination of qualitative research conducted through interviews with industry professionals, linear regression and a Monte Carlo analysis, it was concluded that bitcoins would grow in value by 301 per cent to $2,550 in the next five years i.e. from 2016 to 2021.

The paper talked of an incredible growth in cryptocurrencies like bitcoin and Ether:

> When examining the trends in both sets of prices, the five year forecast for bitcoin is $2,550 which represents a growth of 301 per cent, while Ethereum's forecasted value is approximately $88, which represents a growth of 634 per cent.[1]

However, within one year of such a forecast, we saw bitcoin attain an increase in value of 1,500 per cent and reach a mind-boggling $19,000 in December 2017. So, bitcoins grew at a rate ridiculously beyond the imaginations and hopes of scientific predictions as well as bitcoin yaysayers and naysayers. Going by this complete disjunct between prediction (even if its scientific) and reality, I'll desist from making any Nostradamus-like forecasts on the increase or decrease in the value of 'digital gold'. Suffice it to say that some optimistic bitcoin fans have predicted that the value will go up to $100,000 and even the more cynical dissenters have acknowledged that the value will go up to $40,000. Instead of playing God, I will elaborate on the development, acceptability and growth of bitcoin as a concept. Considering that bitcoin is only in its ninth year of growth, the best, as they say, is yet to come. 'Good software takes 10 years. Get used to it,'[2] says Joel Spolsky and this is as true for the bitcoin software as for any other good software. Jeff Garzik, founder of Bloq and core developer of bitcoin rightly says:

> This is still the very early days of bitcoin's life. The base layer protocol is now stable (TCP/IP). Now engineers are building the second layer (HTTP) that makes bitcoin usable for average people and machine.[3]

Timothy Lee, in an article published on 3 December 2013, cautions against judging bitcoin by its contemporary application base:

> Judging bitcoin by its current applications is making the same mistake as dismissing the early internet because Usenet and FTP were clunky.[4]

On the other end of the spectrum, there are those who think bitcoins and other cryptocurrencies have no future as they are deflationary on account of their limited availability and would not offer an anchor during a financial crisis. Bitcoins would not be the lender of last support in a financial crisis. Paul De Grauwe in an article posted on 11 January 2018 on the website 'Social Europe' in a well-reasoned argument opines that bitcoins have no future as a currency or a unit of account. De Grauwe's argument hinges around his belief that the supply of bitcoins is fixed 'asymptotically' and would therefore veer towards permanent deflation. He reasons that as the world economy grows, it requires an increased supply of money to make financial transactions possible. The only way that the bitcoin economy can move in tandem with the world economy scenario is by reducing bitcoin prices of goods and services i.e. by negative inflation. The other alternative, as provided by the quantity theory of money, would be increased velocity of bitcoin usage. That latter situation is not possible on account of the cap on bitcoin generation. In other words, only a negative inflation would allow a synchronised movement of the global economy and bitcoin economy. De Grauwe, in fact, goes one step ahead and confidently announces to the world that bitcoin is a dangerous currency. The logic here is somewhat skewed. He believes that if the world accepts bitcoin as a legal currency, banks will start lending to households and firms. Subsequently, if bank credit dries up, there would be no institution to bail the banks out of a crisis. He says:

> The problem is that as the supply of bitcoins will be fixed, there will be no lender of last resort support in times of banking crises. And these are certain to occur. Even if the supply of bitcoins or of other cryptocurrencies could be subjected to a constant Friedman growth rule it would not solve this problem.[5]

However, most observers of the cryptocurrency market are not quite so damning in their approach to bitcoins. They believe that the evolution of bitcoins could in equal parts be progressive or regressive and the direction of this growth would make or break the cryptocurrency conundrum. According to Siim Õunap, an Estonian who trades the FX and cryptocurrency markets, much will depend on the media coverage around bitcoin and its long-term prospects will depend on alternatives and how efficient and cost effective they are in terms of exchange and carrying out transactions.[6]

That the bitcoin economy has grown and matured in the last nine years is undeniable. I came across a very interesting paper, 'The Evolution of the Bitcoin Economy: Extracting and Analysing the Network of Payment Relationships'[7] published on 1 July 2016 by Paolo Tasco (UCL Centre for Blockchain Technologies), Shaowen Liu (Deutsche Bundesbank) and Adam Hayes (University of Wisconsin). The scholars gathered together the minimum units of bitcoin identity (the individual addresses) and grouped them into approximations of business entities called 'super clusters'. While these clusters remain largely anonymous, the researchers were able to ascribe many of them to particular business categories by analysing some of their specific transaction patterns, as observed during the period from 2009 to 2015. From the data at hand, Paolo and his co-workers were able to extract and create a map of the network of payment relationships among them and analyse transaction behaviour found in each business category. In doing so they were able to identify three marked regimes that have evolved as the bitcoin economy has grown and matured. The first stage is classified as the early prototype stage. The second stage, synonymous with 'sin' enterprise, is the stage when the bitcoin became associated with unlawful activities like sale of drugs, arms, etc. Then comes the third stage that is marked by a sharp veering away from illicit activities toward legitimate enterprises. From January 2009 to March 2012 can be dubbed as the 'proof-of-concept' period which was dominated by miners with very little commercial activity. This period was followed by the 'early adopter' phase, or 'the period of sin' (as some call it) from April 2012 until October 2013. According to research data, '51 per cent of all transaction inflows on the bitcoin blockchain' came from gambling and black-market businesses. The unique features of bitcoin, such as its 'relative anonymity, lack of regulatory and legal oversight and borderless transactions'[8] attracted these types of businesses first. The shutdown of the Silk Road in October 2013 brought an end to this era of predominantly illicit activities. The third period fortuitously started in November 2013 and is characterised by the maturing of the bitcoin economy by diversifying into legitimate payments, commerce and services. This is furthermore supported by looking at VC investments into the bitcoin space, which has risen from $2 million in 2012 to $95 million in 2013, followed by $361.5 million in 2014 and more than $500 million in 2015. The paper concludes with the observation that bitcoin has indeed matured rather than continuing to be volatile, if not unreliable, as many economists have suggested in the past. It reads:

> The result of this work is to show that the bitcoin economy, rather than being a fleeting and frivolous pursuit, has grown and matured over the few years that it has been operational, with distinct patterns of behaviour among its most influential entities and participants.[9]

The trend thus has been towards a steady progression and evolution of the bitcoin protocol.

There are coders and developers all over the world who are working passionately to make the technology powering bitcoins faster and at the same time less expensive. There is also talk about companies working on a software that will allow building of a 'full-stack infrastructure' for bitcoin from silicon to software. A company called 21 Bitcoin has been claiming that they have developed a 'dev kit' to introduce developers to bitcoins. It is believed by some that as the design of the chips is improved, there is the possibility of the rollout of a router that perpetually mines for the user. A tiny miner in a mobile is another future possibility that is being worked on.

Coders and developers are now working on what has been dubbed as the 'Lightning Network' that targets instant payments, scalability, low cost and cross blockchains. A paper entitled 'The Bitcoin Lightning Network: Scalable Off-Chain Instant Payments'[10] by Joseph Poon and Thaddeus Dryja addresses the problem of scalability of the bitcoin ecosystem. The bitcoin payment network compares unfavourably with payment networks like Visa, for instance. Let's compare figures. The payment network Visa achieved 47,000 peak transactions per second (tps) on its network during the 2013 holidays and currently averages hundreds of millions per day. Currently, bitcoin supports less than 7 transactions per second with a 1 MB block limit. If we use an average of 300 bytes per bitcoin transaction and assume unlimited block sizes, an equivalent capacity to peak Visa transaction volume of 47,000/tps would be nearly 8 gigabytes per bitcoin block, every ten minutes on average. Continuously, that would be over 400 terabytes of data per year. Clearly, achieving Visa-like capacity on the bitcoin network isn't feasible today. No home computer in the world can operate with that kind of bandwidth and storage. If bitcoin is to replace all electronic payments in the future and not just Visa, it would result in the outright collapse of the bitcoin network, or at best, extreme centralisation of bitcoin nodes and miners to only the ones who could afford it. This centralisation would then defeat aspects of network decentralisation that make bitcoin secure, as the ability for entities to validate the chain is what allows bitcoin to ensure ledger accuracy and security.

So, Poon and Dryja have proposed a network of micropayment channel to solve the problem of scalability. The logic is simple enough. In the blockchain, if only two participants care about an everyday recurring transaction, it's not necessary for all other nodes in the bitcoin network to know about that transaction. It is instead preferable to only have the bare minimum information on the blockchain. By deferring telling the entire world about every transaction, doing net settlement of their relationship at a later date enables bitcoin users to conduct many transactions without bloating up the blockchain or creating trust in a centralised counterparty. An effectively trustless structure can be achieved by using time locks as a component to global consensus. The focus is on lightning-fast blockchain payments without worrying about block confirmation times. Security is enforced by blockchain smart contracts without creating an on-blockchain transaction for individual payments. It is claimed that in such cases, payment speed measures in milliseconds to seconds. The network envisages ability to cope with billions of transactions per second across the network. Attaching payment per action/click is now a distinct possibility without custodians. Poon and Dryja make it clear that:

> Micropayment channels create a relationship between two parties to perpetually update balances, deferring what is broadcast to the

> blockchain in a single transaction, netting out the total balance between those two parties.[11]

By transacting and settling off-blockchain, the Lightning Network allows for exceptionally low fees. Poon and Dryja explain that the fees are largely derived from the time-value of locking up funds for a particular route, as well as paying for the chance of channel close on the blockchain. These would be significantly lower than on-chain transactions as many transactions on a Lightning Network channel can be settled into one single blockchain transaction. It is hoped that such a network would result in almost negligible fees and make it possible to build 'scalable micropayments, even amongst 42 high-frequency systems such as Internet of Things applications or per-unit micro-billing'.[12]

Cross-chain atomic swaps can occur off-chain instantly with heterogeneous blockchain consensus rules. So long as the chains can support the same cryptographic hash function, it is possible to make transactions across blockchains without trust in third-party custodians. In essence, Lightning Network is a decentralised network using smart-contract functionality in the blockchain to enable instant payments across a network of participants. The Lightning Network is dependent upon the underlying technology of the blockchain. By using real bitcoin/blockchain transactions and using its native smart-contract scripting language, it is possible to create a secure network of participants which are able to transact at high volume and high speed.

Let me try and simplify this some more. Lightning Network works on the principle of bidirectional payment channels. So, in such a network, both parties create transactions that are reflected as a ledger entry in their individual accounts, but such an entry is not broadcast by them to the blockchain. They can update their individual allocations for the ledger entry by creating many transactions spending from the current ledger entry output. Only the most recent version is valid, which is enforced by blockchain-parsable smart-contract scripting. This entry can be closed out at any time by either party without any trust or custodianship by broadcasting the most recent version to the blockchain. By creating a network of these two-party ledger entries, it is possible to find a path across the network similar to routing packets on the internet. The nodes along the path are not trusted, as the payment is enforced using a script which enforces the atomicity (either the entire payment succeeds or fails) via decrementing time-locks. Sounds incomprehensible? A little. What all that technical jargon simply means is that it is possible to conduct transactions off-blockchain without limitations. Transactions can be made off-chain with confidence of on-blockchain enforceability. This is similar to how one makes many legal contracts with others, but one does not go to court every time a contract is made. By making the transactions and scripts parsable, the smart contract can be enforced on-blockchain. Only in the event of non-cooperation is the court involved—but with the blockchain, the result is deterministic. Poon and Dryja turn up their technically sound nose at the traditional financial market transactions where ownership is transferred through a central hub. They point out that bank wire and fund transfer systems (such as ACH and the Visa card network), or equities clearing houses (such as the DTCC) operate in this manner. But, bitcoin transactions under the micropayment umbrella behave differently in that they can execute transactions without a third party:

> As bitcoin enables programmatic money, it is possible to create transactions without contacting a central clearinghouse. Transactions can execute off-chain with no third party which collects all funds before disbursing it—only transactions with uncooperative channel counterparties become automatically adjudicated on the blockchain.[13]

RootStock (RSK) is another, somewhat similar, attempt to address the issues of scalability faced by the bitcoin ecosystem. RSK is nothing but an open-source smart-contract platform with a two-way peg to bitcoin that also rewards the bitcoin miners via merge-mining. The website asserts that RSK's goal is to add value and functionality to the bitcoin ecosystem by enabling smart contracts, near instant payments and higher-scalability. It claims to plug in the lack of smart contracts in the bitcoin protocol. The website goes on to declare that RSK scales to 100 transactions per second, which is the same as that of PayPal, without sacrificing decentralisation and reducing storage and bandwidth usage using probabilistic verification and fraud proofs, as well as blockchain sharding techniques.[14] RSK parameters and new theoretical protocols (such as DECOR+GHOST) allow creating blocks at 10 seconds average interval, with no additional centralisation incentives.

Scalability has always been a burr in the bitcoin developers' side. The history of bitcoin has been witness to the frequent attempts made to address this problem. From the BIP 100 (Bitcoin Improvement Proposal) and BIP 101 to the BU (Bitcoin Unlimited) and SegWit, developers have tried to arrive at a consensus on how to resolve scalability. But with Lightning Network and RSK, some semblance of a solution is in sight. However, consensus is still to be achieved. Mike Hearn, a former Google engineer who now works on a variety of bitcoin projects thinks it would take more than 10 years to fix bitcoin's scalability problem. I'm not so pessimistic. Proposals like Lightning Network and RSK platforms suggest that the problem will be resolved in the near future.

However, my reading is that it is not the technological glitches that will harm the future development and growth of bitcoin as a currency of choice but rather a monopolistic financial regime. Despite being high profile, bitcoins have not been accepted by information technology giants like Apple and Google. These companies do not support bitcoin on their mobile platforms. Recently, Apple has decided to ban bitcoin wallets on the App Store. Google too does not allow in-app payments with bitcoin. This may not have deterred the bitcoin fraternity but it has put a spade in the bitcoin works. An article by 'Unocoin' posted online alleges that many leaders in the tech-space are using their power to restrict the growth of bitcoin which is a convenient mode of remote payment and works well as a credit card alternative:

> These larger technology companies do not want to have any dealings with bitcoin. So they emulate what restrictive governments do and use their power as leaders in the tech-space to regulate the use of bitcoin at least within their platform.[15]

The metaphor is clear enough. If the article is to be believed, all the big tech fish in the pond is ready to devour this newbie currency through restriction of innovations and active suppression by banning its use. Such an accusation sounds a little extreme and perhaps a teeny-weeny bit motivated but there is a grain of truth in this. Politics rather than technology is the single largest factor that will decide the future fables of bitcoin.

Chapter 17

The Chat Room

Virtual currencies and bitcoin technology are being talked about on different platforms. Fans and critics are both vociferously expressing their opinion about varied facets of this newbie technology. This chapter brings together the opinions of persons from different sectors and strata of society. So, the views of bankers, blockchain-technology users, taxation experts, economists, academicians, legal luminaries, etc. jostle for attention in this chapter. The intention is to ensure that no aspect of this fledgling technology is left out. So, sit back and enjoy the intellectual by-play.

Dr Charan Singh is visiting professor, Anderson School of Management, UCLA. He was former RBI Chair and teaches at IIM Bangalore. Dr Singh has authored two highly acclaimed books, *Public Debt Management: Separation of Debt from Monetary Management in India (2016)* and *Debt Management in India (2018).*

An economist widely respected for his opinions, this is what Dr Charan Singh has to say about bitcoins:

> Bitcoins have caught the imagination of many young people and the prices have fluctuated wildly in the past few years. In a few cases, businesses have started to accept bitcoins as a currency for transactions and trading.
>
> My view is that in modern times, unlike pre-1971 era, fiat currency is popular. As the name suggests, fiat currency has to have

a legal backing. To earn legal backing by the government, there has to be strict control of either the government or its authorised agent, the central bank of the country. Money serves three major purposes—transactions, unit of account and store of value. In each of these functions, legal support is necessary. Bitcoin, mined elsewhere would not be able to enjoy that level of confidence and credibility in geographical jurisdiction of any country. Also, fear of insecurity of technology would prevail and legal support for bitcoin to become a legal tender seems to be difficult.

Money also generates substantial amount of seignorage for the government, which bitcoins cannot. In countries like India, where poverty, illiteracy and digital banking penetration is low, bitcoins cannot be used extensively. Therefore, the future of bitcoins seems bleak.

Dr Harmeet Singh is a doctor by qualification and a taxman by profession. With more than 25 years of taxation experience, Dr Singh, Commissioner of Income Tax, believes that the officers of the Income Tax Department are not equipped to monitor or implement taxation of cryptocurrencies. Training officers in the basics of blockchain technology and cryptocurrencies is the need of the hour.

Crypto technology has created a paranoia in the minds of the Reserve Bank of India as well as the Finance Ministry. From issuing repeated advisories against trading in cryptocurrencies to banning bank transactions the central bank is crying itself hoarse in an attempt to stop cryptocurrency trade. The technical ignorance of the Income Tax Department regarding cryptocurrencies was on display when teams surveyed crypto exchanges and issued notices calling for information instead of looking at the 10 GB of entire bitcoin blockchain data and identifying the Indian transaction trail.

Perhaps they do not want to repeat the mistake of Mohammad Bin Tughlak who started leather coins (*chamm de sikke*) and everyone started minting them in their homes and the whole currency collapsed. Or perhaps it is the overhang of present day demonetisation exercise (where we actually ended up demonetising more currency than was actually issued by the central bank), that makes them do what they are doing.

The twenty-first century is the century of a tech-savvy borderless society which lives in a global village. Facebook and Google have melded geographies in a unified whole. To transact in this tech ecosystem, a currency is needed which has similar characteristics. Crypto technology fits the bill and is being increasingly adopted all over the world. It provides anonymity, security of transaction and is devoid of any central bank control. It is in fact the currency minted by the people for their use and controlled by them. Sooner the Indian authorities come around to accepting this idea, better it would be for them and for the people.

Here I am reminded of the oft cited quote of French dramatist Victor Hugo from *The History of a Crime*, 'One resists the invasion of armies; one does not resist the invasion of ideas.'

If that be the case, it would be the better part of valour to understand this nascent technology and its positive as well as negative fallouts. The only way to do that would be to create a task force within the Ministry of Finance to train officers to understand this new technology and its ramification. Institution of regulations and clear taxing policies for virtual currencies would also create the right ecosystem.

Professor Jayant Varma is a professor in the Finance and Accounting area at the Indian Institute of Management, Ahmedabad where he teaches courses in capital markets, fixed income, alternative investments, risk management and corporate finance. Professor Varma was a full time member of SEBI and has been the chairman of the Secondary Markets Advisory Committee. He was a member of the Raghuram Rajan Committee on Financial Sector Reforms and of the Financial Sector Legislative Reforms Commission.
Professor Varma is of the view that blockchain technology, like all new technologies, will take many decades to realise its full potential:

The second half of the twentieth century saw the creation and growth of large centralised systems (especially in the financial sector), but the twenty-first century has seen an erosion of trust in institutions

> and governments around the world in the aftermath of the global financial crisis and the Eurozone sovereign debt crisis. As a result, the pendulum has started to swing back towards decentralisation, and there is a rising interest in systems like the blockchain that are decentralised, operate with minimal trust and also offer high degree of resilience to failure. Blockchain is still an evolving and therefore immature technology, but history teaches us that radically new technologies take many decades to realise their full potential.

Shri Amitav belongs to the 1990 batch of the Indian Revenue Service and is currently working as Additional Director General in the Directorate of Risk Assessment, Central Board of Direct Taxes, New Delhi. He was a member of the core team of officers that conducted the study phase of Business Process Re-engineering of the Income Tax Department (ITD). He has been a senior faculty member at the National Academy of Direct Taxes, Nagpur, the apex training institute of the ITD. He has also worked in the Financial Intelligence Unit and has been keenly following the cryptocurrency market landscape in India since demonetisation. He has authored a book on the investigation of bitcoin transactions for the officers of the Investigation Directorates of the ITD.

Shri Amitav believes that the need of the hour is to take calibrated steps towards regulation as this was the only way to mitigate risks arising out of use of cryptocurrencies. He opines:

> Bitcoin has fallen short of the expectation of a currency for which it was conceived by its creator. Plagued by the serious limitations of lack of consumer protection, wild price fluctuations, slow throughput and voracious appetite for electricity, bitcoin has failed to establish itself as an alternative to traditional financial system. In India, bitcoin caught the imagination of people more prominently after demonetisation. There was an exponential growth of participants on bitcoin exchanges that facilitated the sale and purchase of cryptocurrencies including bitcoin. However, the demand was too insignificant to have made any impact on the price of bitcoin. The recent development of the half-ban on cryptocurrencies has pushed the market towards underground

cash traders whose presence has conspicuously increased. This would render the country's law enforcement agencies insulated from information from intermediaries which is so critical for investigating the misuse of cryptocurrencies for serious offences like drug trafficking, money laundering and terror financing, besides tax evasion. With countries fragmented in their approach towards regulation of cryptocurrencies, the need of the hour is to take calibrated steps for regulation that helps in developing an inter-agency community of interest and expertise to formulate strategies for mitigating the risks arising from cryptocurrencies.

(The views expressed by Shri Amitav are his own and do not necessarily represent the views of CBDT or the government.)

Ms Prabhpreet Chopra is an IT professional with over 25 years of experience and has worked in several multinational corporations in a variety of roles ranging from IT consultant to team manager for IT solution design, build and delivery. She holds MCA and MBA degrees and has a rich working experience in various IT related functions including business intelligence and analytics. She has authored two books, *IT Tools and Applications (2005)* and *Fundamentals of Information Technology (2006)*. Ms Chopra's book *IT Tools and Applications* was awarded the 'Book Award' by the Federation of Educational Publishers in India. Her second book was prescribed as a course book for Punjab Technical University. Ms Chopra is very optimistic about the salutary impact of blockchain in the financial sector:

> Ignoring bitcoin's challenges, blockchain, the underpinning technology for cryptocurrency, has the potential to revolutionise the world's economy!
>
> The transparency offered by the open-source distributed database using state-of-the-art cryptography to facilitate collaboration and tracking of transactions and interactions makes it a 'platform of truth and trust'. Its distributed nature also makes it harder for the hackers to attack!
>
> If banks and other financial institutions started sharing data using blockchain, it could speed up transactions, take costs

> (manual processing, middlemen costs, etc.) out of the system, and hence provide cheaper and more efficient services for the common man. Access to an open, transparent ledger of bank transactions would also benefit regulators, and could help governments tackle tax fraud.

Ms Vani Gopal Sharma is an additional district and session judge, Haryana. A legal luminary, Ms Sharma strikes a note of cryptocurrency caution when she opines that cryptocurrency's benefits are its shortcomings. She stresses the need for legal monitoring of virtual currencies:

> With any form of business or investment, come the loopholes, thieves and punters. The problem with cryptocurrency is that its benefits are its shortcomings. There are obvious benefits of making transactions using cryptocurrencies over cash, as you can choose how much information to disclose, so no one can steal your money. But at the same time, there are no legal safeguards for people trading in cryptocurrencies. The legal status of cryptocurrency remains uncertain at best. Though cryptocurrency continues to develop and remains a promising financial system with many prospects for a bright future, the investors continue to play at their own risk. Some law is definitely required to deal with this futuristic currency.

Ankush Sharma, a senior platform engineer currently working with Koinex, believes that virtual currencies can gain widespread acceptance only in a completely digital world. Like the crypto geek he is, he dreams of a world based on blockchain technology but without its 'black mirror' reflection. On a more immediate and pragmatic note, this IIT alumnus asserts that the only way to curb money laundering is by creating a global KYC norm.

> Initially, most of the cryptocurrencies had a fixed supply. The fixed supply can be well understood considering the proof-of-work method used for minting new tokens on the network. With time, the number of minted tokens will limit to the fixed supply. Once

the minted number hits the supply cap, there will be little incentive for the miners. So, these currencies are deflation-based with value increasing over time. If you compare them with the fiat currencies we have at this time, most of them are inflation-based with the value fixed and supply increasing overtime. Inflation makes more sense as compared to deflation as the value of fiat currency is pegged to some physical asset like gold, bonds, land, etc. and inflation rates are adjusted accordingly. In case the government is not able to pay back the fiat holders they need to dilute the assets which is not the case in cryptocurrencies like bitcoin as there is no central authority holding physical assets. Unarguably, money without intrinsic value is difficult to understand and fixed value currencies are easy to understand and operate with (you won't like new denomination notes in the market). And you won't like to hold a volatile asset yourself. There has been the advent of stable coins like Tether, Dia, etc. which are issued by private companies. These stable coins are backed by physical assets keeping their values fixed. Considering the advent of such asset-backed cryptocurrencies, we may very well see a global company providing a stable coin through which we can transact around the world. Cryptocurreny, as a national currency, does not make any sense until the world becomes completely digital and people know how to manage their private keys.

Cryptocurrency exchanges are doing KYC using the identification documents according to the region they are based in or the fiat pairs they allow trading in. They only allow bank accounts linked with the documents supplied for deposit/withdrawal. This should be made mandatory in all exchanges as it prevents money laundering and helps governments to impose taxes as well. On the other hand, there are bitcoin wallets (or other crypto wallets). Bitcoin wallets can be created by anyone just running a small piece of software. So, you basically own a bitcoin address that can be tracked only by analysing the blockchain history. A major loophole is created by privacy coins like Monero and ZCash, as there is no way to track the addresses of senders in transactions using such privacy coins. Some global exchanges allow trade in cryptocurrencies without asking for KYC documents, just with an

> email account which is pretty easy to fake. One can easily buy from a KYC regulated exchange using fiat currency and transfer privacy coins to some unregulated exchange and convert those to bitcoins. Then these bitcoins can be used for illegal activities. The reason why most of the exchanges are cutting out privacy coins is because they are acting as a facilitator for money laundering and are consequently coming under scrutiny very often. So, there is a requirement of global KYC on each international exchange.

As you can see, dear reader, there are interesting but varied views aired by a miscellany of sectoral representatives. However, not surprisingly these opinions are characteristic of the global stance towards cryotocurrency. There is some excitement about a new though disruptive technology mixed with large measures of caution. The future of cryptocurrencies like bitcoin may be uncertain but the blockchain technology definitely has the contemporary generation dreaming big dreams. I'll leave you with Ankush's dream of a new blockchain technology world to savour, mull over or shrug away disparagingly:

> I dream of a world when you will be earning from multiple sources at the same time. You will be doing a full-time job as well as participating in multiple shared economies around the world. With blockchain, it is getting easier to put value on a thing without realising its physical existence. Blockchain will lead to the generation of a vast number of virtual and physical economies around the world. For example, consider a healthcare institute that sources health data from individuals around the world to study genes or diseases. Currently, they are bound by a geographical area and can only ask locals to come up and participate. The same is the case of paid surveys. With blockchain and IoT (internet of things) most of these sectors will be automated and will allow global participation.

SECTION VI

A Twist in The Tale

Chapter 18

The Future of Blockchain

> *The internet is entering a second era that's based on blockchain. The last few decades brought us the internet of information. We are now witnessing the rise of the internet of value.*
>
> —'Realizing the Potential of a Blockchain'

Blockchain technology, with its concept of public distributed ledger, is of recent origin. So naturally one would expect that people (other than the coder community) would be clueless about this peer-to-peer technology. But the colourful profile of the blockchain-based cryptocurrency bitcoin brought this technology into the 'sitting rooms' of the common man. It became the subject of discussion in bars, cafes and parties. But despite its popularity, the technology that powers the bitcoin is still regarded as programming gibberish by most people who consider it simply as a mode of transacting cryptocurrencies. And yet this technology has the potential to change the very face of the future. It has the ability to impact not only finance and banking segments but also governance, entertainment, healthcare, etc. Let us see what this technical debutante has to offer.

A Fillip to Good Governance

Emerging economies and welfare states are structured to provide services like healthcare, education, justice, policing, etc. However, most governments farm out services like education and healthcare to private or semi-government organisations. Blockchain technology has a lot to offer in this sphere. Land titles were perhaps the first area where blockchain technology planning and potential deployment took place in a developing country. In 2015 the Government of Honduras signed an agreement with Factom, a US start-up, to use blockchains to manage land title registration and help manage fraud and corruption. Similar initiatives were also launched in Georgia and Ghana. Georgia signed up BitFury, a blockchain start-up, to implement documentation of land records. Ghana teamed up with a local non-profit start-up, Bitland, using bitcoin's blockchain to manage land titles and settle land disputes. Bitland is an experimental platform in Ghana using a blockchain to bridge the gap between the government and the undocumented areas lacking land titles. Unfortunately, these initiatives in Georgia and Ghana fizzled out. Sweden is also dabbling in its own blockchain-based land titles project, that has already moved beyond the proof-of-concept stage. In India, the state of Andhra Pradesh has shown pragmatic and progressive sense in accepting and using blockchain technology for good governance. The state, in partnership with Indian start-up Zebi, is collating land records. Also, it is working on blockchain-based solutions for vehicle registration with Swedish firm Chroma Way. The chief minister of the state has mooted a proposal to make Fintech Valley Vizag the largest repository of blockchain use cases in transport, finance and digital security. There is also a proposal to build a blockchain stack that will make data available on an API (Application Programming Interface) platform which will allow users to build a customised application for use. So, if an individual is looking to buy property, he can—through a customised app—pull out the history of all transactions pertaining to such a property. Things seem to be really looking up in the blockchain-based governance sector.

Blockchain could also play a significant role in creating and running data pertaining to individual identities. The year 2011 saw the arrival of Namecoin (NMC), a blockchain-based domain name register. This prevents governments, domain name services, servers, or any other third party from interfering with the ownership of a domain. The goal behind Namecoin was to create an environment that cannot be censored, manipulated, or illegally obtained by governments. This seems to be one of the most promising fields for the successful application of blockchain technologies. Blockchain technology-based identity can be effectively used for managing passports, birth and wedding certificates, national and electoral IDs and handling e-residence programmes, among others. However, some critics argue that existing digital ID technologies are working fine and are far more scalable than those using blockchain platforms. Blockchain technology scalability limitations could prevent massive deployments in countries with large populations such as India and China. Some critics also point out the failed attempts made in this sphere. An attempt was made to use Namecoin blockchain to manage domain names and personal identities. However, in the absence of scalability, the Namecoin blockchain was not able to deal with large DNS registers. A white paper published by the Canadian Government entitled 'Blockchain: Unpacking the Disruptive Potential of Blockchain Technology for Human Development' explains this struggle:

> The platform only catered to .bit domains which in turn can only be reached via specific add-ons...Given the immutability inherent to blockchains, issues related to DNS squatting, domain names without relevant Internet Protocol addresses and potential name seizures, Namecoin was struggling.[1]

Scalability is undoubtedly a roadblock today but the continuing evolution in the field of blockchain technology would, in all likelihood, plug this technical glitch.

For those who have a quarrel with scalability, it would do well to remember that although the existing ID technologies are scalable, they are prone to frequent hacks and security lapses. The 'Aadhar' imbroglio in India is a case in point. In November 2017 there was a strong rumour of data lapses in the UIDAI (Unique Identification Authority of India) platform that stores the biometric data of all Indians. The rumour was given a quick burial by UIDAI officials who asserted that 'Aadhaar data is fully safe and secure and there has been no data leak or breach at UIDAI.' However, in January 2018, a national daily managed to 'purchase' a service that offered unrestricted access to information of about more than one billion Aadhaar numbers. This service was offered on WhatsApp for a measly ₹500 and delivered within 10 minutes after payment through a Paytm account. An extra ₹300 allowed the 'purchaser' of the data to download a software to print the Aadhaar card after entering the Aadhar number of any individual. The immutable and secure parameters provided by the blockchain would not allow such lapses and illegitimate access to data.

Blockchain technology also has the capacity to change the very face of the electoral processes. Most elections of the world are marred by allegations of misconduct. A recent news item was a bit disconcerting. Apparently, the FBI searched the residential premises of Trump's lawyer and details of payoff to a woman who claimed intimacy with Mr Donald Trump had surfaced. Indian elections are always riddled with accusations of ballot theft, 'fixing' of EVMs (Electoral Voting Machines) and ballot box theft. So, what is needed is a platform that can provide free and transparent election framework. Ergo, we have Follow My Vote, a start-up using distributed ledgers to run voting processes and prevent fraud and identity theft. Follow My Vote builds on the frustration of the citizen who is ignorant of the fate of the votes cast by him. So, we have more and more citizens abstaining from voting simply because they feel their votes do not count. This is adversely impacting the democratic process all over the world. The website of Follow My Vote claims that it allows the voter to not only track his vote and its ultimate status but also watch the entire voting process in real time as the votes are cast. The website lays down some salutary objectives:

> Using a webcam and a government-issued ID, voters can remotely and securely log in and vote for their desired candidates. After they have selected their candidates, they can use their unique voter ID to quite literally open the ballot box, locate their vote and check that it is both present and correct.[2]

So here we have a transparent and cost-effective blockchain technology that will put an end to the manipulation of the voting public by the political parties through their paid hooligans. It also has the advantage of allowing the voter to keep track of his vote. Ukraine has been experimenting with such technology. The plan is to use e-Vox, an Ethereum-based distributed ledger, for local elections. Implementation has already started in a couple of towns. As in most such protocols, there is always a downside. There is still a possibility of a hack that looms large. Hackers may be able to acquire private keys from voters through payoffs or voters could offer to loan or sell their private keys for economic benefit. This again would mean incorporating more stringent security protocols that can discourage such a trade-off.

Evolving Social Mores

Blockchain will also help cause a shift in the social paradigm, if applied correctly. You may wonder how a technological innovation could manage that. Let's see now. There are some blockchain-based start-ups that are working on promoting freedom of speech. FlorinCoin is one of them. It is basically a scrypt-based cryptocurrency that has augmented the blockchain by adding the transaction comment feature to the blockchain. This text field can store 528 characters per transaction. Transaction comments are included when sending coins over the network. This can be used simply as a greeting or a thank you note, or on a business level, express important details about the transaction. However, the transaction comment capability can be used in more complex ways. For instance, a platform can be built using the text function to store records of payment, such as the hash of a receipt, which will forever be associated with this transaction. It can be a permanent record of receipts for every bitcoin, Litecoin and Florincoin transaction. It can also be used to create a perfect freedom of speech application, harnessing hundreds of mining computers as well as wallet clients as a peer-to-peer network of decentralised free-speech nodes. Florincoin has, in fact, created a distributed ledger application (Dapp) called Alexandria that aims to be a decentralised repository of knowledge and information managed directly by end users. One of its applications is the preservation of Namecoin and resolution of certain issues faced in internet governance.

Florincoin, like I said before, augmented the blockchain by introducing the possibility of attaching comments to blocks in the chain, thus allowing free speech nodes. Publicism, another start-up, offers support to journalists that face censorship in many countries, allowing journalists to use pseudonyms to protect their identities. MazaCoin, a US-based start-up, is working on supporting native and indigenous US communities and is using its platform to protect freedom of speech and store protest photos on the blockchain. So there is a lot happening in the free-speech arena.

Lending a Helping Hand

Some blockchain platforms are working for the larger good of humanity. Aid:Tech, a London-based blockchain technology start-up is supporting humanitarian and development efforts in the Middle East. The company provides a voucher system that can be used in even the most challenging circumstances and helps ensure that financial resources securely reach their final destination. Bitnation is another blockchain-based start-up that has made huge strides in innovating and structuring the blockchain technology to ensure a helping end. In 2015, Bitnation kickstarted a Bitnation Refugee Emergency Response (BRER). This was a humanitarian aid project to facilitate and provide emergency services and humanitarian aid to refugees during the refugee crisis in Europe. Bitnation utilised the blockchain to authenticate and validate identification through a Blockchain Emergency ID (BE-ID) and locate and provide needed services to refugees. It also attempted to provide economic and political solutions to refugees in the receiving states. The founder Susanne Tarkowski Tempelhof explained:

> We're proud at Bitnation to be able to help alleviate the challenges these people are facing, through providing IDs, greater financial mobility and over time, we'll be able to add things like our basic income protocol etc. to help them live better...[3]

A similar effort has been made by 9Needs, which in tandem with UNDP has ensured cash transfers and financial tools in Serbia and

Moldova. UNWFP (UN World Food Programme) announced a blockchain technology pilot using Ethereum to disburse financial support to those in need in Jordan, building on the results of a smaller initiative in Pakistan. In January 2017, WFP initiated a proof-of-concept to confirm basic assumptions around the capabilities of blockchain in authenticating and registering transactions in Sindh, Pakistan. Learning from the experience, WFP built and implemented a more robust blockchain system in refugee camps in Jordan. As of January 2018, more than 100,000 people residing in camps redeem their WFP-provided assistance through the blockchain-based system. Blockchain technology has made it possible for WFP to have a full, in-house record of every transaction that occurs at that retailer, ensuring greater security and privacy for the Syrian refugees. It also allows for improved reconciliation and significant reduction of third-party costs.[4]

A Manna for the Entertainment Industry

Blockchain technology is not just about aiding humanitarian programmes or improving governance. Blockchain technology is turning out to be a godsend for the entertainment industry as well. For too long artists in the entertainment industry, be it a musician or a singer or an actor or a comedian, were being sucked dry by a plethora of recording studios, film directors, film and music distributors, sponsors—the list is endless. Profits from publishing rights and distribution profits went to industry insiders. The artists ended up with a tiny piece of the generous financial pie. These artists also had to contend with piracy that whittled down their returns. These writers and artists need to look beyond the limited boundaries of the old business models if they need to set the balance right. There is a strong possibility that blockchain-technology applications will put an end to this exploitation of the artists' vulnerability. Tech-savvy artists have already seen the opportunity and are making use of it. Imogen Heap, a Grammy winner, has embraced blockchain technology in a big way. She joined Ujo, an all-in-one music distribution company and released her first song on the Ethereum blockchain. Ethereum works on the concept of a smart contract that allows a musician to have complete control over collaborators as well as over all aspects of a musical track release like buying licences to download, stream, sync or remix the song.

In 2016, Spotify settled a licensing dispute with the National Music Publishers Association (NMPA) in the United States over unpaid royalties. According to the NMPA, Spotify had failed to obtain mechanical licences—which refer to a copyright holder's control over the ability to reproduce a musical work—for a large number of songs on its service. The issue would obviously have a domino effect as it would impact other streaming services as well. Spotify agreed to pay over $20 million to music publishers as a result of this settlement, in addition to a $5 million penalty. While the company managed to avoid class action lawsuits as a result of the settlement, it was the tip of the iceberg. The crux of the problem was that Spotify had claimed that it didn't pay out the royalties because it simply didn't have the necessary data to help it figure out whose claims were legitimate, or even how to locate the parties. It said it lacked an authoritative database that covered all existing music rights. This opens it up to litigation, which is obviously not the ideal way of managing these payments. To resolve this problem, Spotify has now teamed up with Mediachain, a decentralised blockchain-based company that manages digital rights. Mediachain in a blog post clarified that its vision for the problem is using a shared data layer, which 'is key to solving attribution, empowering creators and rights owners and enabling a more efficient and sustainable model for creativity online'.

Two start-up companies, CEEK and StreamSpace have also jumped into the entertainment arena. CEEK, a developer based in Florida, is attempting to use a virtual reality platform to distribute access to live performances. The CEEK team hopes to revolutionise the concert experience along with other types of live events. The CEEK-enabled VR (virtual reality) headset hopes to create the concert experience at home. Imagine an experience that rivals a ringside view of a match or front-row seats to a Coldplay concert or a bird's-eye view of a book launch. Using smart contracts and a digital-currency payment platform, consumers can connect with artists in a whole new way, confident that their money is going directly to the content creator or performer. CEEK envisages use of blockchain technology to provide such an experience as well as facilitate payments to access such an experience.

StreamSpace is another company with similar objectives, except that their focus will be on connecting filmmakers to their audience on a decentralised storage platform and blockchain-based networks to share content. For the moment, it is virtually impossible for film artists to connect with fans or an audience outside of film festivals or other film studio sponsored events. Netflix, Amazon and other streaming platforms offer access to a wide audience of potential viewers, but it's hard for most films to break through into the mainstream. StreamSpace allows filmmakers to raise money using their digital coins and connect to a wider audience using a scalable, decentralised distribution network.

A company building out the necessary platform for blockchain-based payments is Stem, which hopes to be the payment distribution platform for creators. They allow creatives to publish content, manage contracts and transact payments all from one easy-to-use portal. While micropayments are far from the norm in content consumption today, a promise of lower transaction fees and more secure records of sale and consumption could make it an interesting business model for artists, authors and filmmakers.

This nascent technology would also have a salutary impact on collation and registration of intellectual property rights. As a decentralised, immutable, distributed and transparent platform, blockchain technology would be a perfect fit for the protection of intellectual property rights. The creation of blockchain-based IP (intellectual property) registries would be an ideal solution. It could contain all the details of patents or other IP certificates along with a narration of royalties received on this account. Smart contracts for ensuring timely payment of royalties could also be programmed into the base code. Not a lot of work seems to have been done in this field. Only one start-up seems to be working on this. Ascribe, the start-up in question, is focusing on using an open-source protocol that interacts with the artists and allows them to register intellectual property and obtain certificates of attribution and ownership and also manage licensing of their work to third parties.

A Game Changer

When we talk about entertainment, we cannot in all honesty ignore online games that are a favourite with GenNext. We saw the success of games like Farmville which was a farming simulation social network game. Purchases could be made online with fiat currency and the game could be played on Facebook. In 2009, it was the most 'addictive' game on Facebook. It won the 'Best New Social/Online game' in the Game Developers Conference in 2010. These games worked on a centralised framework. Obviously, gaming has a lot of potential to earn money. Some innovators decided to use the blockchain technology for online gaming. And so 'CryptoKitties' was born. It allows users to buy, own, trade and breed digital collectible cats (with their own particular brand of genotype and phenotype) on the Ethereum blockchain using Ether as the unit of currency. Smart contracts administer every aspect of CryptoKitty creation and trading. As a result, there's no central authority that can change, remove, or otherwise alter a CryptoKitty once it has been created. The website informs that the genesis cat was born and adopted on 2 December 2017. Since then, a new cat has been born every 15 minutes. This will continue until November 2018, at which point no new generation zero CryptoKitties will exist. According to the 'white pa purr' (Don't smirk! That's what it's is called) titled 'CryptoKitties: Collectible and Breedable Cats Empowered by Blockchain Technology'[5], only 50,000 generation zero kitties will ever exist. The founders claim that the motivation behind this game was not to set up a revenue-earning model (which it is) but to educate the common user about blockchain technology by:

1. Gamifying features that use blockchain's unique applications.
2. Using an approachable, consumer-facing brand based on genuine passion for blockchain technology.
3. Implementing an open platform inclusive to users of all levels of technical knowledge.
4. Setting in motion a sustainable, revenue-based model (as opposed to ICOs)

CryptoKitties is, thus, a salutary attempt to 'empower everyday consumers with a basic fluency in distributed ledger technology'.[6]

Good thinking. Killing two birds with one stone. Education (blockchain technology is trending) and earning (some kitties have sold for more than six figures) go hand in hand. There are other contenders in the gaming market. Video game developers EverdreamSoft and their partner 'All 4 Games' officially launched their flagship blockchain-based mobile title 'Spells of Genesis'. According to the developers, Spells of Genesis takes advantage of the bitcoin blockchain by allowing users to store cards on it. The website explains the game:

> Spells of Genesis is a mobile game that is a mix of a trading card game (TCG), bringing in deck collection and strategy, along with arcade-style gaming aspects. The game is based on blockchain technology, which is also the main source of inspiration for the story line.[7]

A new project with huge potential in the gaming sector is the 'Game Protocol'.[8] It is an upcoming ICO that plans a decentralised gaming store, where rankings will impact visibility and placement. It will be a platform for video game developers and will provide any aspiring developer with tools required to develop video games as funding through a crypto-based crowdfunding programme. Such projects may in the future become the waterloo for existing gaming giants.

Unikrn, a similar gaming project, claims on its website that it provides eSports fans with a safe and legal place to gather, game and bet on eSports, covering games such as League of Legends, Counter-Strike: Global Offensive, Dota 2 and more.[9] If the website is to be believed, Unikrn runs a fully regulated and licensed eSports betting platform that allows users to bet legally anywhere in the world using Unikoins, the platform's virtual tokens. The company also holds licences to conduct real-money wagering in Australia and the Isle of Man, with several other pending jurisdictions. Through its partnership with Tabcorp (an integrated gambling and entertainment company), Unikrn employs industry-leading practices and technology to handle account verification, KYC, anti-money laundering, problem gambling, etc. Unikrn is also on the founding board of the eSports Integrity Coalition (ESIC), which addresses threats to the integrity of match results, such as from hacking, scripting, match-fixing, DDOS, or hardware manipulation. The company previously raised $10 million from investors including Ashton Kutcher, Mark Cuban, Shari Redstone, Elisabeth Murdoch and others.

A Tipping Point for Banking and Finance

More than governance and entertainment, blockchain technology will prove to be a game-changer for the banking and financial sector. Despite what one might call sovereign protection, banks are being undermined by a slew of frauds. Here, I would like to refer to the beleaguered banking sector in India. The Punjab National Bank fraud, often referred to as the 'Nirav Modi scam', made headlines in early 2018. The modus operandi has become clear after extensive investigations. Nirav Modi, the CEO of Gitanjali Gems had been obtaining Letters of Undertaking (LoUs) akin to bank guarantees by colluding with certain rogue bank officials. The issue of these LoUs and their subsequent renewal (they were valid for 3 months only) was not recorded in the bank ledgers. These guarantees were used to obtain loans abroad, ostensibly to pay for imports. According to investigators, Nirav Modi and his cohorts would submit forged papers regarding imported jewellery. Once the funds were released to suppliers overseas, the suppliers, believed to be fronts for Nirav Modi would send money into the shell companies owned by the group through fictitious transactions. The transfer of money happened through SWIFT i.e. The Society for Worldwide Interbank Financial Telecommunication that provides a network that enables financial institutions worldwide to send and receive information about financial transactions in a secure, standardised and reliable environment. Despite such checks and balances, the fraud continued for almost 12 years and cost the Indian public sector bank about ₹ 12,000 crore. Had there been a decentralised, immutable and transparent blockchain bank model keeping tabs on financial transactions, the arm of law would have caught up faster with the fraudsters. The cosmetisation of non-performing assets (NPAs) that has become the norm today would also be considerably reduced. Small steps to redress such problems are being made. Infosys has joined hands with six banks to set up a blockchain-based trading network called Trade Connect. The network functionalities will include bill collection, issuing letters of credit, customer-to-customer transactions, invoice financing, etc. This may look like a small step but may turn out to be a 'giant leap for mankind'.

It is also a fact that financial intermediaries like exchanges and banks are subject to cyberattacks. A blockchain model has a high probability of making financial transactions safer. Also, banks and other financial institutions are spending a large amount of money in complying with KYC norms. A Thomson Reuters survey in 2016[10] threw up some disconcerting results. It showed that the average cost of financial firms on KYC and Customer Due Diligence (CDC) varied anywhere between $60 million to $500 million. A blockchain KYC model can put an end to this cost incurred by financial institutions.

Blockchain technology can also help with financial inclusion. In developing countries or emerging economies, a large chunk of the population has no bank accounts. A Kenya-based start-up, BitPesa supports transactions and payments between African businesses and the rest of the world using bitcoin blockchain. BitPesa is active in Congo, Kenya, Nigeria, Tanzania and Uganda and has partners in the United States and China. In addition to payments, BitPesa also exchanges bitcoins into local currencies, as well as US dollars and other currencies. BitSoko is another Kenyan start-up that furnishes an Android-based bitcoin wallet and a transparent platform by capitalising on the benefits of bitcoin blockchain. In 2015, BitSoko received support from the Gates Foundation to create a portfolio of services. BitPesa takes bitcoin payments and exchanges them for local currencies which are then deposited into bank accounts or mobile money wallets. BitPesa promises to be a cheap way to transmit money and remittances internationally, especially for underserved markets in the mobile money space in Africa.

An Elixir for Agriculture

The agricultural sector in developing countries will also benefit from blockchain technology. Looks like this technology is the panacea for all ills. A bit exaggerated but not so far from the truth. There are several blockchain start-ups in this sector. Common applications include tracking products and supply chains, facilitating payments to producers, keeping an eye on prices to ensure fair payment for produce and enhancing community supported agriculture. There is Skuchain, a start-up that uses smart contracts to keep track of agriculture supply chains. Farm Share, a US non-profit, supports community-based agriculture which promotes communal forms of property and collaborative labour processes for developing local economies. Farm Share also uses smart contracts and Dapps to promote local products and ensure payments are distributed among participating communities. BitMari, another African bitcoin wallet service for sending money, is supporting an accelerator and trust for female farmers in Zimbabwe. The project is using crowdfunding to collect bitcoins and then provide funding to 100 women farmers who are expected to receive technical assistance from experts.

Going by the enthusiasm with which blockchain technology applications have been embraced, it is obvious that this fledgling technology has a bright future. The Hyperledger project, initiated by Linux Foundation to encourage and support the collaborative development of blockchain-based distributed ledgers, is another feather in its cap. More on that in the next chapter.

Chapter 19

Steering the Titan

> *Bitcoin is a car going down the road at 1,000 mph. Developers are not the drivers of this car, yet they are tasked with repairing and upgrading this car without turning it off, stopping it or rebooting it.*
>
> —Matthew Roszak, Co-Founder of Bloq Inc.

Bitcoin and the underlying blockchain technology are not without their own set of problem burrs. As we have discussed in the preceding chapters, scalability, security, internal programming community skirmishes, government clampdowns, etc., are making users wary and at times sceptical about the future of blockchain technology. Blockchain technology, by any standard, is extraordinary. However, there is a likelihood that it may be hijacked by disruptive forces who have a stake in ensuring that it fails big time. We need leaders and progressive thinkers to pilot this new paradigm to a successful finale. The future growth and evolution of this decentralised, immutable and transparent public distributed ledger 'concept' depends upon how we steer the concept towards its ultimate goal. It would, of course, require generous inputs from its multiple stakeholders and a reappraisal of the challenges faced in the implementation and governance of this revolutionary and 'disruptive' technology. The white paper of the World Economic Forum entitled, 'Realizing the Potential of Blockchain: A Multistakeholder Approach to the

Stewardship of Blockchain and Cryptocurrencies' (June 2017) expresses the fear that the absence of proper stewardship would mean the end of a promising technology.

Any talk about stewardship naturally brings us into the realm of governance. Governance, in the contemporary political scenario, is perceived as a top-down power structure of control with a distinct pecking order. However, the contemporary digital ecosystem requires, nay demands, identification of common goals and a collaboration to achieve the objectives. A top-down control structure and governance would be hara-kiri for the blockchain technology. At this juncture it would be appropriate to take stock of the governance challenges at three levels: platform, application and ecosystem. This is an appropriate and all-encompassing demarcation that I would also stick to while attempting to find solutions to the impediments faced by a fledgling but challenging technology.

The challenges at the platform level are immense and varied. We have 1,368 currencies working on as many platforms. There is obviously little or no consensus among developers and coders of different platforms. The bitcoin developers with their proof-of-work (PoW) concept do not see eye to eye with the Ethereum programmers who have switched to a proof-of-stake (PoS) system to incentivise honesty among the various nodes of a network. Even within these coder fraternities there is dissension. This has resulted in soft and hard forks. So, we now have Bitcoin Cash as well as bitcoin. We have Ethereum Classic as well as Ethereum. There is a lot of sound and fury within the community on how to handle the problem of scalability. Some bitcoin developers are talking about Bitcoin Unlimited (BU) with an unlimited increase in the block size (currently 1 MB) while others are rooting for SegWit to increase the number of transactions within the 1 MB block. Discussions on such technicalities are not quite cordial and verge on open public warfare. Let us look at some tweets on 6 May 2018 regarding Bitcoin Cash:

Roger Ver (@rogerkver), a well-known angel investor and strong proponent of cryptocurrencies, tweets on 06.05.2018

> Bitcoin Cash is a better currency and therefore a better store of value than Bitcoin Core.

Jameson Lopp (@lopp), the infrastructure engineer at Casa, creator of statoshi.info and founder of bitcoinsig.com responded with

> In the past 6 months, exchanges rates have fluctuated between
> BTC: 46,000-419,000
> BCH: $600-$3,600
> So you're saying that the more volatile asset is a better store of value?

EnkiTek (@Enkitek), a global systems integrator specialising in the Oracle platform, responded with

> Oh Roger you are so played. First it was better payment system, that did not work now it is better store of value. Such a fraudster.

This angry exchange of words is a telling example of the open duelling within the bitcoin ecosystem. And such lack of consensus or absence of an arbiter to channel or resolve differences is perhaps one of the biggest roadblock in the bitcoin and blockchain growth story.

Ethereum, is a good example of how Ethereum protocol was tweaked through consensus that saved the Ethereum from a heist of Ether valued at $70 million. May 2016 saw the advent of the decentralised autonomous organisation (DAO). The DAO was nothing more than a collection of smart contracts that ran on the Ethereum blockchain. Its stakeholders were authorised to review and vote on proposals about fund allocation for DAO. The DAO used a 'split function' that allowed users to get back the Ether they sent to the DAO. This function was misused by a charlatan hacker in June 2016. The hacker put in multiple requests for return of Ether before DAO could update its balance. As a result, the hacker was able to siphon off about $70 million of Ether from the DAO into a separate DAO. The saving grace was that the hacker could not transfer the Ether from this account for 28 days as per the terms of the contract. This gave the Ethereum fraternity time to decide on a course of action. Members came up with proposals of a soft fork as well as a hard fork. The soft fork would leave DAO open to a denial-of-service attack. The hard fork, on the other hand, would allow reversion of the lost Ether. So, six classes of stakeholders were identified. They were developers, exchanges, miners, mining pools, token holders and other community members. The issue was put to vote and 89 per cent voted for a hard fork. So now we have Ethereum (ETH) and Ethereum Classic (ETC).

Consensus, is thus, indispensable to the growth and development of the bitcoin as well as blockchain ecosystem. So how to ensure this consensus? Perhaps, it would be smart to set up a representative group of stakeholders who can vote on any proposed change in protocol or application. The proposed changes can be decided on the basis of a majority (say 85 per cent) vote. The World Economic Forum has also recommended setting up of a task force, appropriately named Bitcoin Engineering Task Force (BETF), to develop, test and implement new protocols. Sensibly and pragmatically, the recommendation does not talk about a formal body in a straitjacket with a long list of membership criterion, but proposes a flexibly structured organisation of stakeholders under the aegis of IETF or W3C. An informal organisation of this nature, could then be tasked with establishing advisory standards for blockchain technology, examining various protocols and codes, testing them before and their implementation.

But what we need to remember is that any changes in the cryptocurrency environment would require the consensus of all stakeholders. It is not enough for coders to write the code. It is also important to envisage the social and financial fallout of a code. All this requires active participation by the stakeholders from different fields. Primavera de Filippi, a faculty associate at the Berkman-Klein Center for Internet and Society at Harvard University and a visiting fellow at the Robert Schuman Centre for Advanced Studies at the European University, puts this succinctly:

> When it comes to governance, we cannot expect a small group of engineers to figure out a perfect protocol for economic transactions and social interactions...It requires involving all relevant stakeholders across diverse disciplines in a neutral forum.[1]

Attempts are already in the pipeline to do just that. One such attempt is ColliderX. It provides an independent R&D hub for core technical research, which will be peer-reviewed and open access. To maintain impartiality, it's crowdfunding its operations and administering the funds to researchers via grants. Iliana Oris Valiente, founder of ColliderX, happily announced that:

> The ColliderX initiative has been received with great enthusiasm from the blockchain tech community, academics and industry partners alike. All stakeholders are rallying behind...a new model to fund and promote core technical research to move the blockchain industry forward.[2]

To find a solution to the scalability problem, Yale Law School Professor Elizabeth Stark organised 'Scaling Bitcoin' convening developers, industry players, thought leaders, government officials and other stakeholders in Montreal and collaborated on the Bitcoin Lightning Network. In the financial and banking sector, both R3 CEV and Hyperledger are analysing and finding a solution to critical standards issues. The Hyperledger website explains the end goal of the Hyperledger project. The objective of the Hyperledger project[3] is to advance cross-industry collaboration by developing blockchains and distributed ledgers, with a particular focus on improving the performance and reliability of these systems so that they are capable of supporting global business transactions. The Hyperledger founders and proponents believe that the project will integrate independent open protocols and standards by means of a framework for use-specific modules, including blockchains with their own consensus and storage routines, as well as services for identity, access control and smart contracts. The website makes it crystal clear that it is not supporting bitcoin or any other cryptocurrency but acknowledges that bitcoin technology has immense potential to 'build a new generation of transactional applications that establishes trust, accountability and transparency at their core while streamlining business processes and legal constraints'.[4]

R3 (R3CEV LLC) is a distributed database technology company. It leads a consortium of more than 70 of the world's biggest financial institutions in research and development of distributed ledger usage in the financial system. It is headquartered in New York City. The consortium's joint efforts have created an open-source distributed ledger platform called Corda, geared to the financial world as it handles more complex transactions and restricts access to transaction data. Although it is inspired by blockchain databases and is expected to have many of the benefits of blockchains, it is not a blockchain. The aim of Corda is to provide a platform with common services to ensure that any services built on top are compatible between the network participants, whilst still fostering innovation and faster time to market as the underlying infrastructure would be accepted and understood by at least the founding firms.

So, we have different organisations attempting to resolve different glitches in the blockchain system but they all share a common goal—to make the blockchain technology not only faster and more secure by developing common standards and adequate infrastructure but acceptable to the large majority.

Other than inclusion of multi-stakeholders to build consensus regarding protocol changes, regulation and common standards, we also need to build a robust blockchain ecosystem. This would mean bringing under a common umbrella the various aspects of governance and stewardship. This would include educating the users as well as ensuring that the blockchain technology attracts the best talent. At the user level, the 'CryptoKitties' initiative has not only brought the common user into the distributed ledger sphere, it has educated the user about the intricacies of the blockchain model. Learning through play, is perhaps the most appropriate teaching tool. However, to steer this technology to its complete potential, we need a more skilled workforce. This could be done if universities and colleges of repute start formal courses on this amazing technology. Online courses by credible education hubs will add to the knowledge base. So, in essence we need to collate and collaborate on our 'knowledge networks'. In this regard, I completely concur with the recommendation of the World Economic Forum that suggests that every university should be organising blockchain courses and there should be online courses available for credit and certification. Thankfully, notable universities such as Stanford, Princeton, Duke and NYU have started courses on blockchain, bitcoin and cryptocurrencies. Such courses could also be replicated on commercial as well as non-profit education platforms.

Online academies like Khan Academy, Udacity, Coursera could take a leaf out the Stanford-Princeton book and also offer courses on blockchain technology and cryptocurrencies.

Another aspect that needs to be addressed immediately and with fervour is the networking between the blockchain stakeholders and the governments and regulators. Unfortunately, there seems to be a major disjunct between the law enforcement agencies and the blockchain community. This has resulted in the governments across the world taking on a rather restrictive role. The governments regard this new technology as disruptive and a refuge for illicit activities. An open dialogue between the two opposing factions would help to bridge the yawning chasm between the two. The Blockchain Alliance is a good start in this direction. The Blockchain Alliance is a partnership between law enforcement, NGOs, trade organisations and the private sector and is the first true advocacy network to form in the space. Coin Center and the CDC, with support from Bitfury, Bitfinex, BitGo, Bitnet, Bitstamp, Blockchain, Circle, Coinbase and others have partnered with US law enforcement agencies, such as the Department of Justice, the Federal Bureau of Investigation, the Secret Service and the Department of Homeland Security. De Filippi established the Coalition of Automated Legal Applications (COALA) with her colleagues, Constance Choi of Seven Advisory and Amor Sexton of Adroit Lawyers' of Australia. COALA, also happens to be a part of the Internet Governance Forum. They have kick-started a series of blockchain workshops at Harvard, MIT and Stanford, as well as in the cities of London, Hong Kong and Sydney. The COALA platform is now being used to have an open dialogue with key stakeholders, regulators and policymakers. The objective is to bridge the knowledge gap between legal, political and financial institutions and the coder community. In an interview with the authors of the white paper of the World Economic Forum, De Filippi said, 'We invite them to contribute to the elaboration of policies, regulations and standards for this emergent ecosystem'.[5]

Coin Center, a non-profit policy group in Washington DC, is making a dedicated endeavour to educate stakeholders on five core verticals: innovation, consumer protection, privacy, licensing and anti-money laundering/know your customer. Similarly, CDC

(Chamber of Digital Commerce), a trade organisation, is targeting a wider acceptance of digital currencies. When the Chamber opened its doors in 2014, the public policy community was sceptical, even fearful, of bitcoin and blockchain. A US senator was calling for a ban on bitcoin. The CDC founder, Perianne Boring, rightly points out that these misconceptions were on account of highly publicised events like Silk Road and Mt Gox that led the common man as well as policymakers to believe that bitcoin was a currency that encouraged only illegal activities. Such impressions need to be rectified and that is possible only if the policymakers are educated in the technology of blockchain. CDC has taken some definite steps in this direction:

> In the past 12 months, we have held over 100 briefings for policymakers at the state, federal and international level. Today, we have many bitcoin and blockchain champions through the world's policy community; we even have a Congressional Blockchain Caucus.[6]

COALA's mission is to create a global dialogue involving multiple stakeholders (governments, academia, industry, civil society) in the blockchain ecosystem. The website narrates the objective clearly:

> As a coalition, we intend to collaboratively analyse and scrutinise the various technical and legal nuances of blockchain technologies so as to ultimately contribute to the formation and evolution of best practices, policies and regulations for these emerging classes of paradigmatic blockchain technnologies.[7]

It has launched initiatives such as COALA-ID, a blockchain-based framework for credentials management and access control in collaboration with MIT; COALA LEX, an interface between smart contracts and legal contracts is aspiring to breach the gap between traditional legal frameworks and blockchain technologies. The Coalition intends to elaborate upon 'meta-languages for hybrid techno-legal agreements' and develop 'an open-source library of standardised and certified smart-contract modules'.[8] It has representation at technical standards setting bodies such as W3C and

IETF and has partnered with such academic institutions as Harvard, Stanford, Cambridge, Oxford, University of California at Berkeley, University College London, National Center of Scientific Research and Hong Kong University of Science and Technology, all 'to drive scientific and fact-based research for the blockchain ecosystem'.[9]

The current global policy scenario is a bit disjointed. So, some countries have a laissez faire approach to virtual currencies while others have a somewhat despotic approach to the digital currencies. Resolution of such inconsistencies is possible only with international collaboration among different countries of the world. Coming together of strong voices in the policy arena will ensure that blockchain has a better chance of fulfilling its potential. It will also help in establishing regulations and policies that are consistent globally.

However, the blockchain fraternity needs to remember that it has to ensure a mechanism where all protocol changes and applications are monitored to ensure that the strict rule of law is not violated. Frequent violations would cause a government-instituted regulatory clampdown which will harm the future of the blockchain technology. Cryptocurrencies will attain a degree of credibility only if they have the stamp of approval of the government. Bitcoins have achieved a modicum of acceptability as the Parliament of Japan has passed a law accepting bitcoins as legal tender. Adam Draper, a prolific VC in the industry, reluctantly acknowledged, 'government endorsement creates institutional endorsement, which has value'.[10] For government acceptability, it is necessary to iron out the differences within the crypto and blockchain community. This requires forums for frequent interactions between the miners, coders and other active stakeholders. The ongoing public skirmish about block size has taken its toll. It has caused some element of distrust in the blockchain technology and its proponents. This distrust needs to be assuaged quickly. This can be only done through open dialogue at forums where the issue can be thrashed out to the satisfaction of the majority of the blockchain community, so that a united front is presented to the world at large.

'There should be a forum to present proposals or ideas,' Tyler Winklevoss of Winklevoss Capital opined.[11] Knowledge dispersal has to be pursued through formal as well as informal networks. Digital

Currency, an MIT initiative, has brought together digital experts and universities in an enthusiastic cause to further develop blockchain technology. Informal gatherings like the San Francisco developer meetup and the New York developer meetup are a necessary link in the blockchain collaboration network. Blockchainworkshops.org has convened stakeholders to share key lessons. Reddit, the online community, has become a medium for debate in the space, a bit like GitHub which is a repository of conversations about programming code. The Blockchain Research Institute is commissioning research on various aspects of blockchain. It has also instituted a publishing programme that will ensure publication of white papers, case studies and conferences. Joichi Ito of the MIT Media Lab underscored the need for basic research that was solution neutral. Ito has gone on record to say that he divested all his shares in bitcoin-related companies, like Guardtime and Blockchain, because he felt that he had to be able to speak without having a conflict [of interest] and with neutrality. He believes that:

> It's important to have people who can have non-financially motivated, non-conflicted points of views on both the technology and the standards.[12]

So, we need forums for shared research on blockchain that encourage consensus-based decisions on code protocol. We also need a continuous exchange of information with regulators and policymakers so that the regulations and policies on bitcoins do not strangle the growth of a new and game-changing technology. At the same time, we need to educate the common man about this technology, so that he can perceive its evolution without being hemmed in by uninformed narrative. This would make for a robust ecosystem and open up the possibility of a future that works on a decentralised, self-regulated and immutable paradigm. Nerve-wracking but extremely exciting.

The Final Word

As I look blankly at the page, I find myself vacillating between mild consternation and a state of surrealistic calm. Is there a final word on bitcoins? I wrack my brains. I think not. Bitcoin is barely nine years of age. And yet its intellectual, financial and social growth has far exceeded its short existence. It is probably one of the greatest techno-socio-economic innovations since the 'wheel'. Wait. It's more. It is a global revolution that has changed our way of handling financial transactions. While the world is still grappling with its widespread impact, the technology underlying bitcoins, is constantly spreading its wings for another flight into the unknown. A plethora of experiments on blockchain applications are being made in sectors as varied as gaming (remember CryptoKitties), healthcare, government aid, electoral processes, etc. If the stewardship is right, blockchain technology will breach frontiers and 'boldly go where no man has gone before' (yes, the opening line of Star Trek!). However, if the multiple stakeholders get their calculations wrong we may be writing an epitaph to a brilliant technology. What I am saying, with a lot of unnecessary prelude, is that there can be no epilogue to bitcoins and blockchain technology. In a decade, we will either be living a life made more technically advanced, secure, accurate, decentralised and self-regulated or we will continue our puny struggles with policies of a centralised diktat. In either case, I would be sitting my grandchildren down to a storytelling session narrating either the birth and evolution of blockchain technology or chronicling the sad demise of bitcoins. No Nostradamus-like prophecies here. We can only wait and watch with bated breath for the final denouement of the exciting bitcoin tale.

Before I sign off, one teeny-weeny authorspeak. Some of my readers would feel short-changed by what they think is an incomplete finale to the bitcoin saga. They must be wondering why there is no 'To Do' chapter in my book. How to set up a bitcoin wallet? How to trade on a bitcoin Exchange? How to maintain anonymity? The book does not answer such questions. Absolutely right. I offer no apology on that count as it was a deliberate oversight. The aim of the book was to hand hold the reader through the technical, social and financial intricacies of bitcoin and ignite a sense of excitement in the journey. Altcoin portfolio managers would be the right option for those who were looking for a quick tutorial on how to trade in cryptocurrencies.

Glossary

(Names and Terms)

Adam Back (born July 1970) is a British cryptographer and cryptohacker. He is the inventor of Hashcash and the proof-of-work system used by several anti-spam systems. A similar system is used in bitcoin. Hashcash has also been used in a number of other protocols such as combating blog spam and defending against user namespace pollution. Today, he is the CEO of Blockstream, a company that seeks to further the development of bitcoin and blockchain technology. (https://en.wikipedia.org/wiki/Adam_Back)

Algorand is a scalable, secure and decentralised digital currency and transactions platform.

Asymptotic—in mathematical analysis, asymptotic analysis or asymptotics is a method of describing limiting behaviour. As an illustration, suppose that we are interested in the properties of a function $f(n)$ as n becomes very large. If $f(n) = n2 + 3n$, then as n becomes very large, the term $3n$ becomes insignificant compared to $n2$. The function $f(n)$ is said to be '*asymptotically equivalent* to $n2$, as $n \rightarrow \infty$'. This is often written symbolically as $f(n) \sim n2$, which is read as '$f(n)$ is asymptotic to $n2$'.
(https://en.wikipedia.org/wiki/Asymptotic_analysis)

The Bear Stearns Companies Inc. was a New York-based global investment bank, securities, trading and brokerage firm that failed in 2008 as part of the global financial crisis and recession and was subsequently sold to JP Morgan Chase. Its main business areas before its failure were capital markets, investment banking, wealth management and global clearing services and it was heavily involved in the subprime mortgage crisis. In the years leading up to the failure, Bear Stearns was heavily involved in securitisation and issued large amounts of asset-backed securities. In March 2008, the Federal Reserve Bank of New York provided an emergency loan to try to avert a sudden collapse of the company. The company could not be saved however and was sold to JP Morgan Chase for $10 per share, a price far below its pre-crisis 52-week high of $133.20 per share. The collapse of the company was a prelude to the risk management meltdown of the investment banking industry in the United States and elsewhere that culminated in September 2008 and the subsequent global financial crisis of 2008–09. (https://en.wikipedia.org/wiki/Bear_Stearns)

Bettina Warburg-Johnson is a blockchain enthusiast, researcher and educator. She is also the co-founder and managing partner of Animal Ventures, a venture studio and consultancy firm. The company focuses on tech companies operating in verticals such as blockchain technology, digital platforms, artificial intelligence and augmented intelligence and the internet of things.
(hta://everipedia.org/wiki/bettina-warburg/)

bit gold—in 1998, Szabo designed a mechanism for a decentralised digital currency he called 'bit gold'. Bit gold was never implemented, but has been called 'a direct precursor to the bitcoin architecture'. In Szabo's bit gold structure, a participant would dedicate computer power to solving cryptographic puzzles. In a bit gold network, solved puzzles would be sent to the Byzantine fault tolerant public registry and assigned to the public key of the solver. Each solution would become part of the next challenge, creating a growing chain of new property. This aspect of the system provided a way for the network to verify and timestamp new coins, because unless a majority of the parties agreed to accept new solutions, they couldn't start on the next puzzle. (https://en.wikipedia.org/wiki/Nick_Szabo)

Bitnation, or '**cryptonation**', is a 'voluntary nation' that records vital records, identity and other legal events using blockchain technology. Bitnation was founded in 2014 using Ethereum smart-contract technology. As of 2018, it has about 15,000 'citizens'. Its 2018 white paper describes Bitnation as 'the world's first Decentralised Borderless Voluntary Nation'. Bitnation organised the world's first Blockchain Marriage and World Citizenship ID, Blockchain Land Title, Birth Certificate and Refugee Emergency ID during 2014 and 2015. Bitnation seeks to provide open-source governance which includes DIY smart contracts mainly on governance, security and law. The subsidiary services include constitutions, secure ID/Reputation systems, dispute resolutions, security, insurance, marriages, notary service and birth certificates, etc.

Charles Hoskinson is a Colorado-based technology entrepreneur and mathematician. His professional experience includes founding three cryptocurrency related start-ups—Invictus Innovations, Ethereum and IOHK. He was the founding chairman of the Bitcoin Foundation's education committee and established the Cryptocurrency Research Group in September of 2013. His current projects focus on education of cryptocurrency, evangelism of decentralisation and making cryptographic tools easier to use for the mainstream. This includes leading the research, design and development of Cardano, a third-generation cryptocurrency that launched in September 2017.

David Lee Chaum (born 1955) is an American computer scientist and cryptographer. He is famous for developing ecash, an electronic cash application that aims to preserve a user's anonymity. He has also invented many cryptographic protocols and founded digicash, an electronic money corporation. His 1981 paper, 'Untraceable Electronic Mail, Return Addresses and Digital Pseudonyms', laid the groundwork for the field of anonymous communications research. He was the founder of the International Association for Cryptographic Research (IACR) that currently organises academic conferences in cryptography research. (https://en.wikipedia.org/wiki/David_Chaum)

The Dodd-Frank Wall Street Reform and Consumer Protection Act is a massive piece of financial reform legislation passed by the

Obama administration in 2010 as a response to the financial crisis of 2008. Named after sponsors, US Senator Christopher J. Dodd and US Representative Barney Frank, the Act's numerous provisions, spelled out over roughly 2,300 pages, were implemented over a period of several years and were intended to decrease various risks in the US financial system. The Act established a number of new government agencies tasked with overseeing various components of the Act and by extension various aspects of the banking system. President Donald Trump pledged to repeal Dodd-Frank and on 22 May 2018, the House of Representatives voted to roll back significant pieces of Dodd-Frank. (https://www.investopedia.com/terms/d/dodd-frank-financial-regulatory-reform-bill.asp)

DigiCash Inc. was an electronic money corporation founded by David Chaum in 1989. DigiCash transactions were unique in that they were anonymous due to a number of cryptographic protocols developed by its founder. DigiCash declared bankruptcy in 1998 and subsequently sold its assets to eCash Technologies, another digital currency company, which was acquired by InfoSpace on 19 February 2002.

Emergent Consensus Algorithm is a proposed replacement for the bitcoin consensus algorithm used and promoted by Bitcoin Unlimited that makes miners the centralised controllers of bitcoin; rather than having a system based on rules enforced by everyone. The way it works is that miners war with each other over the rules of the system by orphaning each other's blocks. If a chain of invalid blocks gets enough of a lead, you accept it even though its invalid because its longer. (https://www.reddit.com/r/bitcoin/comments/6beqxv/eli5_request_what_is_emergent_consensus/)

Fannie Mae and Freddie Mac—the Federal National Mortgage Association (FNMA), commonly known as Fannie Mae, is a US government-sponsored enterprise (GSE) and, since 1968, a publicly traded company. Founded in 1938 during the Great Depression as part of the New Deal, the corporation's purpose is to expand the secondary mortgage market by securitising mortgages in the form of mortgage-backed securities (MBS), allowing lenders to reinvest their assets into more lending and in effect increasing the number of

lenders in the mortgage market by reducing the reliance on locally-based savings and loan associations. Its brother organisation is the Federal Home Loan Mortgage Corporation (FHLMC), better known as Freddie Mac.
(https://en.wikipedia.org/wiki/Fannie_Mae)

Game theory is 'the study of mathematical models of conflict and cooperation between intelligent rational decision-makers'. Game theory is mainly used in economics, political science and psychology as well as in logic and computer science. Originally, it addressed zero-sum games, in which one person's gains result in losses for the other participants. Today, game theory applies to a wide range of behavioural relations and is now an umbrella term for the science of logical decision making in humans, animals and computers.
(https://en.wikipedia.org/wiki/Game_theory)

Hal Finney and reusable proof-of-work (RPOW)—Harold Thomas Finney II (4 May 1956–28 August 2014) was a developer for PGP Corporation. In his early career, he was credited as lead developer on several console games. He also was an early bitcoin user and received the first bitcoin transaction from bitcoin's creator Satoshi Nakamoto. RPOW was an invention by Hal Finney intended as a prototype for digital cash based on Nick Szabo's theory of collectibles. RPOW was a significant early step in the history of digital cash and was a precursor to bitcoin. Although never intended to be more than a prototype, RPOW was a very sophisticated piece of software that would have been capable of serving a huge network, had it caught on. Some proposals for digital collectibles circulated on the cypherpunk mailing list, including b-money by Wei Dai and bit gold by Nick Szabo. RPOW was the only digital collectible to ever function as a piece of software. The double-spending problem is fundamental to all digital cash. RPOW solves this problem by keeping the ownership of tokens registered on a trusted server.
(https://nakamotoinstitute.org/finney/rpow/)

Iliana Oris Valiente, a Certified Bitcoin Professional (BCP), is widely credited for being a trailblazer in the blockchain space, having been among the first to recognise the tremendous impact of this

traditionally 'hacker' technology on the enterprise world. Her focus has been on exponential technology, entrepreneurship and bridging the gap between the corporate world and the start-up communities. Prior to founding ColliderX, Iliana was the catalyst in getting Deloitte actively involved with all things blockchain and founded the Rubix by Deloitte Blockchain practice in 2014. Iliana has experience providing advisory services and has overseen projects to conceptualise and prototype proof-of-concept related to the impact of blockchain technology across industries, with a focus on FSI, healthcare and the public sector. Iliana has strong views on how the network effects of this technology will impact multiple industry verticals and how it will radically change status quo business models. Iliana is a sought-after speaker, having presented at a number of North American and European conferences and events.
(https://www.collider-x.org/team-iliana-oris-valiente-marc-lijour/)

Jackson Palmer is an Australian entrepreneur and technologist best known for creating the infamously successful 'joke' cryptocurrency Dogecoin. Currently based out of San Francisco, Jackson works as a product manager but is still active in the cryptocurrency space.

John David McAfee (born 18 September 1945) is a British-American computer programmer and businessman. He founded the software company, McAfee Associates, in 1987 and ran it until 1994, when he resigned from the company. McAfee Associates achieved early success as the creators of McAfee, the first commercial antivirus software and the business now produces a range of enterprise security software.

Joichi 'Joi' Ito (born 19 June 1966) is a Japanese activist, entrepreneur, venture capitalist and director of the MIT Media Lab. Ito is a professor of the practice of media arts and sciences at MIT and a visiting professor of law from practice at the Harvard Law School. Ito has received recognition for his role as an entrepreneur focused on internet and technology companies and has founded, among other companies PSINet, Japan, Digital Garage and Infoseek, Japan. Ito is the chairman of the board of Pure Tech Health, a strategic advisor to Sony Corporation and a board member of The New York Times Company. Ito writes a monthly column in the 'Ideas' section of *Wired*. (https://en.wikipedia.org/wiki/Joi_Ito)

Julian Oliver is a New Zealander, critical engineer and artist based in Berlin. He is the co-author of the 'Critical Engineering Manifesto' and co-founder of CryptoParty in Berlin. He is an advocate of free and open-source software and is a supporter of and contributor to, initiatives that reinforce rights of privacy and anonymity in networked and other technologically-mediated domains. He has recently been in the news for his 'harvest' project, where he uses wind power to mine Zcash, a bitcoin cousin.
(https://julianoliver.com/output/category/about)

Lehman Brothers was one of the first Wall Street firms to move into the business of mortgage origination. In 1997, Lehman bought Colorado-based lender Aurora Loan Services, an Alt-A lender. In 2000, to expand their mortgage origination pipeline, Lehman purchased West Coast subprime mortgage lender BNC Mortgage LLC. Lehman quickly became a force to be reckoned with in the subprime market. By 2008, Lehman had assets of $680 billion supported by only $22.5 billion of firm capital. In 2008, Lehman faced an unprecedented loss due to the continuing subprime mortgage crisis. It was believed that Lehman Brothers were in talks with Bank of America and Barclays for a possible sale of the company but the talks petered out. Lehman Brothers filed for Chapter 11 bankruptcy protection on 15 September 2008.
(https://en.wikipedia.org/wiki/Bankruptcy_of_Lehman_Brothers)

Matthew Roszak is the co-founder and chairman of Bloq, a leading blockchain technology company. He is also founding partner of Tally Capital, a private investment firm focused on cryptocurrencies and blockchain-enabled technology. He also serves as chairman of the Chamber of Digital Commerce, the world's largest trade association representing the blockchain industry. In addition, Roszak serves on the board of BitGive, a non-profit foundation targeting public health and the environment. Roszak was a producer of the industry's first ever documentary, *The Rise and Rise of Bitcoin*. He is a sought after thought leader on blockchain technology and has presented at TEDx, been featured on CNBC and often quoted in *The Wall Street Journal*, *Bloomberg* and *Financial Times*.
(https://www.linkedin.com/in/matthewroszak)

Nash Equilibrium is a solution concept of a non-cooperative game involving two or more players in which each player is assumed to

know the equilibrium strategies of the other players and no player has anything to gain by changing only their own strategy. If each player has chosen a strategy and no player can benefit by changing strategies while the other players keep theirs unchanged, then the current set of strategy choices and the corresponding payoffs constitutes a Nash equilibrium. The Nash equilibrium is one of the foundational concepts in game theory. Nash equilibrium was propounded by American mathematician, John Forbes Nash Jr. Stated simply, Alice and Bob are in Nash equilibrium if Alice is making the best decision she can, taking into account Bob's decision while Bob's decision remains unchanged and Bob is making the best decision he can, taking into account Alice's decision while Alice's decision remains unchanged. Likewise, a group of players are in Nash equilibrium if each one is making the best decision possible, taking into account the decisions of the others in the game as long as the other parties' decisions remain unchanged.
(https://en.wikipedia.org/wiki/Nash_equilibrium)

New York Agreement—The Bitcoin Scaling Agreement at Consensus 2017, better known as the New York Agreement, was a scaling proposal made jointly by over 50 companies. The agreement intended to put an end to bitcoin's long-lasting scaling debate by increasing the block capacity through activating Segregated Witness and then doubling the block size.
(https://en.bitcoin.it/wiki/New_York_Agreement)

Nick Szabo is a computer scientist, legal scholar and cryptographer known for his research in digital contracts and digital currency. He graduated from the University Of Washington in 1989 with a degree in Computer Science. He earned a JD from George Washington University Law School and holds an honorary professorship at the Universidad Francisco Marroquín.
(https://en.wikipedia.org/wiki/Nick_Szabo)

Patrick L. Young is an entrepreneur and a leading thinker about financial markets and investment. Originally a derivatives analyst and broker, Young has experience running an exchange and a boutique investment bank as well as working in private equity markets. Patrick is the author of several books, namely, *Capital Market Revolution*, *New Capital Market Revolution* and *The Promiscuous Investor*—all of which have proven prescient in their analysis of developments in everything from fees through stock exchange structure via the rise of hedge funds to the use of technology in commerce. He is considered a financial visionary and lateral thinker.

Primavera De Filippi is a permanent researcher at the National Center of Scientific Research (CNRS) in Paris, a faculty associate at the Berkman-Klein Center for Internet and Society at Harvard University and a visiting fellow at the Robert Schuman Centre for Advanced Studies at the European University Institute. She is a member of the Global Future Council on Blockchain Technologies at the World Economic Forum and co-founder of the Internet Governance Forum's dynamic coalitions on Blockchain Technology (COALA). Her fields of interest focus on legal challenges raised by decentralised technologies, with a particular focus on blockchain technologies. She is investigating the new opportunities for these technologies to enable new governance models and participatory decision-making through the concept of governance-by-design. Her book *Blockchain and the Law* was published in 2018 by Harvard University Press (co-authored with Aaron Wright).

Roger Keith Ver (born 27 January 1979) is an early investor in bitcoin-related start-ups. He has been a prominent supporter of bitcoin adoption and saw bitcoin as a means to promote economic freedom. He now promotes Bitcoin Cash, a hard fork of the cryptocurrency created with the intent to fix issues such as high fees and long transaction confirmation times. He identifies as a libertarian, an anarcho-capitalist, peace advocate and advocates for individualism and voluntarism. Also called 'Jesus Bitcoin' as he was an open advocate of bitcoin for many years.
(https://en.wikipedia.org/wiki/Roger_Ver)

See Saw Reward Mechanism—block rewards received by the staker and winning masternode vary based on the amount of coins held for masternodes vs amount of coins available for staking on the network allows for variable rewards based on needs of the

network to keep the network services (masternodes) and the security of the network (staking wallets) evenly distributed. When there are fewer as the number of masternodes rises the portion of the block reward that they earn is reduced, it increases when the number of masternodes declines.
(https://pivx.org/knowledge-base/see-saw-rewards-mechanism/)

Wei Dai is a computer engineer and cypherpunk best known as creator of b-money and the developer of the Crypto++ library. In 1998, Dai helped to spark interest in cryptocurrencies with the publication of 'b-money, an anonymous, distributed electronic cash system'. In the paper, Dai outlines the basic properties of all modern-day cryptocurrency systems: '...a scheme for a group of untraceable digital pseudonyms to pay each other with money and to enforce contracts amongst themselves without outside help'. Described as 'money which is impossible to regulate', Dai's b-money described the core concepts later implemented in bitcoin.
(https://en.bitcoin.it/wiki/Wei_Dai)

The Wolf of Wall Street is Jordan Ross Belfort (born 9 July 1962) an American author, motivational speaker and former stockbroker. In 1999, he pleaded guilty to fraud and related crimes in connection with stock-market manipulation and running a boiler room as part of a penny-stock scam. Belfort spent 22 months in prison as part of an agreement under which he gave testimony against numerous partners and subordinates in his fraud scheme. He published the memoir, *The Wolf of Wall Street*, which was adapted into a film and released in 2013.

Zero-knowledge proof—in cryptography, a zero-knowledge proof or zero-knowledge protocol is a method by which one party (the prover Peggy) can prove to another party (the verifier Victor) that she knows a value *x*, without conveying any information apart from the fact that she knows the value *x*. (https://en.wikipedia.org/wiki/Zero-knowledge_proof)

Endnotes

Chapter 2

1. Hughes, E. (1997). A Cypherpunk's Manifesto. The Electronic Privacy Papers. 285–287. Retrieved from https://keatsmoodledevtest.kcl.ac.uk/pluginfile.php/1251665/course/section/414599/hughes-cypherpunks-manifesto1.pdf
2. Diffie, W. and Hellman, M. (1976). New Directions in Cryptography. *Journal IEEE Transactions on Information Theory*, 22(6), 644–654. Retrieved from https://ee.stanford.edu/~hellman/publications/24.pdf
3. Chaum, D.L. (1981). Untraceable Electronic Mail, Return Addresses and Digital Pseudonyms. Retrieved from https://www.freehaven.net/anonbib/cache/chaum-mix.pdf
4. Chaum, D.L. (1985). Security Without Identification: Transaction Systems to Make Big Brother Obsolete. *Communications of the ACM,* 24(2), 84–88. Retrieved from https://www.cs.ru.nl/~jhh/pub/secsem/chaum1985bigbrother.pdf
5. Hughes, E. (1997). A Cypherpunk's Manifesto. The Electronic Privacy Papers. 285–287. Retrieved from https://keatsmoodledevtest.kcl.ac.uk/pluginfile.php/1251665/course/section/414599/hughes-cypherpunks-manifesto1.pdf
6. Ibid.

7. Dai, W. (1998). B-money. Retrieved from http://www.weidai.com/bmoney.txt
8. Szabo, N. (2005). bit gold. Retrieved from http://unenumerated.blogspot.com/2005/12/bit-gold.html
9. Ibid.

Chapter 3

1. Buck, J. (26 January 2018). Coincheck: Stolen $534 Mln NEM Were Stored On Low Security Hot Wallet. Retrieved from https://cointelegraph.com/news/coincheck-stolen-534-mln-nem-were-stored-on-low-security-hot-wallet
2. Melendez, S. (7 December 2007). Bitcoin Heist Adds $77 Million to Total Hacked Hauls of $15 Billion. Retrieved from https://www.fastcompany.com/40505199/bitcoin-heist-adds-77-million-to-hacked-hauls-of-15-billion

Chapter 4

1. Retrieved from https://en.wikipedia.org/wiki/Satoshi_Nakamoto
2. Nakamoto, S. (October 2008). Bitcoin: A Peer-to-Peer Electronic Cash System. Retrieved from https://bitcoin.org/bitcoin.pdf

Chapter 5

1. Reddit post of 2015. Retrieved from https://www.reddit.com/r/Bitcoin/comments/2lvaiw/bitcoins_phoney_baloney_internet_currency_that_a/
2. Thaler, R. (25 January 2018). 'Bitcoin and Its Sisters Seem Like a Bubble.' Retrieved from https://www.ccn.com/bitcoin-sisters-seem-like-bubble-says-nobel-prize-winner-richard-thaler/
3. Suberg, W. (24 January 2018). 'Regulate It Out of Existence': Stiglitz and Swiss Bank Bash bitcoin at Davos. Retrieved from https://cointelegraph.com/news/regulate-it-out-of-existence-stiglitz-and-swiss-bank-bash-bitcoin-at-davos
4. Tae, K. (9 January 2018). Jamie Dimon Says He Regrets Calling Bitcoin a Fraud and Believes in the Technology Behind It. Retrieved from https://www.cnbc.com/2018/01/09/jamie-dimon-says-he-regrets-calling-bitcoin-a-fraud.html

5. Sanghvi, N. (18 January 2018). Bitcoin Prices Have Fallen Every January Since 2015: Is it Connected to Chinese New Year. Retrieved from https://coincrunch.in/2018/01/18/bitcoin-prices-fallen-every-january-chinese-new-year/
6. Biggs, J. (8 December 2017). Why is Bitcoin's Price So High? Retrieved from https://www.msn.com/en-gb/money/news/why-is-bitcoins-price-so-high/ar-BBGp7Pj
7. Norry, A. (19 November 2017). The History of the Mt Gox Hack: Bitcoin's Biggest Heist. Retrieved from https://blockonomi.com/mt-gox-hack/
8. Wieczner, J. (19 April 2018). Mt Gox and the Surprising Redemption of Bitcoin's Biggest Villain. Retrieved from http://fortune.com/longform/bitcoin-mt-gox-hack-karpeles/
9. 'I Accidentally Killed It': Parity Wallet Bug Locks $150 Million in Ether. (9 November 2017). Retrieved from https://www.ccn.com/i-accidentally-killed-it-parity-wallet-bug-locks-150-million-in-ether/
10. O'Leary, R.R. (15 November 2017). Parity Team Publishes Postmortem on $160 Million Ether Freeze. Retrieved from https://www.coindesk.com/parity-team-publishes-postmortem-160-million-ether-freeze/
11. Baraniuk, C. (24 October 2017). TV News 'Hack' Sees Bitcoins Snatched. Retrieved from https://www.bbc.com/news/technology-41737248
12. Hieleman, G. and Rauchs, M. (2017). Global Cryptocurrency Benchmarking Study. Page 88. Retrieved from https://www.jbs.cam.ac.uk/fileadmin/user_upload/research/centres/alternative-finance/downloads/2017-global-cryptocurrency-benchmarking-study.pdf
13. Why Cryptocurrency Mining is an Environmental Hazard. (24 December 2017). Retrieved from https://www.thenational.ae/business/technology/why-cryptocurrency-mining-is-an-environmental-hazard-1.690059
14. Zhao, W. (4 January 2018). Dogecoin Market Cap Hits $1 Billion, to Its Creator's Dismay. Retrieved from https://www.coindesk.com/dogecoin-market-cap-hits-1-billion-creators-dismay/

15. Norry, A. (29 November 2017). The History of Silk Road: A Tale of Drugs, Extortion & Bitcoin. Retrieved from https://blockonomi.com/history-of-silk-road/
16. Ibid.

Chapter 6

1. Zimbabwe Offers New Exchange Rate: $1 For 35,000,000,000,000,000 Old Dollars. (25 June 2015). Retrieved from https://www.theguardian.com/world/2015/jun/12/zimbabwe-offers-new-exchange-rate-1-for-35000000000000000-old-dollars
2. Chorzempa, M. (31 January 2018). China's Central-backed Currency is the Anti-Bitcoin. Retrieved from https://piie.com/blogs/china-economic-watch/chinas-central-bank-backed-digital-currency-anti-bitcoin
3. Chinese Money Dominates Bitcoin, Now Its Companies Are Gunning For Blockchain Tech. (1 October 2017). Retrieved from https://qz.com/1072907/why-china-is-so-hot-on-bitcoin/
4. Oberoi, R. (26 April 2017). Bull Run or Ferrari Ride With Failed Brakes? Where Do We Go From Here. Retrieved from https://economictimes.indiatimes.com/markets/stocks/news/bull-run-or-ferrari-ride-with-failed-breaks-where-do-we-go-from-here/articleshow/58376245.cm
5. Despite RBI Warning, 2,500 Indians Investing in Bitcoins Daily. Here is All You Should Know About Its Usage and Dangers. (17 May 2017). Retrieved from https://economictimes.indiatimes.com/industry/banking/finance/2500-indians-investing-in-bitcoins-daily-here-is-all-you-should-know-about-bitcoins-its-usage-dangers/arti

Chapter 7

1. Warburg, B. TED Summit. (June 2016). How the Blockchain Will Radically Transform the Economy. Retrieved from https://www.ted.com/talks/bettina_warburg_how_the_blockchain_will_radically_transform_the_economy
2. Cannucciari, C. (2016). *Banking on Bitcoin* (Documentary). US: Netflix Original

3. Wang, K. (17 July 2017). Cryptoeconomics: Paving the Future of Blockchain Technology. Retrieved from https://hackernoon.com/cryptoeconomics-paving-the-future-of-blockchain-technology-13b04dab971
4. Castor, A. (4 April 2017). No Incentive? Algorand Blockchain Sparks Debate at Cryptography Event. Retrieved from https://www.coindesk.com/no-incentive-algorand-blockchain-sparks-debate-cryptography-event/
5. Ibid.

Chapter 8

1. Harper, J. (12 February 2016). Why Bitcoin Governance is a Competition (And That's a Good Thing). Retrieved from https://www.coindesk.com/bitcoin-governance-as-competition/
2. Wang, K. (8 August 2017). Governance in Blockchain Part I: The Bitcoin Experiment. Retrieved from https://itnext.io/governance-in-blockchain-part-i-the-bitcoin-experiment-a8c633791e6d
3. Mow, S. (7 August 2017). The Bitcoin Cash Fork Was a Dangerous Trick. Retrieved from http://fortune.com/2017/08/07/bitcoin-cash-bch-hard-fork-blockchain-usd-coinbase/
4. Cryptobattle: Bitcoin vs. Bitcoin Cash. (15 November 2017). Retrieved from https://en.insider.pro/analytics/2017-11-15/cryptobattle-bitcoin-vs-bitcoin-cash/

Chapter 9

1. Pullen, J.P. (26 December 2017). Bitcoin's Real Value Could Be Zero, Morgan Stanley Analyst Says. Retrieved from http://fortune.com/2017/12/26/bitcoin-price-value-bubble-crash-says-morgan-stanley-analyst/
2. Kharpal, A. (8 February 2018). Bitcoin Price Will Crash to Zero, Nouriel Roubini Says. Retrieved from https://www.cnbc.com/2018/02/06/bitcoin-price-will-crash-to-zero-nouriel-roubini-says.html

3. Murphy, D. (8 December 2017). Bitcoin is a 'Dangerous Speculative Bubble,' Yale Expert Says. Retrieved from https://www.cnbc.com/2017/12/04/bitcoin-is-a-dangerous-speculative-bubble-yale-expert-says.html
4. Minsky, H.P. (1986). *Stabilizing an Unstable Economy.* New Haven: Yale University Press.
5. Shiller, R.J. (8 December 2013). Speculative Asset Prices. Retrieved from https://www.nobelprize.org/nobel_prizes/economic-sciences/laureates/2013/shiller-lecture.pdf

Chapter 10

1. Helms, K. (2 March 2018). 16 Government-Approved Crypto Exchanges Forming Self-Regulatory Body in Japan. Retrieved from https://news.bitcoin.com/government-approved-crypto-exchanges-self-regulatory-body-japan/
2. Hanada, Y. (15 December 2017). Japan's Bitcoin Trading Platforms Extend to Asia and Beyond. Retrieved from https://asia.nikkei.com/Spotlight/Bitcoin-evolution/Japan-s-bitcoin-trading-platforms-extend-to-Asia-and-beyond
3. Helms, K. (15 December 2017). Major Japanese Automotive Group and Dealerships Embracing Bitcoin. Retrieved from https://news.bitcoin.com/major-japanese-automotive-group-and-dealerships-embracing-bitcoin/
4. Japanese Retailers Quickly Embracing Bitcoin Payments. (5 April 2017). Retrieved from https://asia.nikkei.com/Business/Japanese-retailers-quickly-embracing-bitcoin-payments
5. Kano, Y. (5 January 2018). Japan: The New Heart of Bitcoin. Retrieved from https://www.coindesk.com/japan-new-heart-bitcoin/
6. Partz, H. (4 March 2018). South Korean Government Bans Officials From Crypto Holding and Trading. Retrieved from https://cointelegraph.com/news/south-korean-government-bans-officials-from-crypto-holding-and-trading
7. Ibid.
8. How South Korea is Keeping Its Officials From Insider Trading. (22 February 2018). Retrieved from http://www.cryptalnews.com/south-korea-officials-insider-trading/

9. Bitcoin: UK and EU Plan Crackdown Amid Crime and Tax Evasion Fears. (4 December 2017). Retrieved from https://www.theguardian.com/technology/2017/dec/04/bitcoin-uk-eu-plan-cryptocurrency-price-traders-anonymity
10. Ibid.
11. Ibid.
12. Ibid.
13. Rosenfeld, E. (6 February 2015). Ecuador Becomes the First Country to Roll Out Its Own Digital Cash. Retrieved from https://www.cnbc.com/2015/02/06/ecuador-becomes-the-first-country-to-roll-out-its-own-digital-durrency.html
14. Bangladesh Says Bitcoin Users Could be Jailed For up to 12 Years. (16 September 2014). Retrieved from https://www.news18.com/news/india/bangladesh-says-bitcoin-users-could-be-jailed-for-up-to-12-years-714254.html
15. Legality of Bitcoin by Country and Territory. Retrieved from https://en.wikipedia.org/wiki/Legality_of_bitcoin_by_country_or_territory
16. Hieleman, G. and Rauchs, M. (2017) Global Cryptocurrency Benchmarking Study. Page 36, 49, 69. Retrieved from https://www.jbs.cam.ac.uk/fileadmin/user_upload/research/centres/alternative-finance/downloads/2017-global-cryptocurrency-benchmarking-study.pdf

Chapter 11

1. Bank Secrecy Act, Anti-Money Laundering and Office of Foreign Assets Control. Retrieved from https://www.ffiec.gov/bsa_aml_infobase/documents/fdic_docs/bsa_manual.pdf
2. FinCEN (Financial Crimes Enforcement Network). Retrieved from https://www.fincen.gov/resources/fincens-mandate-congress
3. FinCEN (Financial Crimes Enforcement Network) Guidance Note. (18 March 2013). Retrieved from https://www.fincen.gov/sites/default/files/shared/FIN-2013-G001.pdf
4. Registration of Money Services Business (RMSB) Electronic Filing Instructions. Retrieved from https://www.fincen.gov/sites/default/files/shared/FinCENRMSB_ElectronicFilingInstructions.pdf

5. Davidson, J. (18 July 2014). New York Proposes Bitcoin Regulations. Retrieved from http://time.com/money/3004751/new-york-bitcoin-regulations-benjamin-lawsky/
6. New York State Department of Financial Services. New York Codes, Rules and Regulations. Title 23. Department of Financial Services. Chapter 1. Regulations of the Superintendent of Financial Services. Part 200. Virtual Currencies. Retrieved from https://www.dfs.ny.gov/legal/regulations/adoptions/dfsp200t.pdf
7. Canada's Proceeds of Crime (Money Laundering) and Terrorist Financing Act. Retrieved from http://www.fintrac-canafe.gc.ca/reg/1-eng.asp
8. Commonwealth Bank Accused of More Anti-Money Laundering Law Breaches. (14 December 2017). Retrieved from https://www.theguardian.com/australia-news/2017/dec/14/commonwealth-bank-accused-of-more-anti-money-laundering-law-breaches
9. Anti-Money Laundering and Counter-Terrorism Financing Amendment Act. (2017). Retrieved from http://gesellberg.com/wpcontent/uploads/2017/10/report.pdf
10. Financial Action Task Force (FATF) Guidance Note. (2015). Retrieved from http://www.fatf-gafi.org/publications/fatfgeneral/documents/je-yoon-shin-speech-japanese-regulatory-summit.html
11. Guidance Note on the Japanese Virtual Currency Legislation and Overview on Registration Requirement thereunder. (4 July 2017). Retrieved from http://www.so-law.jp/wp-content/uploads/2017/07/Japanese_VC_Act_and_Registration-Overview_170704.pdf
12. Lagarde, C. (16 April 2018). An Even-Handed Approach to Crypto Assets. Retrieved from https://blogs.imf.org/2018/04/16/an-even-handed-approach-to-crypto-assets/

Chapter 12

1. IRS Virtual Currency Guidance: Virtual Currency is Treated as Property for US Federal Tax Purposes; General Rules for Property Transactions Apply. (25 March 2014). Retrieved from https://www.irs.gov/pub/irs-drop/n-14-21.pdf

2. Retrieved from http://www.canadiantaxlitigation.com/wp-content/uploads/2014/01/2013-051470117.txt
3. Retrieved from http://www.canadiantaxlitigation.com/wp-content/uploads/2014/04/2014-0525191E5.txt
4. Global Legal Monitor. (13 March 2018). Retrieved from http://www.loc.gov/law/foreign-news/article/germany-federal-ministry-of-finance-publishes-guidance-on-vat-treatment-of-virtual-currencies/
5. Retrieved from http://www.fatf-gafi.org/media/fatf/documents/reports/Guidance-RBA-Virtual-Currencies.pdf
6. Retrieved from http://www.fatf-gafi.org/media/fatf/documents/reports/Guidance-RBA-Virtual-Currencies.pdf
7. Accounting for Virtual Currencies. (March 2018). Retrieved from https://www.asb.or.jp/en/wp-content/uploads/20180315-01_e.pdf
8. Japan's New Bitcoin Law. (30 March 2017). Retrieved from https://bit-media.org/news/japans-new-bitcoin-law/
9. Tax Treatment of Cryptocurrencies. Retrieved from https://www.ato.gov.au/General/Gen/Tax-treatment-of-crypto-currencies-in-Australia-specifically-bitcoin/ and https://www.ato.gov.au/misc/downloads/pdf/qc42159.pdf
10. Reserve Bank of India Act, 1934. Retrieved from https://rbidocs.rbi.org.in/rdocs/Publications/PDFs/RBIAM_230609.pdf
11. Foreign Exchange Management Act, 1999. Retrieved from http://www.icaiknowledgegateway.org/littledms/folder1/chapter-3-the-foreign-exchange-management-act-1999.pdf
12. The Coinage Act, 2011. Retrieved from https://rbidocs.rbi.org.in/rdocs/Publications/PDFs/COIN281114.pdf
13. Income Tax Act, 1961. Retrieved from https://www.incometaxindia.gov.in/pages/acts/income-tax-act.aspx
14. Retrieved from https://indiankanoon.org/doc/1411881/

Chapter 13

1. Central Bank Digital Currency: Motivations and Implications. Retrieved from https://www.bankofcanada.ca/wp-content/uploads/2017/11/sdp2017-16.pdf

2. Bernsden, R. 'If Blockchain is the Answer, What is the Question?' Speech at the Dutch Blockchain Conference. Retrieved from https://www.dnb.nl/binaries/Speech%20Ron%20Berndsen_tcm46-342846.pdf
3. Ibid.
4. Ibid.
5. Ibid.
6. Breaking: Russia's Central Bank is Developing a National Digital Currency. (2 June 2017). Retrieved from https://www.ccn.com/russia-national-digital-currency/
7. Williams, G. (16 November 2016). Sweden Could Become the First Major Country to Issue a National Digital Currency. Retrieved from https://www.businessinsider.in/Sweden-could-become-the-first-major-country-to-issue-a-national-digital-currency/articleshow/55453626.cms
8. Move Over Bitcoin, These Countries are Creating Their Own Digital Currencies. (13 September 2017). Retrieved from https://www.verdict.co.uk/bitcoin-countries-digital-currency/
9. Njeri, K. (6 June 2017). Senegal Launches National Digital Currency on the Blockchain. Retrieved from http://bitcoinafrica.io/2017/06/06/senegal-launches-digital-currency-on-the-blockchain/
10. Five ways Businesses are Using Blockchains. (1 January 2017). Retrieved from http://gcba.world/bitcoin-news/this-country-may-launch-its-own-virtual-currency/
11. Ulmer, A. and Buitrago, D. (4 December 2017) Enter the 'Petro': Venezuela to Launch Oil-Backed Cryptocurrency. Retrieved from https://in.reuters.com/article/venezuela-economy/enter-the-petro-venezuela-to-launch-oil-backed-cryptocurrency-idINKBN1DY081
12. Applications of Blockchain Technology: To Banking and Financial Sector in India. (5 January 2017). Retrieved from http://www.idrbt.ac.in/assets/publications/Best%20Practices/BCT.pdf
13. Ibid.

Chapter 14

1. List of Cryptocurrencies. (10 April 2018). Retrieved from https://en.wikipedia.org/wiki/List_of_cryptocurrencies
2. Popper, N. (28 March 2016). 'Ethereum, a Virtual Currency, Enables Transactions that Rival Bitcoin's'. Retrieved from https://www.nytimes.com/2016/03/28/business/dealbook/ethereum-a-virtual-currency-enables-transactions-that-rival-bitcoins.html
3. Retrieved from https://ripple.com/company/
4. Schuster, B. (9 December 2017). The Ripple Currency Problem: Why Permissioned Blockchains Will Devalue XRP. Retrieved from https://hackernoon.com/the-ripple-currency-problem-why-permissioned-blockchains-will-devalue-xrp-d79aef84c074
5. Top Ten Altcoins: All You Wanted to Know About Bitcoin's Contenders. Retrieved from http://bitcoinfree365.blogspot.com/2017/04/top-10-altcoins-all-you-wanted-to-know.html
6. Seesaw Reward Balance System White Paper. (24 January 2017). Retrieved from https://bravenewcoin.com/assets/whitepapers/pivx-seesaw-whitepaper-v.7-1.pdf
7. Ibid.
8. Retrieved from https://www.decred.org/
9. Xie, L. (17 October 2017). The Beginner's Guide to Decred. Retrieved from https://medium.com/@linda.xie/a-beginners-guide-to-decred-2fc61670d67c

Chapter 15

1. BTC-e Domain Seized by US Law Enforcement. (30 June 2018). Retrieved from https://news.bitcoin.com/btc-e-domain-seizure-by-u-s-law-enforcement-sparks-jurisdiction-questions/
2. Bonneau, J. and Goldfeder, S. (15 December 2017). Five Myths About Bitcoins. Retrieved from https://www.washingtonpost.com/outlook/five-myths/five-myths-about-bitcoin/2017/12/15/7a506742-e044-11e7-8679-a97
3. Meiklejohn, S., Marjori, P., Jordan, G., Levchenko, K., McCoy, D., Voelker, G.M. and Savage, S. A Fistful of Bitcoins: Characterizing

Payments Among Men with No Names. University of California, San Diego and George Mason University. Retrieved from https://cseweb.ucsd.edu/~smeiklejohn/files/imc13.pdf

4. Orcutt, M. (11 December 2017). Criminals Thought Bitcoin Was the Perfect Hiding Place, But They Thought Wrong. Retrieved from https://www.technologyreview.com/s/608763/criminals-thought-bitcoin-was-the-perfect-hiding-place-they-thought-wrong/
5. Ibid.
6. Noack, R. (17 February 2018). Cryptocurrency Mining in Iceland is Using so Much Energy, the Electricity May Run Out. Retrieved from https://www.washingtonpost.com/news/worldviews/wp/2018/02/13/cryptocurrency-mining-in-iceland-is-using-so-much-energy-the-electricity-may-run-out/?utm_term=.1f7cd29fa58b
7. Will Crypto Replace Fiat Currencies in The Future? (17 June 2018). Retrieved from https://medium.com/boosto/will-crypto-replace-fiat-currencies-in-the-future-433953e89119
8. Bonneau, J. and Goldfeder, S. (15 December 2017). Five Myths About Bitcoins. Retrieved from https://www.washingtonpost.com/outlook/five-myths/five-myths-about-bitcoin/2017/12/15/7a506742-e044-11e7-8679-a97
9. Mehra, S. (17 November 2017). Busting the Myths on Bitcoins. Retrieved from https://www.moneycontrol.com/news/trends/expert-columns-2/busting-the-myths-on-bitcoins-2435473.html

Chapter 16

1. D'Alfonso, A., Langer, P. and Vandelis, Z. (17 October 2016). The Future of Cryptocurrency an Investor's Comparison of Bitcoin and Ethereum. Retrieved from https://www.economist.com/sites/default/files/the_future_of_cryptocurrency.pdf
2. Spolsky, J. (21 July 2001). Good Software Takes 10 Years. Get Used to it. Retrieved from https://www.joelonsoftware.com/2001/07/21/good-software-takes-ten-years-get-used-to-it/
3. Donnelly, J. (14 February 2016). Here's What the Future of Bitcoin Looks Like—And It's Bright. Retrieved from https://venturebeat.com/2016/02/14/heres-what-the-future-of-bitcoin-looks-like-and-its-bright/

4. Rice, D. (26–28 February 2017) Bitcoins: Their Future in Worldwide Commerce. ITTech Law Asia-Pacific Conference. Retrieved from http://asia.itechlaw.org/assets/ITECHLAW/2-Denis-Rice.pdf
5. De Grauwe, P. (11 January 2018). Bitcoin is Not The Currency Of The Future. Retrieved from https://www.socialeurope.eu/bitcoin-not-currency-future
6. Aitken, R. (6 December 2017). Bitcoin Could Fall 'Big Time' But Not Just Yet, Says Crypto Trader. Retrieved from https://www.forbes.com/sites/rogeraitken/2017/12/06/bitcoin-could-fall-big-time-but-not-just-yet-says-crypto-trader/#6d133c41668e
7. Tasca, P., Liu, S. and Hayes, A. (13 July 2016). The Evolution of the Bitcoin Economy: Extracting and Analyzing the Network of Payment Relationships. https://papers.ssrn.com/sol3/papers.cfm?abstract_id=2808762
8. Ibid.
9. Ibid.
10. Poon, J. and Dryja, T. (14 January 2016). The Bitcoin Lightning Network: Scalable Off-Chain Instant Payments. Retrieved from https://lightning.network/lightning-network-paper.pdf
11. Ibid.
12. Ibid.
13. Ibid.
14. Retrieved from https://www.rsk.co/#about
15. What Challenges Will Bitcoin Have to Overcome? (13 February 2018). Retrieved from https://blog.unocoin.com/what-challenges-will-bitcoin-have-to-overcome-a88be58973ff

Chapter 18

1. Zambrano, R. (August 2017). Blockchain: Unpacking the Disruptive Potential of Blockchain Technology For Human Development. White Paper by International Development Research Centre (IRDI), Canada. Retrieved from https://idl-bnc-idrc.dspacedirect.org/bitstream/handle/10625/56662/IDL-56662.pdf
2. Retrieved from https://followmyvote.com/
3. Lace, E. (18 September 2015). Bitnation Registers First Refugees on the Blockchain. Retrieved from https://cointelegraph.com/news/bitnation-registers-first-refugees-on-the-blockchain

4. World Food Programme. Building Blocks. Retrieved from https://innovation.wfp.org/project/building-blocks
5. CryptoKitties: Collectible and Breedable Cats Empowered by Blockchain technology (White paper).
6. Ibid.
7. Retrieved from https://spellsofgenesis.com/
8. A Decentralised Economy for Creating Games. The Game Tech Team. Retrieved from https://www.gameprotocol.io/white paper
9. Retrieved from https://unikrn.com/
10. Thomson Reuters. (9 May 2016). Know Your Customer Surveys Reveal Escalating Costs and Complexity. Retrieved from https://www.thomsonreuters.com/en/press-releases/2016/may/thomson-reuters-2016-know-your-customer-surveys.html

Chapter 19

1. Realizing the Potential of Blockchain: A Multi-Stakeholder Approach to the Stewardship of Blockchain & Cryptocurrencies. (June 2017). Retrieved from http://www3.weforum.org/docs/WEF_Realizing_Potential_Blockchain.pdf
2. Ibid.
3. Retrieved from https://www.hyperledger.org/projects
4. Ibid.
5. Realizing the Potential of Blockchain: A Multi-Stakeholder Approach to the Stewardship of Blockchain & Cryptocurrencies. (June 2017). Retrieved from http://www3.weforum.org/docs/WEF_Realizing_Potential_Blockchain.pdf
6. Ibid.
7. Retrieved from http://coala.global/whatwedo.html
8. Ibid.
9. Realizing the Potential of Blockchain: A Multi-Stakeholder Approach to the Stewardship of Blockchain & Cryptocurrencies. (June 2017). Retrieved from http://www3.weforum.org/docs/WEF_Realizing_Potential_Blockchain.pdf
10. Ibid.
11. Ibid.
12. Ibid.

About the Author

A littérateur and a number cruncher, Dr Rachna Singh is an unusual blend of literary panache and financial acumen. With a masters and MPhil degree in English Literature and three gold medals for academic excellence under her belt, Singh was awarded the Nehru centenary scholarship to pursue a doctorate degree at Cambridge University. However, capricious fate beckoned and Singh joined the Indian Revenue Service in 1991. Dr Singh is well-versed in the intricacies of taxation, finance, economics, regulations and law, which she has been handling for 27 years. She is currently posted as Commissioner Income Tax in Delhi.

The travails of a demanding career notwithstanding, Dr Singh has been penning articles for various national dailies. She has authored two books on economic issues, *Penny Panache: Piecing the Economic Puzzle* (2016) and *Financial Felicity: Making Sense of Money Matters* (2017). *Myriad Musings* (2016) is a collection of her published articles and travelogues.